365 Days Of Dessert

"365 Celebrity Chef Caliber Desserts Easy Enough For Even Raw Kitchen Rookies"

Written by

Nora Even   Ryan Even

Dedicated to Gail and Betty who taught us that making dessert can be just as fun as eating it!

"When we no longer have good cooking in the world, we will have no literature, nor high and sharp intelligence, nor friendly gatherings, no social harmony."

- Marie-Antoine Carême

All Rights Reserved © 2010 Nora Even & Ryan Even.

Disclaimer and Terms of Use: No information contained in this book should be considered as physical, health related, financial, tax, or legal advice. Your reliance upon information and content obtained by you at or through this publication is solely at your own risk. The author assumes no liability or responsibly for damage or injury to you, other persons, or property arising from any use of any product, information, idea, or instruction contained in the content provided to you through this book.

Table of Contents

Introduction 16
Day 1 – 30 Pieces Of Kourabiedes 18
Day 2 – 4 Layer-Easy As Pie 19
Day 3 – 5 O'Clock Cobbler 20
Day 4 – ABC Apple Pie 21
Day 5 – After Dinner Grasshopper Pie 22
Day 6 – Afternoon Pecan Chocolate Rum Pie 23
Day 7 – Afternoon Spoon Pecan Delight 24
Day 8 – Ali's Chocolate Turtle Pie 25
Day 9 – All Aboard Heavenly Express 26
Day 10 – All For You Pumpkin Dessert 27
Day 11 – Almond Joy Cherry Pie 28
Day 12 – Aloha Pumpkin Pie 29
Day 13 – Amazing Butter Cookies 30
Day 14 – Amazing Glazed Fruit Pie 31
Day 15 – Anna's Anytime Rum Balls 32
Day 16 – Apple Pie Applause 33
Day 17 – Atop The Mantel Huckleberry Cobbler 34
Day 18 – Backyard Summer Pandowdy 35
Day 19 – Baked Grape Pie 37
Day 20 – Bakers Fried Peach Pie 38
Day 21 – Barbie's Plum Pie 39
Day 22 – Be-My-Valentine Pie 40
Day 23 – Beg For More Sugar Cream Pie 41
Day 24 – Berlinerkranzer 42
Day 25 – Berry Merry Cobbler 43
Day 26 – Best Berry Fest Fried Pies 44
Day 27 – Betty's Double Pecan Pie 45

Day 28 – Betty's Mousse Chocolate Frozen Pie 46
Day 29 – Bingo-Blaster Freedom Fruit Cake 48
Day 30 – Blended Custard Pie................................... 49
Day 31 – Block Party Whoopie Pies 50
Day 32 – Boo Boo's Banana Meringue Pie 51
Day 33 – Boo's Ready Pumpkin Light Pie 52
Day 34 – Border Ecclefechan Tarts.......................... 53
Day 35 – Bourbon Street Pie.................................... 54
Day 36 – Bourbonation Sweet Potato Pecan Pie....... 55
Day 37 – Bow To Queen Mary's Tart 57
Day 38 – Bright Gooseberry Pie............................... 58
Day 39 – Brilliant & Easy Mince Pie........................ 59
Day 40 – Bring It On Honey Crunch Pecan Pie 60
Day 41 – Broomstick Pumpkin Pie 61
Day 42 – Brunch for The Bunch Egg Pie - No Crust ... 62
Day 43 – Butter Have It Tart Pie 63
Day 44 – Captain Norm's Noodle Kugel 64
Day 45 – Care Pear Pie 65
Day 46 – Care To Dance Coconut Pie 66
Day 47 – Celebration Confetti Pie 67
Day 48 – Celebrity Waffle Cone 68
Day 49 – Cheesy Apricot Jam Pastries 69
Day 50 – Cherida's Basic Graham Cracker Pie Crust 70
Day 51 – Cherida's Basic Graham Cracker Pie Shell. 71
Day 52 – Chocolate Bite Brownie Pie 72
Day 53 – Chocolate Chip Nut Pie Kentucky Derby Pie 73
Day 54 – Chocolate Chocolate Pie 74
Day 55 – Chocolate Effortless Crumb Pie Shell 75
Day 56 – Cinnamon Ginger Cookies 76
Day 57 – Cinnamon Halvas Politikos 77

Day 58 – Cinnamon Savor Zwetschgendatschi 78
Day 59 – Classic Boston Cream Pie 80
Day 60 – Clear Cloud Pie 82
Day 61 – Coconut Pie At Ease 83
Day 62 – Coconut Pie For Everyone 84
Day 63 – Coconut Smurk Pie 85
Day 64 – Conquering Chocolate Cream Pie 86
Day 65 – County Fair Cream Puffs 87
Day 66 – Cozy Christmas Pie 88
Day 67 – Crowd Pleasing Pecan Tarts 89
Day 68 – Crumbs A Top Rhubarb Custard Pie 90
Day 69 – Crunch Crunch Coconut Crunch 91
Day 70 – Crust Basics 101: 92
Day 71 – Crust Basics 102: 93
Day 72 – Crust Basics 103: 94
Day 73 – Crust Basics 104: 95
Day 74 – Crystals' Creamy Honey Pie 96
Day 75 – Crème de Menthe Ice Cream Pie 97
Day 76 – Crème Of The Crop Apricot Tart 98
Day 77 – Custom Baked Crumb Crust 99
Day 78 – Dance To Pavloval 101
Day 79 – Daydream Walnut Horns 102
Day 80 – Delicious Buttermilk Pie 103
Day 81 – Delicious Kolache Slovakian Pastry 104
Day 82 – Delightful Carrot Cake 105
Day 83 – Diabetic Cherry Moon Pie 107
Day 84 – Diabetic Easy Popovers 108
Day 85 – Diabetic-Crumb Pie Shell 109
Day 86 – Double Chocolate Brandy Pie 110
Day 87 – Double Chocolate Kiss Pie 111

Day 88 – Double Trouble Berry Pie 112
Day 89 – Dried My Apricot Pie 113
Day 90 – Easiest Coconut Custard 114
Day 91 – Easy Peanut Butter Pie w/ Fudge Topping. 115
Day 92 – Easy Scrounge Up Chiffon Jam Pie 116
Day 93 – Easy Street Peanut Butter Pie 117
Day 94 – Edgy Chocolate Crusted Peanut Butter Pie 118
Day 95 – Effortless Crumb Pie Crust 119
Day 96 – Escape Your Mind Margarita Pie 120
Day 97 – Everything Waits Pumpkin Ice-Cream Pie. 121
Day 98 – Family First Pecan Pie 122
Day 99 – Family's Here Toffee Bar Crunch Pie 123
Day 100 – Family's Near Chocolate Chip Pie.......... 124
Day 101 – Fancy Pants Baklava 125
Day 102 – Fast Peanut Butter Delight Cookies 128
Day 103 – Father's Day Peanut Butter Chip Pie 129
Day 104 – Favorite Banana Split Cake 130
Day 105 – Ferris Wheel Peaches and Cream Pie 132
Day 106 – First Date Pie 133
Day 107 – First Kiss Strawberry Pie 134
Day 108 – Floating Orange-Almond Pastries Lite.... 135
Day 109 – Fluffy & Crispy Peanut Butter Pie........... 136
Day 110 – Fold'em Rum Pie 137
Day 111 – Four Seasons Berry Pie 138
Day 112 – Fourth Of July Lemon Pie 139
Day 113 – Fresh Red Raspberry Pie 140
Day 114 – Frozen Chocolate-Peanut Butter Pie 141
Day 115 – Frozen Tapioca Time Peach Pie 142
Day 116 – Fruit And Jello Pie 143
Day 117 – Fruitful Fast Skillet Pie 144

Day 118 – Fudgey Chocolaty Pie 145
Day 119 – Fun Mixed Oatmeal Fudge Cookies 146
Day 120 – G-Force Rhubarb Pie 147
Day 121 – Gail's Great German Chocolate Pie 148
Day 122 – Get To The Party Pumpkin Pie 149
Day 123 – Glazed Fresh-Strawberry Pie 150
Day 124 – Good Morning Fruity Frozen Yogurt 151
Day 125 – Grandma Betty's Oatmeal Bars 152
Day 126 – Grandma Bev's Best Carrot Cake 153
Day 127 – Grandma's Thanksgiving Pecan Pie 155
Day 128 – Grasshopper Pie 156
Day 129 – Great Cream Cheese Pound Cake 157
Day 130 – Great Thanksgiving Pie 158
Day 131 – Gumdrop Dream Cake 159
Day 132 – H2O Crust 160
Day 133 – Hammock Banana Custard Pudding 161
Day 134 – Handpicked Raspberry Pie 162
Day 135 – Harvest Time Pumpkin Pie 163
Day 136 – Heartthrob Cherry-Cream Pie 164
Day 137 – Heaven On Earth Pie 165
Day 138 – Heroic Grape Pie 166
Day 139 – Hide and Seek Pumpkin Pie 167
Day 140 – His And Hers Vegetarian Mince Pies 168
Day 141 – Hobo Apple Pie 169
Day 142 – Holiday Christmas Stars 171
Day 143 – Holiday Party Coconut Meringue Drops.. 173
Day 144 – Homemade Sweet Potato Pie 174
Day 145 – Hot Hot Hot Butternut Rhubarb Pie 175
Day 146 – I'm In Love Cherry Cream Cheese Pie ... 177
Day 147 – Ice Cream Pumpkin Pie 178

Day 148 – If The Shoe Fits Cake 179
Day 149 – Island Chocolate Coconut Crunch Pie 180
Day 150 – It's a Deal! Blueberry & Walnut Pie 182
Day 151 – It's Possible Banana Cream Pie 2 184
Day 152 – Jack O's Pumpkin Cheese Pie (Low Cal).. 185
Day 153 – Jacqueline's Meringue Crust 186
Day 154 – Jay's Venison Mincemeat 187
Day 155 – Jazzy Smooth Velvet Cream Pies 188
Day 156 – Jess's Pumpkin Cheese Pie 190
Day 157 – Jessica's Coffee Cake 191
Day 158 – Joanne's Chocolate Chip Pie 192
Day 159 – JBP's Chocolate Malted-Milk Pie............ 193
Day 160 – Joyful Nesselrode Pie 195
Day 161 – Jump For Joy Popovers 196
Day 162 – Justin's Secret Sweet Potato Pie 197
Day 163 – Keep A Secret Sugar Cookies 198
Day 164 – Key Lime Pie (Nutrasweet) 199
Day 165 – Kids Muddy Pie 200
Day 166 – Lake Superior Whipping Cream 201
Day 167 – Lakeview Strawberry-Rhubarb Pie 202
Day 168 – Lazy River Pie 203
Day 169 – Lemon Cream Cheese Pie 204
Day 170 – Lemon Lips Pie 205
Day 171 – Let's Party Margarita Pie 206
Day 172 – Lingering Blueberry Torte 207
Day 173 – Little Chapel Butterscotch Oat Squares ... 208
Day 174 – Little Elf's Coconut Cream Pie 209
Day 175 – Little Jenna's Sweet Potato Pie 210
Day 176 – Loveable Peaches and Cream Pie 211
Day 177 – Lunch Pail Apple Squares 212

Day 178 – Magical Black Bottom Pie 213
Day 179 – Make Mice 214
Day 180 – Mama Bear's Lime Bars 215
Day 181 – Managers Special Walnut Crumb Crust .. 216
Day 182 – Mardi Gras Pecan Pie 217
Day 183 – Marshawna's Hot Toddy Pie 218
Day 184 – Megan's Chocolate Mousse Pie 219
Day 185 – Megan's Chocolate Mousse Pie -2 220
Day 186 – Memories Of Mincemeat 221
Day 187 – Meringue Cream Peanut Butter Pie 222
Day 188 – Merry Mincemeat 223
Day 189 – Miss Pretty Persimmon Pie 224
Day 190 – Mission Possible Banana Cream Pie 1 225
Day 191 – Modern Mincemeat 226
Day 192 – Mom's Manageable Peanut Brittle Pie 227
Day 193 – Monkey Business Peanut Butter Pie 228
Day 194 – Moonshine Sour Cream Raisin Pie 229
Day 195 – Morning Blend Sour Cream Coffee Cake. 230
Day 196 – Morning Maple Custard Pie 231
Day 197 – Mr. Mississippi Mud Pie 232
Day 198 – Mrs. Mississippi Mud Cake 233
Day 199 – Ms. Love's Butterscotch Custard Pie 234
Day 200 – Never Ending German Friendship Cake... 235
Day 201 – Nice Little Fruit Tarts 237
Day 202 – Nitty-Gritty Pie 238
Day 203 – No Sweat Peanut Brittle Crust 239
Day 204 – Now Serving Boysenberry Syrup Pie 240
Day 205 – Nutty Buddy Macadamia Cream Pie 241
Day 206 – Nutty Caramel Pie 242
Day 207 – Oh Honey Meringue 243

Day 208 – One Of A Kind No Bake Blueberry Pie 244
Day 209 – Original Mint Cream Pie 245
Day 210 – Out Of World No-Bake Strawberry Pie 246
Day 211 – Papa's Up High Papaya Pie 247
Day 212 – Park Peanut Pie with Shortbread 248
Day 213 – Parkside Pineapple Cream Cheese Pie .. 249
Day 214 – Paul's Surprise Coconut Cream Pie 250
Day 215 – Peach Beach Streusel Pie 251
Day 216 – Peach Pie Awakenings 252
Day 217 – Peanut Butter-Chocolate Mini Cutie Pies. 253
Day 218 – Pear Pie In A Deep-Dish 254
Day 219 – Peter's Low-Calorie Pumpkin Pie 255
Day 220 – Pick Me Up Linzer Tart 256
Day 221 – Piece In The Dark Fruitcake 257
Day 222 – Pipsqueak's Double Layer Pumpkin Pie .. 259
Day 223 – Plain Jane's Pastry Pie 260
Day 224 – Please Chocolate Banana Pudding Pie... 261
Day 225 – Please Hold-The-Sugar Apple Pie 262
Day 226 – Please Pass The Butter Cookies 263
Day 227 – Poker Room Rum Cream Pie 264
Day 228 – Presidential Suite Pudding Pies 265
Day 229 – Pretty Super Open-Faced Peach Pie 266
Day 230 – Pristine Praline Pumpkin Pie 267
Day 231 – Proud Pumpkin Pudding 268
Day 232 – Proud Shortbread 269
Day 233 – Pumpkin Pie Perfection 270
Day 234 – Quick Chocolate Cheese Pie 271
Day 235 – Rags To Riches Banana Pie 272
Day 236 – Railroad Cross Sweet Green Tomato Pie 273
Day 237 – Raspberries & Cream Snowflake Pie 274

Day 238 – Ready In A Jiffy Butter Pie Crust 275
Day 239 – Real Spanish Cream 277
Day 240 – Red Carpet Pie Crust 278
Day 241 – Rhubarb Custard Pie 279
Day 242 – Rhubarb Streusel Perfect Pie 280
Day 243 – Rich Taste Poor Man's Pie 281
Day 244 – Riverside Pear-On-Pear Tart 282
Day 245 – Rock The Banana Guava Pie 284
Day 246 – Ronaldo's Passion Fruit Pie' 285
Day 247 – Rosy Cheeks Cherry Almond Mouse Pie..286
Day 248 – Rosy Rhubarb Pie 287
Day 249 – Runnin' Rich Coconut Pie 288
Day 250 – Ryan & Nora's Baked Apples 289
Day 251 – Ryan's Nutty Cocoa-Peanut-Butter Pie.... 290
Day 252 – Sail Away Chocolate Brandy Cream 292
Day 253 – Sally's Best Darn Turtle Pie 293
Day 254 – Santa's Helper Eggnog Pie 294
Day 255 – Satisfying Baklava 295
Day 256 – Saturday Night Vanilla Almond Puff 297
Day 257 – Scary Larry's Berry Pie 298
Day 258 – Scrumptious Cranberry-Apple Cookies ... 299
Day 259 – Senorita Amanda Chocolate Sponge Pie 300
Day 260 – Sherry Fruit Tickle 301
Day 261 – Shoo-Fly Don't Botha Me Molasses Cake 303
Day 262 – Shooting Star Sour Cream Apple Pie...... 304
Day 263 – Shoreline Rhubarb and Banana 305
Day 264 – Show Me The Poppyseed Bundt Cake ... 306
Day 265 – Simple Delight Butterscotch Cookies 307
Day 266 – Simply Maple Syrup Pie..................... 308
Day 267 – Simply Tasty Rhubarb Cream Pie 309

Day 268 – Sinful Cherry Pie 310
Day 269 – Six Item Frozen Peanut Butter Pie 311
Day 270 – Skinny Lemon Lips Pie (Lowfat Version) . 312
Day 271 – Skip The Meeting Pie 314
Day 272 – Sky Rocket Plum Torte 315
Day 273 – Sky's The Limit Vanilla Pie 316
Day 274 – Slap-Happy Peanut Butter Cream Pie 317
Day 275 – Smart & Flakey Pie Pastry 319
Day 276 – Smile For Coconut Pie 320
Day 277 – Smooth And Creamy Fruit Pie Filling 321
Day 278 – Smooth Blackberry Custard Pie 322
Day 279 – Snow Angel Pie 323
Day 280 – So Easy Sugar Pie 324
Day 281 – So Good Banana Caramel Pie 325
Day 282 – So Good South Fried Pies 326
Day 283 – Space Odyssy Reeses Peanut Butter Pie 328
Day 284 – Sparkling Peach Pie with Crumb Topping 329
Day 285 – Specialty Persimmon Pie 330
Day 286 – Spoonfull Blueberry Cream Pie 331
Day 287 – Springtime Nectarine Pie 332
Day 288 – Sqeeky Peachy Peach Pie 333
Day 289 – Starlight Eggnog Pie 334
Day 290 – Stellar Pineapple Cheese Pie (Low Cal) .. 335
Day 291 – Step Ahead Sour Cream Pie 336
Day 292 – Straight To The Point Choco Hazel Tart .. 337
Day 293 – Sugar Free Blueberry Blast Pie 339
Day 294 – Sugar Free Choc. Banana Cream Pie 340
Day 295 – Summertime Lemon Pie 341
Day 296 – Sunny Cranberry -Raz Meringue Pie...... 342
Day 297 – Sunny Southern Pecan Pie 343

Day 298 – Sunroom Strawberry Cream Pie 344

Day 299 – Sunset Chocolate Walnut Pie 345

Day 300 – Surprise Fruit and Cream Pie 346

Day 301 – Surrendering Sugar Cream Pie 347

Day 302 – Susie's Soft Shortbread 348

Day 303 – Sway To Pavlova II 349

Day 304 – Sweet and Sour Milk Cake 350

Day 305 – Sweet As Maple Sugar Pumpkin Pie....... 351

Day 306 – Sweet Little Fruit Tart 352

Day 307 – Sweet Treat Strawberry Glace Pie 353

Day 308 – Sweetheart Cookies 354

Day 309 – Sweetie Pie 355

Day 310 – Take A Bite Of Melomacarona 356

Day 311 – Take Time For Graham Cracker Quickie . 358

Day 312 – Take Two Orange Pound Cake 359

Day 313 – Tang Bang Lemon Meringue Pie 360

Day 314 – Tasty Delight Pecan Pumpkin Pie 361

Day 315 – Tasty Kolachki 363

Day 316 – Tea Party Strawberry Chiffon Pie 364

Day 317 – Teeter Totter Jam & Sour Cream Pie 365

Day 318 – Tempo Tart 367

Day 319 – The Best Creamy Peanut Butter Pie........ 369

Day 320 – The Great Frozen Chocolate-PB Pie 371

Day 321 – The Return Of The Macadamia Nut Pie .. 372

Day 322 – The World's Greatest Meringue............. 373

Day 323 – Time For Lime Summer Pie 374

Day 324 – Ting Tang Pie 375

Day 325 – Tip Toe Twinkie Pie 376

Day 326 – Tis' Chocolate Peppermint Angel Pie 377

Day 327 – To The Rescue Pie Pastry 378

Day 328 – Traffic Jam Oatmeal Cookies 379
Day 329 – Trick Or Treat Pumpkin Pie 380
Day 330 – Twisted Strawberry Lime Pie 381
Day 331 – Ultimate Frozen Peanut Butter Pie 382
Day 332 – Uncle Karl's Caramel Apple Pie 384
Day 333 – Undercover Orange Meringue Pie 385
Day 334 – V.I.P Apple Cinnamon Pie 386
Day 335 – Valley View Vanilla Wafer Crust 387
Day 336 – Variety Fried Pies 388
Day 337 – Victoria's Vine Grape Pie 389
Day 338 – Wafer Crust Pumpkin Pie 390
Day 339 – Warm Butternut Biscuits 391
Day 340 – Warm Elderberry Pie 392
Day 341 – Wedding Vow Cookies 393
Day 342 – Welcome Home Oatmeal Pie 394
Day 343 – West Coast Carrot Raisin Bars 395
Day 344 – Wetzel Lane Raspberry Tart 396
Day 345 – Wheel Barrow Whipped Cream 397
Day 346 – Who's Ready Pumpkin Pie 398
Day 347 – Will You Be My Brown Sugar Pie?........ 399
Day 348 – Winner's Circle Rum/bourbon Balls 400
Day 349 – Winter Wonderland Oatmeal Squares 401
Day 350 – Wisconsin Cranberry Pie 402
Day 351 – Wishful Hazelnut Cherry Tart 403
Day 352 – Yes You Flan 405
Day 353 – You Can Do It Corn Flake Pie Crust 406
Day 354 – Yummy C.C. Peanut Butter Pie 407
Day 355 – Yummy Cream Cheese PB Pies 408
Day 356 – Zesty Bavarian Pie 409
Day 357 – Zesty Lemon Custard Pie 410

Day 358 – Zeta Sorority Apple Pie Cake 411
Day 359 – Zeus Is Loose Dirty South Apple Pie 412
Day 360 – Zig-Zag Apple Cranberry Pie 413
Day 361 – Zippy's Crab Apple Pie 414
Day 362 – Zoltar Baklava 415
Day 363 – Zone 105 Sour Cream Apple Pie 418
Day 364 – Zoo Keeper's Baked Apples 419
Day 365 – Zoom Upside Down Apple Pie 420

Introduction

Have you ever been to a baby's first birthday? This is often the first time some babies ever get to try sweets. You may have seen birthday photographs of a shirtless baby covered in cake and frosting. If you've never seen it before, let me tell you that it is absolutely astounding.

Around the time when a baby turns one they are allowed to move onto the next step of foods, the most curious one being sweets.... A.K.A. sugar! Witnessing a human being eat sugar for the first time is a special moment to savor.

As adults we don't remember the first time we put a delicious sugary dessert to our tongues. Watching a child for the first time gives us a pretty good idea of how most of us probably began handling this inquisitive thing called "dessert".

The baby pauses for a moment to ponder the green and yellow frosting that they just licked off of their hands and then it hits them! Their eyes light up with excitement and they look to mom and dad with a smile that can only say *"mmmm what is this stuff? This is really, really good"*.

It is from this point on that these baby's will be rewarded, indulged and treated with desserts for the rest of their lives. From childhood to adulthood we try so many different desserts. We celebrate life events with dessert, we explore restaurants that create unique desserts, and we bake desserts right at home to give it that *"just made with love"* touch.

We know that you love to treat your family, friends and yourself to delicious desserts you've created in your kitchen and that is why we've dedicated our efforts to an entire book full of 365 desserts that is bound to satisfy your sweet-tooth for years to come!

Some of these great recipes you may have eaten before (maybe even in 5 star restaurants), but never thought you could actually make yourself... Now you can!

Most of the recipes are easy-to-follow and simple-to-make.

The fun thing about desserts is that there are always new combinations and things to try. So go ahead and find a new favorite dessert amongst the following 420 pages of recipes... And a 2nd favorite... And a 3rd favorite...

Make them for your family and friends and feel free to call them your own!

Nobody has to know your "secret" recipes came from this book ☺

30 Pieces Of Kourabiedes

30 Pieces

2 c Butter, unsalted
1 c Sugar, powdered
3   Egg yolks
3 T Brandy
2 t Vanilla extract
6 c Flour
1/2 c Almonds (blanched),
   -chopped
1 lb Sugar, powdered
   -(one package)

Beat the butter with the sugar until it becomes fluffy. Add the egg yolks one by one, beating continuously. Add the brandy and vanilla.

Blend in the almonds and the flour, a cup at a time. Use enough flour to get a firm dough (it may take a bit more or less than the amount mentioned in the ingredients list). Use your hands to do the mixing, as an electric mixer will be useless after the first two or three cups of flour have been added. Place the dough in the refrigerator for at least one hour.

Shape the dough into balls, about one inch in diameter, flatten them and place on greased cookie sheets. Bake at 350 degrees F. for 20 minutes.

Remove from the oven. Roll each cookie (while it is still hot) in the powdered sugar and put it back on the cookie sheet. Repeat this step once more, so that you get a thicker coating.

Place the coated cookies on a platter, liberally sprinkling each layer and the bottom of the platter with powdered sugar. When you are done, there shouldn't be any sugar left. Let them cool and they are ready to eat!

4 Layer Easy As Pie

1 c Flour
1   Cube soft margarine
1 1/2 c Chopped walnuts
8 oz Softened cream cheese
1 c Powdered sugar
16 oz Container Cool Whip
2 sm Pkgs. instant pistachio
Pistachio Instant Pudding (or any flavor desired)

There are 4 layers to this recipe. Use an 8 x 12 inch baking dish.

1ST LAYER: Mix together the following ingredients: 1 cup flour, 1 cube soft margarine and 1 cup walnuts. Press in bottom of dish to make crust. Bake at 350 degrees for 15 minutes. Cool completely.

2ND LAYER: Cream cheese, powdered sugar and 1 cup Cool Whip. Mix together and spread over the crust.

3RD LAYER: Mix pistachio instant pudding mix with 3 cups of milk and spread over 2nd layer.

4th LAYER: Spread remaining Cool Whip on top and sprinkle with fine chopped nuts.

12 servings.

5 O'Clock Cobbler

1/4 c Butter (or margarine,
   -if you must)
1/2 c Sugar
2/3 c Milk
 1 c Flour
 2 t Baking powder
 13 oz Tart cherries
   -(one normal U.S. can)
 2 T Sugar (to sweeten
   -and thicken; use less
   -or more as needed)

Preheat oven to 350 degrees F. Drain cherries, saving liquid.

Cream butter and sugar together. Alternately add in milk and sifted dry ingredients. Pour into a buttered and floured casserole dish. Top evenly with cherries.
Sprinkle sugar on top and cover with saved liquid/juice.
  Bake 45-50 minutes.

The batter will expand and surround the cherries so they're evenly mixed throughout the cobbler. The juice will congeal to fruity and pudding-like.

Serve warm topped with cream, milk or ice cream. (I prefer milk). If any is left, it's good cold, too.

NOTES:
 * As the name implies, this is a very quick recipe to make. Depending on how soft the butter is to start with, or whether or if you use a food processor (I don't, but it should work) this recipe takes only 5 to 10 minutes to mix.

 * You can use any unsweetened canned fruit for this recipe. You can also use frozen fruit, by thawing it before adding to the pan. Berries or peaches are standard substitutes. Yesterday I made one with crushed
  pineapple. I used brown, rather than white sugar atop the fruit. It tasted very much like pineapple upside down cake (though the appearance was a bit different).

ABC Apple Pie

1 Serving

-"This dessert has been a real time-saver when there's a large crowd to be fed. It serves more than an ordinary pie with about the same amount of effort." -

3 3/4 cups flour
1 1/2 tsp. salt
3/4 cup shortening
3 eggs, lightly beaten
1/3 cup milk
8 cups sliced peeling baking apples
1 1/2 cups sugar
1 tsp. ground cinnamon
1/2 tsp. ground nutmeg
1 cup crushed cornflakes
1 egg white, beaten

In a bowl, combine flour and salt. Cut in shortening until mixture resembles coarse crumbs. Add eggs and milk; mix to form dough. Chill for 20 minutes. Divide dough in half; roll one half to fit the bottom and sides of a greased 15x10x1" baking pan. Arrange apples over crust. Combine sugar, cinnamon, nutmeg and cornflakes; sprinkle over apples. Roll remaining dough to fit top of pan and place over apples. Seal edges; cut slits in top.

Brush with egg white.

Bake at 400 degrees for 15 minutes. Reduce heat to 350 degrees and bake for 25-30 minutes or until golden.

After Dinner Grasshopper Pie

20 Chocolate cookies; cream-filled
14 oz Sweetened condensed milk
3 tb Creme de menthe; (green)
2 tb Creme de cacao; (white)
1 c Heavy cream; whipped
 Mint; for garnish

 In a bowl crush 20 cream-filled chocolate cookies to make 1 3/4 cups of cru. Reserve 1/4 cup for garnish. Pat the remaining crumbs on the bottom and sides of buttered 9-inch pie tin. Set the crust aside.

  In a medium bowl combine the condensed milk, crème de menthe, creme de caca and heavy cream. Mix thoroughly. Pour the mixture into the crust. Top with the remaining crumbs. Freeze pie for 6 hours. The pie will not freeze solid. Garnish with mint.

   Makes 8 servings.

Afternoon Pecan Chocolate Rum Pie

1/4 ts Salt
1 1/4 c flour
1/2 c Lard; chilled
3 Eggs; lightly beaten
3 tb Water
1/4 ts Vinegar
1 1/2 oz Unsweetened chocolate
3 tb butter
3/4 c Dark corn syrup
1/2 c Brown sugar
3/4 ts vanilla extract
1 tb Rum
1 1/4 c Chopped pecans

Mix the salt into the flour and cut in the lard. Measure out 1 tablespoon Of the beaten eggs into a small bowl and reserve the remaining eggs. Add the water and vinegar to the bowl and stir. Slowly add the liquid to the flour and lard, just until the mixture holds together to form a dough.

Lightly flour a work surface and rolling pin and roll the dough into an 11-inch circle. Fit it into a 9-inch pie pan and refrigerate it if you plan to finish the pie after several hours, or freeze it if you are completing the recipe at this point. This will prevent shrinkage.

Melt the chocolate and butter together in a heavy saucepan. Set aside and allow to cool.

Stir the corn syrup and sugar into the reserved eggs. Add the chocolate and butter, vanilla, rum and the pecans. Mix well and pour into the pie shell.
Bake in the preheated oven for 1 hour, or until set. The filling will rise and then fall. Remove from the oven and cool on a rack. Serve slightly warm or at room temperature.

Afternoon Spoon Pecan Delight

3 ea Egg whites
20 ea Round buttery crackers; roll
1 c Sugar; fine
1/4 t Baking powder
1 c Finely chopped pecans
1 t Vanilla extract
1 x Whipped cream

  Grease 9" glass piepan. Beat egg whites til stiff; fold in sugar, baking powder, and vanilla extract.
   Beat until stiff. Fold in cracker crumbs & chopped pecans. Pour mix into piepan. Bake at 350 degrees for 20 mins. Top with==>> whipped cream.
  6-8 servings.

Ali's Chocolate Turtle Pie

  1/4 c Caramel ice cream topping
  6 oz Graham cracker crust
  1/2 c Pecans; chopped
  2 pk 4 oz chocolate pudding;
    -cook and serve variety
  3 c Milk
    Cool whip

Spread caramel topping on bottom of crust. Sprinkle with pecans.
Refrigerate. Stir pudding mixes into milk in medium saucepan. Stirring constantly, cook on medium heat until mixture comes to full boil. Remove from heat. Cool 5 minutes, stirring twice. Pour into crust. Place plastic wrap on surface of filling. Refrigerate 3 hours or until set. Garnish with cool whip.

All Aboard Heavenly Express

1 1/4 c Cream, heavy
  2   Bananas (or equivalent amount of soft fruit)
       Broken meringue

Whip the cream. Chop fruit coarsely, but don't crush. Break meringue into large crumbs. Mix everything shortly before serving and pile into glasses.

NOTES:

* Simple dessert for failed Pavlova attempts – My mother used to make the banana variety of this when she cooked her meringues a little too long or too hot.

* I can never make up my mind whether I prefer the strawberry or the banana version. Peach should be pretty good too, though I've never tried it.

* This is a neat way of saving a Pavlova attempt when the meringue part fails: it produces a delicious desert and no-one need ever know...

All For You Pumpkin Dessert

- 1 c Sugar, granulated
- 3   Eggs, beaten
- 29 oz Pumpkin (1 large can)
- 2 t   Cinnamon, ground
- 1/2 t Ginger, ground
- 1/4 t Cloves, ground
- 1/2 t Salt
- 12 oz Evaporated milk
  - -(1 large can)
- 1 lb Cake mix, yellow
  - -(1 standard box)
- 1 c Nuts, chopped
- 4 T Butter (sweet), melted
- Whipped cream

Preheat oven to 350 degrees F. Mix together sugar, eggs, pumpkin, cinnamon, ginger, cloves, salt and milk. Line a 9x13-inch pan with wax paper and pour the mixture in.

Sprinkle the dry cake mix on top, then sprinkle the nuts. Pour melted butter evenly over the cake mix and nuts. Bake at 350 degrees F. for 50-60 minutes.

Cool (very important). Flip over and remove from pan. Remove the wax paper. Top with whipped cream (which would dissolve if the cake weren't cooled first).

Almond Joy Cherry Pie

Ingredients

FOR THE PIE

1 pie shell, 9 inch, unbaked
21 oz cherry pie filling
1/2 tsp cinnamon
1/8 tsp salt (optional)
1 tsp lemon juice

FOR THE TOPPING

1 cup coconut
1/2 cup almonds, sliced
1/4 cup sugar
1/8 tsp salt (optional)
1/4 cup milk
1 tbsp butter, melted
1/4 tsp almond extract
1 egg, beaten

Directions

Preheat oven to 400F. Roll out pie pastry and place in 9 inch pie pan. In large bowl, combine pie filling, cinnamon, salt and lemon juice. Mix lightly. Spoon into crust-lined pie pan. Bake 20 minutes.
Meanwhile, combine all topping ingredients in medium bowl and mix until blended. Remove pie from oven after 20 minutes, spread topping evenly over surface, and return pie to oven. Bake an additional 15 to 30 minutes, or until crust and topping are golden brown.

Servings: 6 servings

Aloha Pumpkin Pie

INGREDIENTS:
2 cups canned pumpkin puree
1 cup milk
1 cup light cream
1/2 cup brown sugar
1/2 cup white sugar
1 1/2 teaspoons ground cinnamon
1/4 teaspoon salt
1/2 teaspoon ground nutmeg
1/4 teaspoon ground ginger
1/4 teaspoon ground cloves
1 tablespoon all-purpose flour
2 eggs, lightly beaten
1 (9 inch) unbaked pie crust

DIRECTIONS:
Preheat oven to 450 degrees F (230 degrees C.)
In a large bowl, combine pumpkin puree, milk, cream, brown sugar and white sugar. Mix in the cinnamon, salt, nutmeg, ginger and cloves. Beat in the flour and eggs. Pour filling into pie shell.
Bake for 10 minutes at 450 degrees F (230 degrees C) then reduce the temperature to 350 degrees F (175 degrees C) and bake for 50 minutes, or until filling has set.

Amazing Butter Cookies

    1/2 c Butter (unsalted),
          -at room temperature
    1/2 c Sugar, granulated
    1 1/2 c Flour, white
      1 lg Egg
      1 t   Vanilla extract
    1 1/2 t Baking powder

Beat the butter with the sugar. Add the egg and vanilla and beat until you get a uniform mixture. Mix the flour and baking powder and gradually blend them into the mixture. When you're done, you should have a rather sticky dough.

Shape the dough into balls, about 1 inch in diameter. Roll them in sugar and place them on an ungreased cookie sheet, leaving about an inch of space between cookies, so that they don't stick together when they expand.

Bake in preheated oven at 350 degrees F. for 20 minutes. Remove from oven, let them cool for a while, and start eating right away.

Amazing Glazed Fruit Pie

3/4 c Finely chopped ginger snaps
1/2 c Finely crushed grah. cracker
 1 T Sugar
 3 T Butter, melted
 1 ea Env. unflavored gelatin
 8 oz Can pineapple slices
 2 ea Small bananas
 2 c Sliced strawberries
 2 ea Kiwi fruit, peeled and slice

Stir together gingersnaps, graham crackers and sugar. Drizzle with margarine, tossing to combine. Press onto bottom and up sides of a 9" pie plate to form a firm, even crust. Bake in a 375-degree oven for 5 minutes. Cool. For glaze, drain pineapple, reserving juice(unsweetened juice). Cut pineapple into small pieces and set aside.

Add enough unsweetened pineapple juice (about 1 1/2 cups) to the reserved juice to make 1 3/4 cups total liquid. In a small sauce pan stir together pineapple liquid and gelatin, then let stand 5 minutes. Stir over low heat until gelatin dissolves. Cover and chill to the consistency of unbeaten egg whites (partially set). Spread 1/3 cup of the glaze over botton of crust.

Slice bananans and arrange over glaze. Top with another 1/3 cup of glaze and arrange strawberries over glaze. Stir together pineapple pieces and remaining glaze, then spoon over strawberries. Chill for 2 to 4 hours or until set.

Before serving, arrange kiwi fruit on pie.

Anna's Anytime Rum Balls

- 2 1/2 c Vanilla wafers, crushed
- 1 c Walnuts, crushed
- 2 T Cocoa
- 3 T Dark corn syrup
- 1/4 c Rum
- 1 c Powdered sugar

Mix all of the above ingredients in a large bowl. Roll the mixture into small balls. Roll the balls in powdered sugar.

You can substitute your favorite spirits for the rum.

Apple Pie Applause

2 c Flour
1 ts salt
3/4 c Shortening
4 tb water, cold (to 5 tbs)

----------------------------FILLING----------------------------
8 c Apples, baking; peeled,
   -thinly sliced
2 tb Juice, lemon
1 c Sugar
1/4 c Flour
1 ts Cinnamon, ground
1/4 ts salt
1/8 ts Nutmeg, ground
2 tb Butter
1 x Eggs; yolk only
1 tb water

In a bowl, combine flour and salt; cut in shortening. Gradually add cold water, 1 tablespoon at a time, tossing lightly with a fork until dough forms a ball. Chill for 30 minutes. On a floured surface, roll half of dough into a 10" circle. Place into a 9" pie pan. In a bowl, toss apples with lemon juice. Combine sugar, flour, cinnamon, salt and nutmeg; add to apples and toss. Pour into crust; dot with butter. Roll out remaining pastry to fit top of pie; cut slits in top. Place over filling; seal and flute edges. [You can also cut dough into strips and lay out a criss-cross lattice work pattern. ~JW] Beat egg yolk and water; brush over pastry. Bake at 425 degrees for 15 minutes. Reduce heat to 350 degrees, bake 40-45 minutes more or until crust is golden and filling is bubbly.

Atop The Mantel Huckleberry Cobbler

    2 lg T. lard
    2 c Flour, sifted
    1/4 ts Baking powder, sifted
    1/2 ts Salt
    1/3 c Water
    2 T   Flour
    2/3 c Sugar
          Huckleberries
          Butter

  Cream lard, 2 c. flour, baking ppowder, salt; add the 1/3 c. of water to make a soft dough. Roll and cover the bottom of a bread pan with part of the dough and sift the 2 T. of flour and 2/3 c. of sugar together over the bottom crust. Place wahed berries over this until pan iis as full as you want it; add a bit of butter and cover with a perforated crust. The pperforations should be large enough to let the juice rise upp. Cook until brown. Serve with shipped cream.

Backyard Summer Pandowdy

1 1/2	lb	Nectarines, pitted, cut -into eighths
1	pt	Fresh blueberries
1/2	c	Packed light brown sugar
1/2	ts	Ground cinnamon
		Grated rind (colored part only) from 1/2 lemon
1 1/2	ts	Fresh lemon juice
1	tb	Cold unsalted butter, cut -into slivers
		-----CRUST-----
2	c	All-purpose flour
3	tb	Granulated sugar
1	tb	Baking powder
5	tb	Cold unsalted butter, cut -into bits
3/4	c	Plus 1 tb whipping cream
1	t	Sugar

    Usually made with a rolled sweet crust baked on top of fruit, the crust is "dowdied" by pushing the crust into the fruit to soften before serving or by inverting the crust during serving to the bottom of the serving bowl. Serve this warm from the oven or at room temperature, with or without ice cream.
    1. Position a rack in the center of the oven and heat the oven to 425 degrees. Butter a deep-dish pie pan or an 8-inch-square baking dish; set aside.
    2. Gently stir together the fruit, brown sugar, cinnamon, lemon rind and juice in a large bowl. Pour the fruit into the prepared pan. Scatter the 1 tablespoon butter slivers over the fruit.
    3. For the crust, put flour, 3 tablespoons sugar and the baking powder in a large mixing bowl. Whisk to combine. Work the bits of butter into the flour mixture with a pastry blender until the mixture resembles coarse meal. Add 3/4 cup of the cream and stir with a fork.
    The mixture will be stringy. Knead with your hand about 45 seconds and it will become smooth.
    4. Roll the dough to 1/4-inch thickness. Trim it to about 1/2 inch larger than the baking dish. Cut a small circle out of the center of the crust to serve as a steam vent,

and carefully place the crust over the fruit. Do not press the crust against the sides of the pan.

Reroll the scraps and cut as decorations if you desire. Brush the crust with the remaining 1 tablespoon of cream and sprinkle with the teaspoon of sugar.

5. Place the pandowdy on a baking sheet with raised sides and bake 10 minutes. Reduce the oven temperature to 350 degrees and loosely cover the crust with a foil tent, shiny side out. Continue baking until the crust is golden and the fruit bubbly, 35 to 45 minutes. Either "dowdy" the crust now by pushing it under the surface of the fruit or serve crust side down in bowls.

Baked Grape Pie

- 2 1/2 c Grape pulp and skins
- 3/4 c Sugar
- 2 T Flour
- 3 T Melted butter
- Pastry for a 10-inch pie

Wash the ripe grapes. Separate the skins and the pulp. Cook the pulp very slowly until it is soft; rub pulp through a sieve. Combine the sieved pulp and skins; set aside. Combine sugar and flour; add to the grape mixture. Stir in butter. Pour filling into an unbaked pastry-lined 10-inch pie pan. Bake at 425F. for 25 minutes

Bakers Fried Peach Pie

```
2 1/2 c  All-purpose flour
    1 tb  Sugar
    1 tb  Baking powder
    1 ts  Salt
  1/3 c  Shortening
    1 ea  Egg; beaten
  3/4 c   Plus 1 tbsp evaporated milk
    1 ea  8 oz package dried peaches
1 1/4 c  water
  1/4 c  To 1/3 cup sugar
         Vegetable oil
```

Combine flour, sugar, baking powder, and salt; cut in shortening until mixture resembles coarse meal. Combine egg and milk; mix well, and stir into flour mixture just until moistened. Cover mixture, and chill 24 hours.

Cut peaches into quarters. Bring peaches and water to a boil; simmer, uncovered, 15 minutes, stirring occasionally. Stir in sugar.

Divide pastry into 22 to 24 portions. On a lightly floured surface, roll each portion to a 3-inch circle.

Place about 1 tablespoon peach mixture on each pastry circle. Moisten edges of circles; fold pastry in half, making sure edges are even.

Using a fork dipped in flour, press edges of pastry together to seal.

Prick pastry 2 or 3 times.

Heat 1 inch of oil to 375F. Cook pies until golden brown, turning only once. Drain well. about 2 dozen.

Barbie's Plum Pie

```
-----crust-----
2 c  Flour
1 pn Salt
1 ts Baking powder
2 tb Sugar
3/4 c  Unsalted butter
1    Egg; beaten
1    Milk
-----filling-----
2 lb Italian plums; quartered
  -and pitted
1/2 c  Sugar
1 ts Cinnamon
2 tb Flour
```

Combine the flour, salt, baking powder and sugar. Cut in the butter until it is very fine. Add the beaten egg and the milk. Work the mixture with fingers until it is smooth. Press it evenly over the bottom and sides of a 9-inch round tart pan with removable bottom.

Place the pitted plums over the crust. Sprinkle 1/4 cup of the sugar over the plums. Combine the remaining sugar with the cinnamon and flour; sprinkle it over the top. Bake at 400 for 40 minutes, or until the plums are bubbling with syrup.

Be-My-Valentine Pie

    1 c Water
    1   3-ounce package - Strawberry
      -Flavored Gelatin
    1 pt Vanilla Ice Cream (2 cups)
    1   Chocolate-flavored crumb
      -pie shell
    Milk chocolate kisses -
    -(optional)

1. In a 4-cup glass measuring cup stir together water and gelatin. Cook, uncovered, on 100% power (high) for 1 1/2 to2 minutes.

2. Add vanilla ice cream to the hot gelatin mixture, stirring till ice cream is melted. Chill mixture for 35 to 30 minutes, stirring twice during chilling (the mixture should mound when you drop it from a spoon.

3. Pour chilled ice cream mixture into pie shell. Chill about 4 hours or till ice cream is set.

4. If desired, arrange milk chocolate kisses in a heart shape atop pie.

Serves 8

Beg For More Sugar Cream Pie

INGREDIENTS
2 c Whole milk
1/4 c Cornstarch
1   Stick butter
1 c Sugar
1 ts Vanilla

Mix and stir over medium heat to boil. Cook until it looks like it will thicken. Then pour into a baked pie shell. Double recipe for 2 pies.

Berlinerkranzer

- 3/4 c Butter (or margarine),
    -softened
- 3/4 c Solid shortening
    -(e.g. Crisco)
- 1 c Sugar
- 2 t Orange peel, grated
- 2 Eggs
- 4 c Flour, all-purpose
- Red cinnamon candies
    -(optional)
- Green food coloring
    -(optional)

Heat oven to 400 degrees F. Mix thoroughly butter, shortening, sugar, orange peel and eggs. Blend in flour. Color with green food coloring, if desired.

Shape dough by rounded teaspoonfuls into ropes, each about 6 inches long and 1/4 inch in diameter.

Form each rope into a circle, bringing one end over the other and through into a single knot. Let about 1/2 inch extend at each end. Place on ungreased baking sheet. Press in red cinnamon candies, if desired.

Bake 10 to 12 minutes or until set but not brown. Immediately remove from baking sheet.

NOTES:

* Norwegian wreath cookies -- These are decorative holiday cookies adding quite a bright, colorful aromatic touch to your plate of cookies.

Berry Merry Cobbler

    1/2 c Sugar (for sprinkling)
       4 c Berries (fresh or frozen)
       1 c Sugar (for the batter)
       1 c Flour, all-purpose
1 1/2 t Baking powder
    1/2 t Salt
    1/2 c Milk
    1/4 c Butter (softened)
           Nutmeg

Preheat oven to 375 degrees F. Sprinkle about 1/2 cup of sugar on the berries and place them in the bottom of a 2-quart baking dish. Combine the remaining dry ingredients (flour, sugar, baking powder and salt).

Add the milk and softened butter and beat well. Spoon the batter over the berries. Sprinkle some nutmeg on top. Bake for about 45 minutes.

NOTES:

* You can use pretty well any type of berry for the base. A favorite of mine is a combination of strawberries, raspberries and blueberries.

* The base of this turns out to be a bit thin and liquidy. If you strain the juice from the fruit, add a couple of tablespoons of flour to the juice, and then pour the juice over the fruit in the baking dish, the base will be semi-firm.

* You do not need to sprinkle the full 1/2 cup of sugar on the berries; with sweeter berries, much less will often suffice.

* If you would like a sweeter, candy-like batter, try adding more sugar to the batter. I wouldn't recommend putting more than about 1 1/4 cups of sugar into the batter, though, the crust of the batter will be very candy-like, but the centre of the batter will not properly bake if you do.

Best Berry Fest Fried Pies

1/2 c Sugar
1 tb Cornstarch
1/2 c water
2 c Blueberries, fresh/frozen

----------------------------DOUGH--------------------------------
2 c Flour
1/4 ts Baking soda
1/4 ts salt
1/2 c Oil
1/3 c Buttermilk
Oil for frying

In a saucepan, combine sugar, cornstarch and water; add berries. Cook and stir over medium heat until the mixture comes to a boil. Cook and stir for 2 minutes; set aside to cool. Combine oil and buttermilk; stir into dry ingredients until mixture forms a ball. Roll on a floured board to 1/8" thickness; cut int 4 1/2" circles. Place 1 tablespoon blueberry filling on each circle. Fold over; seal edges with a fork. In a skillet over medium heat, fry pies in 1/4 to 1/2 inches of hot oil until golden brown, about 1 1/2 minutes per side. Drain on paper towels.

Betty's Double Pecan Pie

   3   Eggs
2/3 c Sugar; granulated
3/4 c Dark syrup
1/8 ts Salt
   3 tb Butter; melted
   2 c Pecans; chopped
   2   Pie shells, unbaked; 8"

1. Preheat oven to 400'F.

2. Beat eggs until blended, add sugar, syrup, salt, and beat thoroughly.
Stir in butter.

3. Put 1 cup of pecans in each pie shell. Pour liquid mixture equally over pecans

4. Place pies on a cookie sheet on middle rack of oven, bake for 10 minutes

Betty's Mousse Chocolate Frozen Pie

```
--------------------------------CRUST---------------------------
    2/3 c  Chocolate wafer crumbs
    1/3 c  Graham cracker crumbs
    1/4 c  Unsalted butter; melted

-----------------DARK CHOCOLATE MOUSSE-----------------
    4 oz Semi-sweet chocolate
       - finely chopped
    2 oz Unsweetened chocolate
       - finely chopped
    6    Egg yolks
    3/4 c  Sugar
    1/2 c  Frangelico liqueur
  1 1/4 c  Chilled whipping cream

------------------WHITE CHOCOLATE MOUSSE--------------
    3/4 c  Whipping cream
     10 oz White chocolate; chopped
    3 tb Frangelico liqueur
  1 1/3 c  Whipping cream; chilled
    2 oz Semisweet chocolate
       - coarsely chopped
    1 tb Unsalted butter
```

For crust: Preheat oven to 350øF. Mix all crumbs in bottom of 9-1/2-inch springform pan. Pour butter over. Mix with fork until well-blended. Press mixture firmly onto bottom of pan. Bake 8 minutes. Cool crust on rack.

For dark chocolate mousse: Stir both chocolates in double boiler over barely simmering water until smooth and melted. Cool to lukewarm. Using electric mixer, beat yolks to blend in large bowl. Gradually add sugar and beat until pale yellow and slowly dissolving ribbon forms when beaters are lifted. Blend in Frangelico, then melted chocolate. Whip cream in another bowl until soft peaks form. Fold 1/3 of cream into chocolate mixture.
  Gently fold in remaining cream. Pour mixture into crust; smooth top. Freeze until set, about 30 minutes.

For white chocolate mousse: Bring 3/4 cup cream to boil in heavy small saucepan. Reduce heat and simmer 2 minutes. Finely chop white chocolate in processor. Pour hot cream through feed tube and blend until mixture is smooth, about 1 minute. Transfer to medium bowl. Cool completely.

Stir Frangelico into white chocolate mixture. Using electric mixer, whip 1 1/3 cups cream in medium bowl until peaks form. Fold 1/3 cream into white chocolate mixture. Gently fold in remaining cream. Pour over dark chocolate mousse; smooth top. Freeze until top of mousse sets.

Cover mousse and freeze at least 24 hours. Run knife around edges of pan to loosen. Release pan sides from mousse. Smooth sides of mousse with icing spatula. Return to freezer.

Stir 2 ounces of semisweet chocolate and butter in heavy small saucepan over low heat until melted and smooth. Cool to lukewarm. Spoon into parchment cone or pastry bag fitted with small plain tip. Pipe chocolate in decorative pattern around edge of mousse. Freeze until chocolate sets.

Bingo-Blaster Freedom Fruit Cake

--------------------------------CAKE--------------------------------
- 1 c   Flour, all-purpose
- 1/2 t   Salt
- 1/4 t   Baking soda
- 1/4 t   Baking powder
- 1/2 t   Allspice
- 1/2 t   Cinnamon
- 1/2 t   Cloves
- 1/2 t   Mace
- 1/2 t   Nutmeg
- 1/2 c   Butter, melted
- 2   Eggs
- 3/4 c   Coffee (black), cold
- 1/2 c   Brown sugar
- 1 c   Raisins
- 1 c   Fruit, mixed
- 1 c   Dates
- 1/4 c   Rum or brandy

--------------------------------GLAZE--------------------------------
- 4 T   Butter
- 1/2 c   Rum or brandy
- 1/2 c   Sugar

Mix the melted butter, eggs, rum and coffee together. Add brown sugar and mix well. Add rest of dry ingredients and place in a buttered loaf pan.

Bake at 300 degrees F. for 2 hours or until done (it will separate from the sides of the pan). Make glaze when almost completely baked: Melt (do not boil) butter. Add rum and sugar. Stir by hand. Remove the cake from the oven and pour half of the glaze over it. Let it cool 25 minutes, then turn it over and pour the remaining glaze on the other side.

Blended Custard Pie

1 servings

-----in blender, com-bine-----
2 c Milk
1/2 c Flour
1/4 ts Baking powder
1 pn Salt
3 tb Unsalted butter; softened
4 lg Eggs
1/2 c Sugar
1 ts Vanilla
-----garnish-----
Coconut flakes

Blend for about a minute. Place in buttered 9 inch pie plate. Sprinkle with flaked or shredded coconut. Bake until knife inserted 1 inch from edge comes out clean (about 30 minutes)

Block Party Whoopie Pies

- 1/2 c Shortening
- 1 c Sugar
- 1 Egg
- 1 c Milk
- 1 ts Vanilla
- 2 c Flour
- 1/2 ts Salt
- 1/2 c Cocoa powder
- 1/2 ts Baking powder
- 1 1/2 ts Baking soda
- -----filling-----
- 1/2 c Shortening
- 1 c Powdered sugar
- 1 c Marshmallow fluff
- 1/2 ts Vanilla
- Few drops of milk

Cream shortening and sugar. Mix in egg, milk, and vanilla. Sift dry ingredients together and add. Drop by teaspoonful on a cookie sheet, flatten with the bottom of a glass and and bake for 8 minutes. Cool and put filling between cakes.

Makes 3 dozen pies.

Boo Boo's Banana Meringue Pie

1 1/4 c All-Purpose Flour
2 tb Granulated Sugar
6 tb Cold Unsalted Butter, diced
1 ea Egg, beaten
6 ea Ripe Bananas
1/2 c Warm Light Cream
1/2 c Granulated Sugar
1 tb Cornstarch
1 t Vanilla
4 ea Egg Whites, room temperature
1 pn Salt
1/3 c Granulated Sugar

To make pastry, combine flour, sugar and butter in a food processor.

Process until the consistency of fine meal. Add beaten egg; continue to process just until dough starts to come together. Gather into a ball, wrap and refrigerate for one hour or place in freezer for 15 minutes to chill.

Roll out dough on a floured surface or roll out between two sheets of plastic wrap to an 11-inch circle. Dough is sticky and falls apart easily; just patch together and fit into a nine-inch flan pan with removable bottom; trim edges. (If you don't have a flan pan, a pie plate can be used.) Chill for 30 minutes. Bake pastry at 375 degrees for 12 minutes until light golden in color. Thinly slice five of the bananas and arrange on bottom of pastry shell. Mash the remaining banana and combine with warm cream, 1/2 cup sugar, cornstarch and vanilla. Pour over banana layer. Bake at 350 degrees for 35 - 40 minutes or until filling is set. Let pie cool slightly. To make meringue, beat egg whites with a pinch of salt until soft peaks form. Gradually beat in 1/3 cup sugar until meringue is stiff and glossy. Spread meringue over warm pie; bake at 350 degrees for 12 – 15 minutes or until browned. Let cool; refrigerate until serving time. Serves 6.

Boo's Ready Pumpkin Light Pie

    3 tb Butter or margarine
    3/4 c Graham wafer crumbs
    1 tb Plain gelatin 1 pkg
    1/2 c Cold water
    3   Eggs, separated
    1/2 c Skim milk
1 1/4 c Canned pumpkin (or cooked)
    1/2 ts Salt
    1/4 ts Nutmeg
    3/4 ts Cinnamon
    1/2 ts Ginger
    1/2 ts Allspice
    1/2 c Granulated artificial sweet.
        OR 2 tb. liquid SugarTwin
    2 tb Sugar

Leftover pie may be frozen.

Melt butter or margarine in a 9 inch pie plate at High for 30 to 40 sec.
Add graham wafer crumbs to pie plate and combine well with a fork. Spread evenly over bottom of pie plate. Microwave at High for 3 to 5 min, watching carefully to prevent scorching. Allow to cool before filling.

Dissolve gelatin in cold water and set aside. Beat egg yolks in a 2 quart measure or mixing bowl. Stir in milk, pumpkin, salt and spices. Mix well.
Microwave at Medium Low 50% for 30 second intervals until thick and smooth, stirring after each interval. Add gelatin and sweetener. Stir until completely dissolved. Refrigerate until the thickness of unbeaten egg whites.

Beat egg whites until soft peaks form. Gradually add sugar and continue beating until stiff and shiny. Fold into pumpkin mixture, being careful to combine thoroughly. Pour into prepared pie shell. Chill overnight.

Border Ecclefechan Tarts

** British Measurements **

---------------------------THE FILLING---------------------------
- 2 oz Butter
- 3 oz Brown sugar
- 2 ts Wine vinegar
- 4 oz Mixed dried fruit
- 1 oz Walnuts; chopped
- 1 Egg

This variation of the border tart is traditionally made into small individual tarts, though it can be made into a larger tart.

Directions:

Make a shortcrust pastry, as for the Border Tart and cut 12 circles to line a patty tin, or line an 8-inch flan ring.

Melt the butter and stir in the sugar and egg. Add the vinegar, fruit and nuts and spoon into pastry cases.

Bake for 20 to 25 minutes at 375øF / 190øC / gas mark 3. Serve either hot or cold.

Bourbon Street Pie

```
1   9 inch pie shell
4   Eggs
3/4 c White sugar
1/4 c Brown sugar
1 tb Vanilla
2 tb Bourbon
3/4 c Light corn syrup
1   Butter; melted
1 tb Flour
1 c Pecans; chopped
1 c Chocolate chips
```

Beat eggs. Add next 7 ingredients to eggs.
Place pecans and ch. chips in a 9 inch pie shell.
pour filling over. Bake at 350 degrees for 40 to 45 mins.

Bourbonation Sweet Potato Pecan Pie

```
1 1/4 c  Cooked, mashed sweet 'taters
         -(about 2 medium potatoes)
  1/4 c  Brown sugar
  1/4 c  Granulated sugar
    1    Egg, lightly beaten
  1/4 c  Heavy (whipping) cream
  1/4 t  vanilla extract
         Pinch of salt
  3/4 t  Ground cinnamon
  3/4 t  Allspice
  3/4 t  Nutmeg
    3 T  Softened butter
    1    Unbaked pastry for a single
         -crust 9"-10" pie shell
         Pecan filling and Bourbon
         -sauce (ingredients below)
```

---------------------------PECAN PIE FILLING------------------

```
1 1/4 c  Sugar
1 1/4 c  Dark corn syrup
    3    Eggs, lightly beaten
    3 T  Unsalted butter, softened
  1/4 t  vanilla extract
         Pinch of salt
  3/4 t  Ground cinnamon
1 1/4 c  Chopped pecans
```

-----------------------------BOURBON SAUCE------------------

```
1 1/2 c  Heavy (whipping) cream
    1 c  Milk
    1    Package instant vanilla
         -pudding mix (4-serving
         -size
    3 T  Bourbon, brandy or rhum
    1 t  vanilla extract
```

Preheat oven to 325 Deg F. Combine mashed sweet potatoes, sugars, egg, cream, vanilla, salt, cinnamon, allspice, nutmeg and butter in an electric mixing bowl and beat at medium-low speed until smooth, do not over mix.

    To assemble pie, spoon sweet potato filling into the pastry-lined pie pan. Fill shell evenly to the top with pecan filling. Bake 1 1/2 hours or until a knife inserted into the center of the pie comes out clean. Store pie at room temperature for 24 hours. Serve pie slices with Bourbon Sauce on top or to the side.

    Prepare Pecan Pie Filling: Combine sugar, syrup, eggs, butter, vanilla, salt and cinnamon in an electric mixing bowl and beat on low speed until syrup is opaque, about 4-5 minutes. Stir in pecans, mix well.

    Prepare Bourbon Sauce: Combine cream and milk in a large mixing bowl.
    Slowly whip in pudding mix. Add bourbon and continue whipping. Add vanilla and whip until mixture is well blended to sauce consistency (should not be as firm as pudding, but should not be runny). Sauce should be made about one hour before use; it will thicken as it sits.

Bow To Queen Mary's Tart

** British Measurements **
Ingredients listed in recipe

The following recipe was introduced to me by the latter name with the story that it had been devised as a treat when Mary Queen of Scots first came to Edinburgh. It was certainly a tea time treat and because it is so easy to make, well worth a try.

Directions:

Line a greased 8 or 9 inch shallow dish, plate or flan ring with puff pastry and into the centre pour the following mixture:

2 ounces of sugar dissolved in 2 ounces of melted butter to which is added
2 ounces of chopped candied peel, 1 ounce of sultanas and 2 beaten eggs.

Bake in a hot oven, 450øF / 230øC / gas mark 8 for about 15 to 20 minutes.
Use a lower shelf. Or reduce the temperature slightly and bake for 20 to 30 minutes.

Bright Gooseberry Pie

    1 ea Unbaked Two Crust Pie Crust
    3 c   Gooseberries
  3/4 c Hot Water
1 1/2 c Granulated Sugar
    6 T   Unbleached All Purpose Flour
  1/4 t   Salt

Line a 9-inch pie plate with the lower crust and set aside. Pick over the gooseberries and then cook, with the water, for 5 to 10 minutes, or until tender. Combine the rest of the ingredients, blending well, and add to the gooseberries, mixing well. Cook, stirring constantly, until thickened.

    Remove from the heat and let cool. Preheat the oven, while the berry mixture cools, to 450 Degrees F. When the filling is cool, pour into the pie plate and add the top crust, adjusting and sealing the two crusts together. Bake in the hot oven, 450 Degrees F., for 10 minutes. Reduce the heat to 350 Degrees F. and cook for another 35 minutes or until done. Cool to room temperature before serving.

Brilliant & Easy Mince Pie

    1 pk   Mincemeat
  1/2 c   Chopped dates
1 1/2 c   Finely chopped apple
  1/2 pk Seedless raisins
1 1/2 c   Water OR juice from spiced
            Peaches

Add all and let boil over moderate heat and boil for about 15 minutes. Col and pour into a pastry lined pie plate, cover with strips of pastry or with a whole pastry top and bake for about 40 minutes in a 375-400 degree oven.
  This makes 1 large and 1 small pie.

Bring It On Honey Crunch Pecan Pie

        Filling
- 4 Eggs; slightly beaten
- 1 c Light corn syrup
- 1/4 c Packed brown sugar
- 1/4 c Sugar
- 2 tb Butter or margarine; melted
- 1 ts Vanilla
- 1/2 ts Salt

        Topping
- 1/3 c Packed brown sugar
- 3 tb Honey
- 3 tb Butter or margarine
- 1 1/2 c Pecan halves

In a medium bowl add filling ingredients and mix. Pour into crust and bake at at 350 degrees.

When pie is baking prepare topping in a medium saucepan over medium heat.
Combine sugar, honey and butter - cook 2-3 minutes until sugar dissolves, stirring constantly.

When pie has baked 40 minutes, remove from oven. Pour topping over filling and return pie to oven baking 10-15 minutes until topping is bubbly and golden brown.

Cover pie crust with foil if necessary to prevent from browning.

Broomstick Pumpkin Pie

-----filling-----
- 3/4 lb Tofu; firm
- 2 c Pumpkin,pureed; cooked
- 3/4 c Fruitsource
- 2 tb Molasses; sorghum or cane
- 1 1/2 ts Cinnamon; ground
- 3/4 ts Nutmeg; grated
- 3/4 ts Ginger; powdered
- 1/2 ts Mace
- 1/4 ts Sea salt

-----sweet crust-----
- 1/2 c Pastry flour; whole-wheat
- 1/2 c Flour; unbleached white
- 3 1/2 tb Soy margarine; cut into bits
- 1/4 ts Nutmeg; grated
- 1 ds Salt(opt)
- 3 tb Water; ice

1. Place flour, margarine, nutmeg and salt in a food processor and process
2. Form the dough into a ball and flatten into a thick dish. Flour your wor
3. Place the rolling pin in the center of the dough. Fold half over the pin
4. Preheat oven to 350'. 5. Blend ingredients for filling until smooth and creamy in a blender or fo 6. Chill and serve.

Brunch for The Bunch Egg Pie - No Crust

    4   Eggs
    2 c Milk
    1 c Sugar
    5 tb Flour
    6 sm Chunks of butter
     ds Salt
       Nutmeg
       Vanilla
       Cinnamon

Add flour and sugar together with other ingredients. Bake at 375 degrees for 45 minutes.

Butter Have It Tart Pie

3		Eggs
3/4	c	Brown sugar -- packed
3/4	c	Corn syrup
3	tb	Butter -- melted
4	ts	Flour -- all purpose
1 1/2	ts	Vanilla
1/4	ts	-salt
2 1/4	c	Currants or raisins
1		Pie shell, 9", unbaked

In bowl, beat eggs lightly. Stir in brown sugar, corn syrup, butter, flour, vanilla and salt until blended. Stir in currants or raisins. Pour in pie shell. Bake in 400F for 5 minutes. Remove heat to 250F. Bake for about 30 minutes longer or till centre is just firm to the touch, covering edges of pastry with foil if browning too much. Let cool completely before cutting.

MAKES:10 Serving

Captain Norm's Noodle Kugel

 1/4 c Butter
 8 oz Noodles, uncooked
 3   Eggs, beaten
 4 oz Cottage cheese
 2 c   Milk
 1/3 c Sugar
 1 1/2 t Vanilla extract
 12 oz Pineapple, crushed,
   -with juice
   Cornflake crumbs, to top

Melt butter in a 9x13 pan. Add noodles.

Combine remaining ingredients, except crumbs, spread evenly over noodles.
Top with crumbs. Bake at 350 degrees F. for about an hour.

NOTES:

* Noodle kugel using uncooked noodles -- This recipe is interesting because you don't cook the noodles first. Serves 6.

* This recipe is very simple, but it does taste a little pastier than recipes that require the noodles to be cooked first. It also comes out very flat -- most of the kugel recipes I've made in the past use twice as many noodles in the same size pan. I found that some of the things can be increased, i.e., add more noodles, more pineapple, more cottage cheese.

Care Pear Pie

3 tb   Cornstarch
1/8 ts Salt
2 tb   Butter Or Regular Margarine
1/2 ts Lemon Rind; Grated
4   Pears; Medium, *
1/4 ts Ginger; Ground
1/2 c Dark Corn Syrup; Karo
1 ts   Lemon Juice
1   Unbaked 9-inch Pie Shell

-----------------------ALMOND TOPPING-----------------------
1 c   Unbleached Flour
1/4 ts Ginger; Ground
1/2 c Almonds; Coarsely Chopped
1/2 c Brown Sugar; Firmly Packed
1/2 c Butter Or Regular Margarine

*   The pears should be pared and thinly sliced. There should be about 4
Combine the cornstarch, ginger and salt in a large bowl. Add the corn syrup, melted butter, lemon juice and lemon rind, stirring until smooth. Add the pears and toss until well coated with the corn syrup mixture. Arrange the mixture into the unbaked pie shell. Prepare the Almond Topping and sprinkle over the pears. Bake in a preheated 400 degree F. oven for 15 minutes, then reduce the heat to 350 degrees F. and bake an additional 30 minutes or until the topping and crust are golden brown. Cool on a wire rack. ALMOND TOPPING: Combine the flour, brown sugar, and ginger in a bowl. Cut in the butter, using a pastry blender, until crumbly. Stir in the almonds.

Care To Dance Coconut Pie

  2 c Milk
1/4 c Grated coconut
1/4 c Sugar
1/4 t Salt
  4   Egg yolks
  3 T Cornstarch
1/2 c Sugar
  1 T Butter
  1 t Vanilla
  2   Drops almond extrace
       Single crust pie shell ckd
  4   Egg whites
1/4 t Cream of tartar
1/2 c Sugar
1/4 t Salt

Mix first four ingredients in the top of a double boiler. Place over, but not touching water. Bring water to a boil. Mix egg yolks, cornstarch and remaining 1/2 c sugar together and add to custard mixture in pan. Bring to a boil and cook until thickened, stirring frequently. (This will take some time, about 15 minutes. As it begins to cook it gets lumpy, but will smooth out as it thickens.) Mix butter, vanilla and almond extract together and add to thickened custard. Pour into baked and cooled pie shell. Top with meringue: Beat egg whites until stiff. Mix salt, cream of tartar and sugar together and add a little at a time to egg whites. Beat mixture until stiff and stands in peaks. Spread over pie being sure to touch crust all around. Bake at 350 degrees until golden brown, about 20 minutes.

Celebration Confetti Pie

3 Servings

1 Graham cracker crust
4 oz Chocolate pudding & pie mix
1/4 c Chopped nuts
2 oz Dream Whip
1 c Multi color miniature Marshmallows

Mix pudding as directed; set aside. Mix Dream Whip as directed and mix with pudding. Combine nuts and marshmallows. Pour in pie shell. Sprinkle more marshmallows on top. Chill and serve.

Celebrity Waffle Cone

    3   Eggs
  3/4 c Sugar, granulated
  1/2 c Butter, melted
    2 t Vanilla
1 1/2 c Flour
    2 t Baking powder

Beat the eggs and gradually beat in the sugar until the mixture is creamy.
Stir in the melted butter and vanilla.

Combine the flour and baking powder, and then add it to the mixture. Blend it in well.

Drop about 4 t of the batter into a heated pizelle iron, and cook both sides over medium-high heat for about 1 minute each, or until golden brown.

Remove the waffle from the pizelle iron and immediately shape it into a cone while it is still pliable.

  * A pizelle iron looks like a round waffle iron. There are "manual" irons and electric ones too. If you don't have a pizelle iron, another idea is to use an ordinary waffle iron and have ice-cream on top of the waffle. Not having either a waffle iron or a pizelle iron, we tried making these on an electric griddle, but since the batter is fairly thick it wouldn't spread into a large enough circle to make cones from.

  * When you form the cones, there will probably be a small hole in the bottom of them that ice-cream can drip out of. One idea for plugging this hole is to put miniature marshmallows in the bottoms of the cones.

Cheesy Apricot Jam Pastries

  2 1/2 c Flour
    1/4 ts Salt
     1 c   Unsalted butter
    1/2 c Sugar
     1 ts Vanilla
     2 tb Milk
     8 oz Cream cheese; softened
           Apricot jam

Mix flour and salt. Cut in butter. Cream sugar, vanilla, milk and cream cheese. Add flour mixture. Chill. Roll out 1/8 inch thick, cut into circles. Place 1 teaspoon jam in center, cover with another circle. Press edges together with a fork. Place on greased cookie sheets and bake in a preheated 400 degree oven 10-12 minutes. Makes 24.

Cherida's Basic Graham Cracker Pie Crust

1 servings

1 pk Graham crackers; crushed
-(about 11)
2 tb Sugar
6 tb Unsalted butter; melted
Cinnamon
Nutmeg

Bake at 350 for 8 minutes.

Cherida's Basic Graham Cracker Pie Shell

7 lg Plain graham wafers; (each
 -2 1/2" X 5")
3 tb Margarine; melted

Break graham wafers into small pieces, place in a plastic bag, fasten opening with a bag tie, and press with a rolling pin or a large jar to make crumbs. Continue until all crumbs are fine (total of 1 1/4 cups). Empty into bowl. Melt the margarine, add to crumbs, and mix well with a fork. Set aside 2 tb to use later as the garnish on the pie filling. Using the back of a spoon, press remainder of crumb mixture evenly on bottom and sides of a 9" pie plate. Chill in refrigerator for 3 hours or longer before filling.

Chocolate Bite Brownie Pie

4		Eggs
1/4	c	Margarine or butter -- melted
4	oz	Chocolate -- cooking
		-melted & cooled
1/2	c	Brown sugar -- packed
1/2	c	Bisquick or baking mix
1/2	c	Sugar -- granulated
3/4	c	Nuts -- chopped

Preheat oven to 350F. grease pie plate 9x1 1/4". Beat eggs, margarine and chocolate till smooth, 10 seconds in blender on high or 30 seconds with hand beater. Add brown sugar, Bisquick and granulated sugar. Beat till smooth, 1 minute in blender on high (stopping occasionally to scrape down sides) or 2 minutes with hand beater. Pour into plate; sprinkle with nuts. Bake till knife inserted in centre comes out clean; about 35 minutes. Cool.

Chocolate Chip Nut Pie (Kentucky Derby Pie)

-VERSION #1:
1 c Softened butter
1/2 c Brown sugar
1/2 c Sugar
1/2 c Flour
2   Eggs
1 c Chopped black walnuts
1 c Chocolate chips

-VERSION #2:
3/4   Stick softened butter
3/4 c White sugar
3/4 c White corn syrup
1 ts Vanilla flavoring
3   Eggs
3/4 c Chopped pecans
1/2 c Chocolate chips

-VERSION #3:
1   Stick butter, softened
1 c Sugar
1/2 c Self-rising flour
2   Eggs
1 ts Vanilla flavor
1 c Chopped pecans
1 c Chocolate chips

Cream butter and sugar together. Add flour. Separately beat eggs until foamy then beat into mixture until foamy. Fold in syrup and vanilla. Fold in nuts and chocolate chips. Pour into 9" deep dish unbaked pie shell. Bake at 325F for 1 hour. Bake at 350F for 45 min - 1 hour.

Chocolate Chocolate Pie

- 1 9" baked pie crust, or crumb Crust.
- 1 Envelope unflavored gelatin
- 1 2/3 c Milk, divided
- 2/3 c Sugar
- 1/3 c Hershey's cocoa
- 2 T Butter or margarine
- 3/4 ts Vanilla
- 1/2 c Chilled whipping cream

In medium saucepan sprinkle gelatin over 1 c. milk; allow to stand 2 minutes to soften. Stir together sugar and cocoa; add to mixture in saucepan. Cook over low heat, stirring constantly until mixture boils.

Remove from heat; add butter, stirring until melted. Blend in remaining 2/3 c. milk and vanilla. Cool; chill, stirring occasionally, until mixture begins to set. Beat whipping cream until stiff; carefully fold into chocolate mixture.

Garnish as desired.

Chocolate Effortless Crumb Pie Shell

1 1/2 c Chocolate cookie crumbs
 1 tb Granulated sugar
 1/4 c Butter; softened

Mix ingredients until thoroughly blended. Press into a 9" pie pan. Bake @ 375

Cinnamon Ginger Cookies

- 3/4 c Butter
- 1 c Sugar
- 1/4 c Dark molasses
- 1 Egg
- 2 c Flour
- 2 t Baking soda
- 1 t Ginger, ground
- 1 t Cinnamon, ground
- 1 t Cloves, ground

Cream the butter and sugar together. Add the egg (beaten) and the molasses.

Sift the rest of the dry ingredients together and add to the mixture. Form into about 1-inch balls and roll in granulated sugar. Place about 2 inches apart on a greased cookie sheet and bake at 350 degrees F. for 10 to 12 minutes.

Cinnamon Halvas Politikos

- 1 c Olive oil
- 2 c Semolina
- 3 c Sugar
- 4 c Water
-       Cinnamon, powdered

Dissolve the sugar in the water and bring it to a boil. At the same time, brown the semolina in the oil on high heat, stirring continuously.

When the semolina has taken a golden brown colour, add the syrup into it (taking care not to burn your hands), turn down the heat and keep stirring until you get a kind of thick porridge. Pour into any kind of mold you can think of (a cake-mold is perfect for the job), and let it cool.

Unmold into a platter and sprinkle with cinnamon. Slice it using a wet knife, serve, and watch your weight go sky high!

Cinnamon Savor Zwetschgendatschi

- 1/4 lb Butter
- 1/3 c Sugar
- 1/2 t Vanilla (or use
    - vanilla sugar)
- 1 Egg
- 1 T Sour cream
- 1 pn Salt (only if you
    - use unsalted butter)
- 1 t Lemon peel
- 1 3/4 c Flour
- 1 t Baking powder
- 2 c Italian plums

-------------OPTIONAL STREUSEL TOPPING----------------
- 6 T Butter
- 3/4 c Flour
- 1/3 c Sugar
- 1/2 t Cinnamon

In a large bowl, cream the butter, add the sugar (and vanilla), add the egg, (salt,) lemon peel and sour cream. Mix the flour and baking powder and add that.

Pit the plums, splitting them into halves or thirds. Grease the pan and spread the dough. Liberally spread plums over the dough, meat side up. If the plums are sour (as opposed to just tart), sprinkle them lightly with sugar.

To make the optional Streusel topping, cream the butter, add flour, sugar and cinnamon. Sprinkle over the plums. Bake for 30-45 minutes in the middle rack at 375 degrees F. Be careful not to let the bottom burn!

Serve liberally topped with freshly-made whipping cream.

NOTES:

* A Bavarian plum delicacy for dessert -- My mother

and grandmother make this Bavarian specialty without a recipe; this recipe is from my mother, after I pressed her to write it down so I could make my own. It also includes variations from a few other folks that you might like to try.

Roughly translated from Bavarian to German, this is Pflaumenkuchen, which, roughly translated from German to to English is Plum cake. However, Zwetschgen aren't ordinary plums, a Datschi isn't really a Kuchen, and a Kuchen is most definitely NOT a cake!

This dessert is made of the slightly tart Italian plums, which are unfortunately only available at certain times of the year. Don't try to make it with ordinary plums; they're too sweet and too juicy. Fills one round cake pan.

Classic Boston Cream Pie

       Cake layers
1/4 c Butter; softened
  1 c Sugar
  3 lg Eggs
2/3 c Milk
  1 ts Vanilla
1 3/4 c All-purpose flour
  2 ts Baking powder
      Custard
2/3 c Sugar
1/3 c Cornstarch
1/4 ts Salt
2 1/2 c Milk
  4 lg Egg yolks; lightly beaten
      Glaze
3 oz Chocolate
1 tb Butter
1/3 c Confectioner's sugar
1/4 c Milk

PREPARE CAKE LAYERS: Heat oven to 350 degrees. Grease and flour two 9" round cake pans. In large bowl with electric mixer at medium speed, beat 1/4 cup butter, 1 cup sugar, eggs, 2/3 cup milk, 1 tsp. vanilla and baking powder about 4 minutes until thoroughly blended and smooth. Spoon batter into prepared pans; bake 30 minutes until wooden pick inserted in center of each layer comes out clean. Remove layers to wire racks to cool completely.

PREPARE EGG CUSTARD: In 2 qt. saucepan, stir 2/3 cup sugar, cornstarch and salt until thoroughly mixed; slowly stir in 2 1/2 cups milk until smooth. Bring to boil over medium heat, stirring constantly; cook 1 minute until mixture boils rapidly and thickens. Remove from heat; very slowly pour lightly beaten egg yolks into hot mixture, stirring rapidly and constantly to blend and keep smooth. Return mixture to low heat; cook 1 minute longer. Do not allow to boil. Remove from heat; stir in 1 tbsp. vanilla. Cool completely, stirring frequently.

PREPARE CHOCOLATE GLAZE: In small heavy

saucepan over very low heat, melt chocolate and 1 tbsp. butter,stirring frequently until blended and smooth. Remove from heat;stir in confectioners sugar and ¼ cup milk until blended and smooth. Keep warm,covered. To assemble: Using sharp serrated knife,carefully cut cooled layers in half horizontally. Place one layer,cut side up,on serving platter; spread with 1/3 cooled custard. Repeat with remaining cake layers and custard, ending with cake layer, cut side down. Spoon warm glaze over top of cake, letting mixture drip down sides.

Makes 12 to 16 servings.

Clear Cloud Pie

----------------------------------CRUST----------------------------
- 2 c Vanilla wafer crumbs
  - (about 50 wafers)
- 5 tb Butter or margarine; melted

---------------------------------FILLING---------------------------
- 2 pt Fresh strawberries
- 8 oz Pkg light cream cheese;
  - softened
- 1 cn Sweetened condensed milk
  -(14 oz can)
- 1/2 c Fresh lime juice (about
  - 6 to 8 limes)
- 1 tb Green creme de menthe
  - liqueur

--------------------DECORATIVE TOPPING-------------------
-
- 1 c Whipping cream
- 3 tb Sugar
- 1/2 ts Vanilla
  - Lime slice; for garnish

Combine crumbs and butter in a small bowl. Press firmly on bottom and up side of a 9 inch pie plate. Refrigerate until firm.

Reserving 3 strawberries for garnish, cut off stem ends of remaining berries so they are no more than 1 inch tall. Arrange, cut ends down, on crust, refrigerate. Beat cream cheese until smooth. Add sweetened condensed milk; beat well. Add lime juice and liquer; blend well. Pour into prepared crust, covering strawberries. Refrigerate at least one hour.

Whip cream until soft peaks form. Gradually add sugar and vanilla and whip until stiff and glossy. Using a pastry bag with a decorating tip, pipe a lattice design on top of the pie. Garnish with the reserved strawberries and lime slice.

Coconut Pie At Ease

- 2 c Milk
- 3/4 c Sugar
- 1/2 c Bisquick
- 4 Eggs
- 1/4 c Butter
- 1/2 ts Vanilla
- 1 c Coconut

Combine everything but coconut in blender on low for 3 minutes. Pour into pie plate, let sit for 5 min. Top with coconut. Bake at 350 for 40 minutes.

Coconut Pie For Everyone

- 1 1/2 c Sugar
- 2   Eggs
- 1/2 ts Salt
- 1/2 c Margarine; softened
- 1/4 c Flour
- 1/2 c Milk
- 1 1/2 c Grated coconut

Beat together sugar, eggs, and salt until lemon colored.

Add margarine and flour and blend well. Beat in milk then fold in 1 cup of coconut. Pour filling into 9" unbaked pie shell.

Top with remaining coconut. Bake in 325 degree oven for 1 hour.

Coconut Smurk Pie

    1 c Coconut
    2 c Milk
    4   Eggs
 1/4 c Butter or margerine
 1/2 c Biscuit mix
    1 c Sugar
1 1/2 ts Vanilla

Sprinkle coconut into the bottom of a 9 inch pie plate. Combine remaining ingredients in a blender and blend until smooth. Pour over coconut and bake at 350 for about 45 to 55 minutes or until a knife come out clean

Conquering Chocolate Cream Pie

    1 c Milk
  1/4 c Margarine, softened
    1 ts Vanilla
    2   Eggs
    2 oz Melted unsweetened chocolate
       Cooled.
    1 c Sugar
  1/2 c Bisquick mix

Heat oven to 350 F. Grease pie plate, 9 x 1 1/4". Place all ingredients in blender container. Cover and blend on high 1 minute. Pour into plate.

Bake until no indention remains when lightly touched in center, about 30 minutes. Cool completely. Top with sweetened whipped cream if desired.

County Fair Cream Puffs

```
-----pastry-----
  1 c  Water
1/2 c  Unsalted butter
  1 c  Flour
  4    Eggs; at room temperature
-----cream filling-----
  2 c  Milk
3/4 c  Sugar
1/2 ts Salt
  3 tb Cornstarch
  3    Egg yolks
  1 ts Vanilla
```

Boil water and butter. Stir in the flour all at once and stir by hand until mixture forms a ball and doesn't stick to the sides of the pot.

Remove pot from the heat. Add the eggs, one at a time, beating well after each addition (this part may be done in the food processor). Drop from a spoon onto an ungreased cookie sheet and bake for 40 minutes. Slice in half, remove part of center, and fill with cream filling.

Cook all but the vanilla until thick, over medium heat. Add vanilla when the mixture has cooled.

Cozy Christmas Pie

3 Servings

1/2 c Sugar
1 3/4 c Milk
1/2 c Sugar
1/4 c Flour
3/4 ts Vanilla
1/2 c Whipping cream, whipped
1   Envelope unflavored gelatin
3   Egg whites
1 c Moist shredded coconut
1/2 ts Salt
1/4 ts Cream of tartar

Blend 1/2 cup sugar, flour, gelatin and salt thoroughly in a saucepan, gradually stir in the milk. Cook over medium heat until the mixture boils, boil for 1 minute. Place the pan in cold water, cool until the mixture mounds slightly when dropped from a spoon. Blend in flavoring. Carefully fold into meringue made of egg whites and 1/2 cup of sugar and cream of tartar, gently fold into whipped cream. Fold in moist coconut. Chill until set. Serve cold. Tastes great topped with crushed strawberries.

Crowd Pleasing Pecan Tarts

----------------------------------PASTRY---------------------------

-
- 6 oz Cream cheese
- 1/2 lb Butter (or margarine)
- 2 c Flour, all-purpose

---------------------------------FILLING----------------------------
- 3 c Brown sugar
- 2 t Vanilla
- 1 c Pecans, chopped
- 4   Eggs, beaten
- 4 T Butter (or margarine),
   -melted

Allow the butter and cream cheese to soften. Mix cream cheese and butter with a mixer until fluffy. Then (using your hands) mix in the flour.

Separate mixture into four equal parts and flatten each into a rectangular shape. Allow the pastry to chill for several hours.

Preheat oven to 350 degrees F. Prepare filling by mixing all ingredients gently. Use a spoon, not a mixer. Refrigerate until muffin tins are ready to fill.

Take one unit of the chilled pastry and cut into 12 equal pieces. Roll each piece into a ball and then form the ball into the muffin tin in the shape of a crust. Fill each tart about 3/4 full. Bake at 350 degrees F. for 20 to 30 minutes.

Bake these until slightly brown. To remove tarts, just turn the tin upside down onto paper towels and then turn the tart right side up on a baking rack to cool.

Crumbs A Top Rhubarb Custard Pie

```
   1 ea  9" pie shell,unbaked
 1 1/2 c  Sugar
    1 x  Dash of salt
  1/2 t  Vanilla
  1/2 c  Flour
  1/4 c  Butter or margarine
 4 1/2 c  Rhubarb, 1/2" pieces
  1/4 c  Flour
   2 ea  Eggs
    1 x  -------------t--------------
  1/2 c  Sugar
```

Prick pastry shell with fork. Bake @ 450 degrees for 5 minutes. Cool. Combine rhubarb with sugar, flour and salt. Let stand 15 minutes. Beat eggs slightly. Add vanilla. Stir egg mixture into rhubarb. Turn into pastry shell. For Topping; stir together flour and sugar. Cut in butter until it resembles coarse crumbs. Sprinkle over pie. Bake in 425 degree oven for 15 minutes, then reduce heat to 350 degrees. Bake for 30 minutes more. Cool completely before serving. Store pie in refrigerator.

Crunch Crunch Coconut Crunch

3 Servings

```
  4   Egg whites
1 c   Sugar
1/2 c Coconut
1/2 c Chopped nuts
  1 c Vanilla wafer crumbs
 1 ts Vanilla
```

  Beat egg whites with a dash of salt, add sugar - beat as if you were making meringue. Stir in coconut, nuts, vanilla wafer crumbs and vanilla. Pour in buttered pie pan and bake at 350 degrees for 45 minutes. Top with whip cream and add sliced bananas on top!

Crust Basics 101:

1 1/4 c Flour
        Pinch of salt
  3 T Butter
  3 T Shortening
  3 To 4 Tb. cold water

Sift the flour and salt together into a bowl. But the butter and shortening into the flour with a pastry blender or two knives until the mixture resembles course meal. Add three Tb. water and mix with a fork and then with your fingertips until the dough can be gathered into a ball.

If the dough is very crumbly, sprinkle a few drops of water over the dough, adding only enough to make the dough stick together. Wrap the dough in wax paper and chill in the refrigerator one hour before rolling out.

ROLLING AND PRE-BAKING : Roll the dough out on a floured board and fit it into a nine to ten inch quiche tin or nine inch pie plate. Cover the pastry with a sheet of aluminum foil, pressing it firmly around the sides and over the edges of the pastry. Fill with uncooked rice or dry beans and bake in a preheated 400 degree oven for 7 minutes. Carefully remove the rice or beans and aluminum foil. Prick the bottom of the crust with a fork and continue baking 5 minutes more. The crust should not brown but should be only partially baked unless otherwise directed in a specific recipe. Let the pastry cool before filling and baking the quiche or pie.

Crust Basics 102:

    2   3-oz. pks. Philadelphia
         Cream cheese
1/4 c Softened butter
  2 T Heavy cream
1 1/4 c Flour
1/4 ts Salt

    Beat the cream cheese and butter together in an electric mixer or by hand until smooth and creamy. Add the cream and beat one to two minutes.
  Gradually add the flour and salt and combine thoroughly. Form the dough into a ball and wrap in wax paper. Chill at least one hour before rolling out.

    ROLLING AND PRE-BAKING: It is easiest to roll this dough between two sheets of wax paper. Place a large sheet of wax paper on a board and place the ball of dough on top. Flatten it slightly and place another sheet of wax paper on top of the dough. Roll the dough as you would for Basic Crust 101, lifting the wax paper from time to time to keep it smooth.
  Fit the pastry into your quiche or pie pan and pre-bake as directed for Basic Crust I

Crust Basics 103:

1 1/4 c Sifted all-purpose flour
1/4 ts Salt
1/2 c   Grated parmesan cheese
4 T   Butter
4   To 5 T. cold water

    Place the flour, salt and parmesan cheese in a bowl. Cut the butter into the flour mixture with a pastry blender or two knives until the mixture resembles course meal. Add 4 T. water and stir with a fork, gathering the dough into a ball with your fingertips. Add a few more drops of water if necessary to make the dough stick together. Wrap the dough in wax paper and chill one hour. Roll out and partially bake as directed for Basic Crust 101.

Crust Basics 104:

- 1 1/2 c Flour
- 1/4 ts Salt
- 3 T   Sugar
- 1/2 c Butter
- 1   Egg
- 2   To 3 T. cold water

Place the flour, salt and sugar in a bowl. Cut the butter into the flour, using a pastry blender or two knives, until the mixture resembles coarse meal. Beat the egg lightly with 2 T. water. Add the egg to the flour mixture and stir with a fork, gathering the dough into a ball with your fingertips. Add water, a few drops at a time, if necessary to make the dough stick together. Wrap the dough in wax paper and chill one hour.

Roll out as directed in Basic Crust 101. Bake in the same way but extend the baking time by about 8 minutes for a fully baked crust. In most cases, you will use this crust with an unbaked filling so it should be crisp and golden brown.

This crust is used for open fruit tarts or dessert pies.

Crystals' Creamy Honey Pie

1 Pie

```
  3    Eggs, separated
1/3 c  Honey
  2 T  Flour
1/2 ts Cinnamon
  1 c  Sour cream
```

Beat egg yolks, add honey and beat again. Add flour and cinnamon. Mix well. Add sour cream. Raisins may be added. Cook in double boiler until thick. Pour into baked pie shell. May be topped with Honey Meringue or Honey Whipped Cream.

Crème de Menthe Ice Cream Pie

3-1/4 cups miniature marshmallows
2 tablespoons milk
1/4 cup green creme de menthe
2 tablespoons white creme de cacao
1 cup whipping cream, whipped
1 pint vanilla ice cream, softened
1 (9-inch) chocolate wafer crust
Additional whipped cream for garnish

Combine marshmallows and milk in top of double boiler; bring water to a boil. Reduce heat to low; cook until marshmallows melt, stirring frequently. Remove from heat; coo, stirring occasionally. Add creme de menthe and creme de cacao; fold in whipped cream.

Spread ice cream evenly in piecrust, and pour marshmallow mixture over ice cream. Freeze at least 6 hours. Garnish with additional whipped cream.

Crème Of The Crop Apricot Tart

```
    8    Leaves phyllo
    1 c  Dried apricots
  1/2 c  Honey
    2 c  Water
  1/2 ts Agar-agar powder
    8 oz Tofu
  1/2 ts Vanilla
    2 tb Lemon juice
   16 oz Can apricot halves
  1/4 c  Apricot jam
    1 oz Melted chocolate, optional
```

Preheat oven to 350F. Spray a 9" pie tin with non-stick spray. Place in a leaf of phyllo pastry & spray it. Fold edges inwards so they don't extend beyond the rim of the pan. Repeat the procedure till the pan is covered.
Bake for 15 to 20 minutes till crispy brown.

Place dried apricots, honey & water in a saucepan & simmer gently till apricots are soft & liquid is a heavy syrup. Dissolve agar-agar powder in 2 tb water & add to mixture, simmering for a couple of minutes. Transfer to a processor. Add tofu, vanilla & lemon juice & process till smooth. Pour into the crust.

Drain canned apricot halves & arrange on the pie. Melt jam & brush on top of tart. If desired, melt chocolate & drizzle over the top in a zig zag fashion. Chill 1 hour at least before serving.

Custom Baked Crumb Crust

1 Pie crust

---------------GRAHAM CRACKERS (ABOUT 16-------------
- 1/3 c Margarine;
- 1/3 c Butter
- 1 1/3 c Graham crackers Crumbs;
- 1/4 c Sugar;

----------------VANILLA WAFERS(ABOUT 24- 2"--------------
- 1/4 c Margarine; -=OR=-
- 1/4 c Butter
- 1 1/3 c Vanilla wafers Crumbs;

--------------CHOCOLATE WAFERS 18 -2-1/4"---------------
- 1/3 c Margarine; -=OR=-
- 1/3 c Butter
- 1 1/3 c Chocolate wafers Crumbs;

----------------GINGERSNAPS (ABOUT 20 -2"----------------
- 1/3 c Margarine; -=OR=-
- 1/3 c Butter
- 1 1/3 c Gingersnaps crumbs;

----------------------------ZWIEBACK----------------------------
- 6 tb Margarine; -=OR=-
- 6 tb Butter
- 1 1/3 c Zwieback crumbs;
- 1/4 c Sugar;

------------CEREAL FLAKES (ABOUT 4 CUPS--------------
- 1/2 c Margarine;
- 1/2 c Butter
- 1 1/3 c Corn Cereal flakes; -=OR=-
- 1 1/3 c Wheat cereal flakes;
- 1/4 c Sugar;

Let butter or margarine soften. Place a long length of waxed paper on pastry board; stack crackers, or pour cereal, down center. Make double fold in paper; tuck ends under. Gently roll fine with rolling pin. In a 2 cup measuring cup, mix 1-1/3 cups of crumbs, sugar, and butter with fork until crumbly. Set aside 3 tablespoons (optional). With the back of spoon, press rest to bottom and sides of 9" pie plate, forming small rim. Bake at 375 F. for 8 minutes. Cool; fill; top with reserved crumbs.

Dance To Pavlova I

    4   Egg whites
        -(at room temperature)
    1 c Sugar, castor
    1 T Vinegar
        Cornflour

With an electric mixer, beat the egg whites until soft peaks form, then gradually add the sugar (about 1 t every 30 seconds). This will take around 15 minutes. Beat until firm. Add the vinegar. When combined, turn out onto a flat baking sheet that has been greased and dusted with cornflour. Shape it so that there will be a hollow in the centre to hold the fruit.

Cook in a pre-heated, warm oven (350-375 degrees F.) for 10 minutes, then at 200-250 degrees F. for 40-50 mins.

When cooked, turn the oven off and allow to cool slowly in the oven for at least an hour, preferably overnight. Gradual cooling is important. Serve cold, topped with whipped cream and fresh fruit such as strawberries, bananas and kiwi fruit.

Daydream Walnut Horns

    2 c Flour
    1 c Butter
    8 oz Sour cream
    1   Egg yolk
    1 c Brown sugar
    1 c Walnuts, ground
  1/2 t Cinnamon, ground
       Butter

Cream the flour and butter. Mix in the sour cream and the egg yolk.

Divide the dough into four parts, wrap in plastic wrap, and chill for several hours.

Mix together the brown sugar, walnuts and cinnamon.

Roll each dough section on a floured surface until about 1/8 inch thick.
Spread about 1/4 of the sugar/walnut/cinnamon mixture over each rolled dough section. Cut the dough into pie-shaped wedges and roll, beginning at the wide end.

Place cookies on an ungreased cookie sheet. Brush with melted butter (about 2 T should be enough). Bake for about 20 minutes at 375 degrees F.
If you remove the cookies from the oven before they turn brown, the dough will be softer and flakier. If you remove them after they have browned slightly, the dough will be crisper.

Remove cookies from cookie sheet before they have cooled completely, or else they stick to the cookie sheet.

Delicious Buttermilk Pie

---------------------------------CRUST----------------------------
- 3 c Flour, all-purpose
- 1 ts Salt
- 1 1/4 c Shortening
- 1   Egg; well beaten
- 1 tb Vinegar
- 5 tb Water

----------------------------BUTTERMILK FILLING---------------
- 6   Eggs
- 3 c Sugar
- 1 c Margarine; (2 sticks)
- 2 ts Vanilla extract
- 1 c Buttermilk

Crust: Cut flour, salt, and shortening together. Combine egg, vinegar, and water and add to first 3 ingredients. Divide into 4 parts and roll out on floured board. They will keep in the refrigerator 4 weeks and can be rerolled. 4 single crusts.

Filling: Mix eggs, sugar, and margarine until light. Add vanilla and buttermilk. Pour into 2 unbaked pie shells. Bake at 350 degrees for 10 minutes. Reduce heat to 325 degrees and bake for 30 more minutes or until firm in the middle. 2-9" pies.

Delicious Kolache Slovakian Pastry

    1   Pkg yeast
1 1/2 c Milk, scalded and cooled
       -to 80F
  1/2 c Sugar
1 1/4 ts Salt
    2   Eggs
  7 c Flour
  1/2 ts Mace
      Grated rind of 1 lemon
  3/4 c Shortening

1. Crumple yeast into bowl
2. Add milk which has been scalded and cooled to 80F
3. Add sugar and salt. Stir to dissolve.
4. Beat the eggs well. Add the beaten eggs.
5. Sift flour once before measuring. Spool lightly into cup to measure.
6. Add the mace and lemon rind to the flour, then add all the flour to the liquid, at once, working it in thoroughly with your hands.
7. Work in the softened shortening.
8. When the dough is well mixed, knead gently in bowl or on lightly floured board until smooth.
9. Round up and set to rise in a well greased bowl. Cover bowl and keep dough at 80-85F until doubled in bulk, about 2 hours.
10. Remove dough from bowl and round up on a lightly floured board. Cover and allow to loosen up for 15 minutes.
11. Shape into desired shapes. (I.e. roll out, wrap the fillings in the dough, etc.)
12. Let the kolache rise again until not quite doubled in bulk, about 30-40 minutes.
13. Brush top with solution of 1 egg yolk slightly beaten and diluted with 1/2 cold water.
14. Bake 20-25 minutes in 400F oven.
15. When done baking, rub the crust with butter.

Delightful Carrot Cake

```
    4   Eggs, separated
1 1/2 c Sugar
    1 c Carrots, grated
    1 c Walnuts, finely grated
1 1/2 c Flour
    1 t Baking powder
  1/4 t Nutmeg
  1/2 t Cinnamon
    1 t Vanilla extract
    1 pn Salt
    1 c Oil
2 1/2 t Water, hot
  1/2 t Baking soda
```

---------------------------------FILLING---------------------------

```
    8 oz Cream cheese
  1/2 c Sugar
  1/2 c Jam (strawberry,
        -apricot or raspberry)
```

---------------------------------FROSTING--------------------------

```
    1 c Whipping cream
    2 T Sugar
```

Preheat oven to 350 degrees F. Cream together egg yolks and about 1 cup of the sugar until the yolk color lightens. Stir in carrots, nuts, flour, baking powder, nutmeg, cinnamon, vanilla, salt and oil. Mix together hot water and soda and stir into flour mixture.

Beat egg whites until foamy. Gradually add remaining sugar. Beat until stiff and glossy. Fold egg white mixture into flour mixture.

Turn mixture into a greased pan, 13 x 9-inch, lined with greased wax paper and bake for 45 minutes or until done. Cool. Slice in half horizontally, to form two layers.

Make the cream cheese filling: soften the cream cheese and beat in the sugar, mixing gradually, until the filling is smooth and fluffy. A food processor works well for this.

Cover bottom layer with cream cheese filling, then cover cream cheese layer with jam. Place the top layer of the cake carefully on top of the jam.

Make the frosting: beat the whipping cream until slightly stiff, then add the sugar and beat the mixture to stiff peaks. Frost the entire cake with whipped cream.

Diabetic Cherry Moon Pie

    9" unbaked pie shell
  2 c Unsweetened cherries
 1/4 c Soft margarine
  1 tb Flour
 1/2 c Sugar replacement
  2 x Egg yolks
 1/4 c Evaporated milk
 1/2 ts Vanilla extract
  2 x Egg whites
  2 ts Granulated sugar replacement

Drain cherries; pout into unbaked pie shell. Cream margarine, flour, and sugar replacement. Add egg yolks and beat until smooth. Add evaporated milk and vanilla extract. Pour over cherries. Bake at 450F for 10 minutes. Reduce heat. Bake at 350F for 30 minutes.

Whip egg whites until soft peaks form. Add granulated sugar replacement; whip until thick and stiff. Top pie filling with meringue, carefully sealing edges. Bake at 350F for 12-15 minutes, or until delicately brown.

Diabetic Easy Popovers

   1 c Flour
1/2 ts Salt
   2   Eggs
   1 c Skim milk

Sift flour and salt together; set aside. Beat eggs and skim milk; add to flour. Beat until smooth and creamy. Pour into heated greased muffin tins, filling half full or less. Bake at 375F for 50 minutes, or until popovers are golden brown and sound hollow. DO NOT OPEN OVEN FOR FIRST 40 MINUTES.

Diabetic-Crumb Pie Shell

1 1/4 c   Fine crumbs(graham cracker,
1 1/2 c   or Dry cereal,zwieback,etc
  3 tb   Margarine (melted)
  1 tb   Water
  1   Spices (optional)
  1   Sugar replacement (optional)

Combine crumbs with melted margarine and water; add spices and sugar replacement, if desired. Spread dough evenly in 8-10 inch pie pan, pressing firmly onto sides and bottom. Either chill until set, or bake at 325F for 8-10 minutes.

Double Chocolate Brandy Pie

   1   10-inch pie shell; baked & cooled
 2 1/2   Sticks butter softened to room temp (about 2/3 lb)
 1 3/4 c Confectioners' sugar; sifted
 1 1/4 c Cocoa powder; sifted
   2 ts Vanilla
   7   Eggs;beaten
       Whipped cream or Chocolate Brandy Cream (see recipe)

In the bowl of an electric mixer, cream together the softened butter and the confectioners sugar until smooth. On low speed, add the sifted cocoa and beat until smooth, scraping the bottom and sides of the bowl often to ensure even mixing. Blend in the vanilla and then add the eggs a few at a time, scraping down the bottom and sides of the bowl carefully after each addition. Beat until smooth. Pour pie filling into backed and cooled pie shell and chill 2 to 4 hours before serving. Top with whipped cream or Chocolate Brandy Cream.

Double Chocolate Kiss Pie

    110 g Butter
      60 g Unsweetened chocolate
    200 g Sugar
        3 Eggs; lightly beaten
    60 ml Creme de cacao liqueur
      15 g All-purpose flour
7 1/2 ml Vanilla extract
  1/2 ml Salt

1. Baked pie shell Vanilla ice cream or sweetened whipped cre Preheat oven to 175 øC. In a medium saucepan over low heat melt butter

2. Blend in sugar, eggs, liqueur, flour, vanilla and salt. Beat until smooth.

3. Pour into the pie shell. Bake for 30 to 35 minutes or until set. Cool

4. Serve with ice cream or whipped cream.

Double Trouble Berry Pie

- 1/3 c Flour
- 1 c Sugar
- 3 c Blueberries
- 1/2 pt Fresh raspberries
- 2 tb Chambord or other raspberry Liqueur
- 1 ts Grated lemon peel
- 2 ts Lemon juice
- 1 tb Unsalted butter, optional
- Pastry for 9" deep dish Pie*
- Milk, for brushing
- Sugar, for sprinkling

Preheat oven to 425F.

Combine flour and sugar. Add berries, liqueur, lemon peel and juice and toss gently. Pile in pie plate.

Top with dough, sealing edges and crimping. Brush with milk and sprinkle with sugar. Cut several steam vents.

Bake 20 minutes; reduce heat to 350F and continue baking until crust is golden brown and juices bubble up, 30 to 40 minutes longer.

Dried My Apricot Pie

   1 pk (6 oz.) dried apricots
   1 c Water
   1 T Gelatine
 1/4 c Cold water
    3 Egg yolks
   1 c Brown sugar
1/4 ts Salt
   1 T Lemon juice
    3 Egg whites
   2 T Sugar
   1 c Whipping cream
   1 Baked pie crust (8 or 9")

Cook apricots in water until pulppy. Soften gelatine in water. Mix egg yolks, brown sugar, salt, lemon juice and apricot pulp. Cook over low heat. Stir constantly until thick. Add gelatine. Chill until firm.

Beat egg whites and sugar until stiff. Whip cream; put 1/2 aside. Fold egg whites into 1/2 the cream, then into filling mixture. Pour into crust. Top with remaining 1/2 of cream.

Easiest Coconut Custard

- 4 Eggs
- 2 c Milk
- 1/2 c Flour
- 1 t Vanilla
- 6 t Margarine
- 1 c Coconut

Put all ingredients in blender for 10-15 seconds on high speed. Grease and flour one 9" pie plate and pour mixture in and bake at 350 degrees for 1 hour. The easiest pie you will ever make!

Easy Peanut Butter Pie with Fudge Topping

Crust:
1 c Graham cracker crumbs
1/4 c Sugar
1/4 c Unsalted butter; cut into 1/
Filling:
8 oz Cream cheese; softened
1 c Creamy peanut butter
1 c Powdered sugar
2 tb Unsalted butter; softened
1 tb Vanilla extract
1/2 c Heavy cream; well chilled
Fudge topping:
1/2 c Heavy cream
6 oz Semisweet chocolate; chopped

Recipe by: Classic Home Desserts Preheat the oven to 350. In a medium bowl, combine the graham cracker crumbs, sugar and butter until well blended.
Press evenly into a buttered 9" pie pan, reaching up to but not over the rim. Bake until lightly browned, about 10 minutes. Cool the crust completely on a wire rack. Beat the cream cheese and peanut butter with an electric mixer at medium speed until well blended. Add the powdered sugar, butter and vanilla and continue beating until fluffy. Whip the cream until not quite stiff. Fold a large spoonful of the whipped cream into the peanut butter mixture to lighten it; gently fold in the remainder. Carefully spoon the filling into the cooled crust, spreading evenly. Loosely cover the pie and refrigerate until firm, about 3 hours. (You can put it in the freezer, if you'd like to speed it up.) Bring the cream to a simmer in a small, heavy saucepan. Add the chocolate and stir until smooth. Set aside to cool to lukewarm. Gently spread the topping over the cooled pie. Refrigerate until firm, about 3 hours. Serve cold.

Easy Scrounge Up Chiffon Jam Pie

  1 1/2 c To 2 cups scum from jam
          Making
   12 oz CoolWhip or equivalent
    1   Graham Cracker crust

Mix cooled jam making scum and carton of COOL WHIP together. Pour into graham cracker crust. Garnish with some of the fruit Jam was made from.
Chill for 2 hours. Serve. Very sweet but tasty.

Easy Street Peanut Butter Pie

  1 c Graham cracker crumbs
1/4 c Melted butter
  2 c Sugar
  2 tb Melted butter
  2 c Whipping cream
  3 tb Coffee plus
  2 ts Coffee
1/4 c Packed light brown sugar
  2 c Creamy peanut butter
16 oz Cream cheese, room
    -temperature
  1 ts Vanilla
  4   Ounces semisweet chocolate

Combine first three ingredients in 9-inch springform pan; mix well. Press into bottom and halfway up sides of the pan. In large bowl, mix peanut butter, sugar, cheese, butter, vanilla. Fold in peanut butter, pour into crust. Refrigerate six hours, melt chocolate with coffee in double boiler over gently boiling water and spread this atop pie and refrigerate until firm. If too thin, add egg white. From: Earl Shelsby

Edgy Chocolate Crusted Peanut Butter Pie

    Crust:
2 c Unsalted peanuts, dry-roasted
1/4 c Sugar
  4 tb Unsalted butter; melted
3/4 c Semisweet chocolate chips
    Filling:
 8 oz Cream cheese; at room temp.
1/2 c Peanut butter
  2 tb Peanut butter
3/4 c Powdered sugar
  2 tb Powdered sugar
1/2 c Milk
  1 c Whipping cream; chilled
1/2 oz Unsweetened chocolate; for g

Preheat the oven to 375. Place all the ingredients for the crust in a large bowl and toss them together with your hands or a wooden spoon. Pat the mixture firmly into a 9" pie plate with your fingers, pushing it as far up the sides of the pan as possible. Place   the crust on the center oven rack and bake for 10 minutes. Place it in the freezer to cool completely, 15 minutes.

For the filling, using an electric mixer on medium speed, cream the cream cheese, peanut butter and powdered sugar together in a medium size mixing bowl until light and fluffy, about 1 1/2 minutes. Scrape the bowl with a rubber spatula. With the mixer on low speed, gradually add the milk and mix until it is incorporated, 10 seconds.

Scrape the bowl and mix several seconds more. Whip the cream in another mixing bowl to soft peaks and fold it into the peanut butter mixture. Scoop the filling into the pie shell and freeze the pie for at least 6 hours. Two hours before serving, move the pie from the freezer to the refrigerator.

Shave chocolate over the top right before serving.

Effortless Crumb Pie Crust

  1 1/2 c Rolled crumbs
    1/3 c Melted margarine or butter
    1/4 c Sugar

Cookies, bread crumbs or graham crackers may be used in this crust.

Mix sugar and crumbs. Mix well with the shortening and press with the palm of your hand against the bottom and sides of the pie pan. It is well to chill this crust thoroughly, but if you are in a hurry, you may bake it at once in a moderate oven about 350 degrees for 15 minutes.

Escape Your Mind Margarita Pie

1 pk Frozen strawberries in syrup
   -thawed (10 ounces)
1 pk Cream cheese, softened (8 oz
1/2 c Thawed Margarita mix conc.
4 oz Cool whip - thawed
1 pk Ready-to-use graham cracker
   -pie crust

Place strawberries, cream cheese and margarita mix concentrate in blender or food processor. Cover and blend on medium speed until well blended.

Pour mixture into medium bowl; fold in whipped topping. Pour into pie crust. Freeze 4 to 6 hours or until firm. Let stand at room temperature 5 to 10 minutes before cutting. Freeze any remaining pie.

Everything Waits Pumpkin Ice-Cream Pie

    1/3 c Butter or margarine, at room
        -temperature
      2 c Cinnamon graham-cracker
        -crumbs (15 double crackers)
        FILLING:
      1 qt Orange sherbert, slightly
        -softened
      1 cn (16 ounces) solid-pack
        -pumpkin
      1 pt Vanilla ice cream, slightly
        -softened
      1 ts Vanilla extract
        For Garnish:
      1 c Heavy cream, whipped stiff
        -(2 cups)

Timing Tip: Can be frozen for up to 2 weeks. Decorate up to 8 hours ahead. Calorie Trimmer: Use reduced-calorie margarine, vanilla nonfat frozen dessert instead of the ice cream and 2 cups thawed frozen reduced-calorie whipped topping for garnish.

CRUST:

candied orange peel, cut in diamonds
1. Heat oven to 375 degrees F. Have a 10-inch deep-dish pie plate ready.
2. Mix butter and cracker
crumbs in a medium-size bowl until evenly moistened. Press over bottom and up sides of pie plate.
3. Bake 8   minutes or until lightly browned. Cool on wire rack.
4. FILLING: Put orange sherbert into large bowl. Fold in pumpkin just until blended. Fold in ice cream and vanilla until blended.
5.Spoon into crust, swirling   top. Freeze until hard, at least 4 hours.
6. Up to 8 hours before serving: Pipe whipped cream in lattice design on pie or garnish with dollops of cream. Decorate with orange peel. Return to Freezer

Family First Pecan Pie

Ingredients
3 egg whites
1 cup sugar
2 tbsp sugar
2 tsp vanilla
1 cup crisp round cracker crumbs
1 1/2 cup pecans (chopped)
1 cup heavy cream
1/4 tsp almond flavoring

Directions

Beat egg whites until foamy. Add 1 cup sugar a little at a time, beating after each addition. Add 1 teaspoon vanilla. Continue beating until mixture holds soft peaks. Mix cracker crumbs and 1 cup pecans. Fold into meringue mixture a little at a time. Spoon mixture into an 8" pie plate tp form a shell. Pull up mixture into peaks around edge of plate with mack of spoon. Spread evenly. Bake in a moderate oven, 350 F, for 30 minutes. Cool thoroughly on a wire cake rack. Mix cream, 2 tablespoons sugar, 1 teaspoon vanilla and almond flavoring. Whip until thick and shiny. Spoon into cold pie shell. Sprinkle remaining 1/2 cup chopped pecans round edge of cream. Using a sharp knife, cut like a pie.

Makes 6 - 8 servings

Family's Here Toffee Bar Crunch Pie

- 1/3 c Caramel ice cream topping
- 1 1/2 c Milk
- 1 pk Vanilla instant pudding; 4
    -serving size
- 8 oz Cool Whip; thawed
- 6 Heath bars; 1.4 oz size,
    -chopped
- 1 Graham cracker crust

Spread ice cream topping on bottom of crust. Pour milk into large bowl.

Add pudding mix. Beat with wire whisk 2 minutes. Let stand 5 minutes. Stir in cool whip and chopped heath bars. Spoon into crust. Freeze 4 hours or until set. Let stand at room temperature 15 minutes or until pie can be cut easily. Store leftovers in freezer.

Family's Near Chocolate Chip Pie

  2   Eggs
1/2 c Flour
1/2 c Sugar
1/2 c Brown sugar; firmly packed
  1 c Butter; * see note
  6 oz Semisweet chocolate chips;
     -(nestle's)
  1 c Walnuts; chopped
  1   9 inch pie shell; (unbaked)

* melted and cooled to room temperature

Preheat oven to 325 degrees. In large bowl, beat eggs until foamy. Add flour, sugar and brown sugar; beat until well blended. Blend in melted butter. Stir in semi-sweet chips and walnuts. Pour into pie shell. Bake at 325 for 1 hour. Serve warm with whipped cream or ice cream. Makes one pie.

If using frozen pie shell, only use deep dish style and thaw completely.
Place on cookie sheet; bake 10 minutes longer.

Fancy Pants Baklava

1 Batch

---------------------------------DOUGH---------------------------
   1 lb Strudel dough
     -(or fillo leaves)
   1 lb Butter, unsalted,
     -well-melted (salted
     -butter (or margarine)
     -is not acceptable)

---------------------------------FILLING---------------------------
   1 lb Walnut meat,
     -chopped medium-fine
   1/4 c Sugar
   1 t Vanilla (or use
     -vanilla sugar)

---------------------------------SYRUP----------------------------
   4 c Sugar
   2 c Water
   1 t Lemon juice

Heat oven to 300 degrees F. to 325 degrees F.

  MAKE THE SYRUP: Boil the water and sugar for 15 minutes. Add lemon juice, boil 10 more minutes, set aside to cool.

  MAKE THE FILLING: Mix all ingredients well. I prefer the walnuts fairly coarse; some people like them quite fine.

  BUILD THE BAKLAVA: Cut the dough with scissors to the size of the tray.
  Handle the dough very carefully; do not press hard on it at any time. Cover with wax paper and damp towel.

  Take out one sheet of dough at a time and place it in the pan. Brush the dough with melted butter between each layer. Continue until you have about 12 sheets buttered. Small and broken pieces of dough can be used in the center, but there must be butter between every two layers.

Spread walnut filling across the tray. Put on a sheet of dough, brush on butter and continue until all the dough is used up.

Cut into diamond shapes: cut into quarters with cuts parallel to the long axis, then cut diagonally across. Don't press hard!

Bake for about 1 1/2 hour, until golden brown. Be careful not to burn the bottom or the walnuts, especially with a glass pan.

Let cool on rack for 5 minutes. Add syrup which should have cooled to room temperature. Let cool for at least two hours before eating.

NOTES:

* An incredibly sweet and wonderful Balkan dessert -- Baklava is claimed by almost every Balkan state as its own invention; most people in the United States first encounter it in Greek restaurants. If the truth were known, it's probably the Turkish who invented it, as is the case for many other "typically Greek" dishes. This recipe comes from my Bulgarian grandmother and follows Bulgarian tradition, in that the filling is very simple. Makes two small pans.

* Probably the hardest thing about this recipe is waiting those last two hours!

* Depending on where you go, you'll hear the name of this dish pronounced different ways. I pronounce the name with all /ah/ sounds, with accents of equal intensity on both the first and third syllable. The second syllable is quite faint. Greek-speaking persons typically put a heavy accent on the second syllable.

* Many variations on the filling are to be found. A simple one was mentioned above, regarding the coarseness of grind of the walnuts in the filling. They may even be ground. Spices such as chopped cloves or cinnamon may be added and the filling may be included

in several layers instead of just one.

  * A large (14 x 10 inch) pan is almost too big to handle. I typically make this recipe in two 7 3/4 x 11 inch pans, which is just about the size of a half sheet of the dough I buy. By the way, if you can make your own strudel dough, it will be even better... but much more effort.

  * It is best to have a partner help you prepare the pans. One person handles the dough and places it in the pan, while the other applies the butter. It is very important that sufficient butter be placed between layers so that each layer gets flaky, rather than having them stick together. Pay particular attention to the edges and corners.

  * In case you haven't noticed, this is very sweet stuff. It goes great with a fine cup of coffee, espresso, or Turkish coffee, even with sugar.
  Two pieces will probably fill anyone up; it refrigerates and freezes quite well. This recipe requires a lot of effort, but it's well worth it.

Fast Peanut Butter Delight Cookies

1 c Peanut-butter
1 c Sugar
1 lg Egg

Beat the egg. Mix everything together. Preheat oven to 325 degrees F.

Place blobs of cookie dough on a greased cookie sheet in the size you like, and flatten with a fork to make the traditional peanut-butter cookie pattern. Put in oven and bake for 8-10 minutes.

NOTES:

* These are very simple peanut-butter cookies -- They turn out a little moist, but are yummy.

* These cookies are a bit moist, so don't worry about that. Don't burn them; they don't taste good when they're burnt.

Father's Day Peanut Butter Chip Pie

- 1 (9") unbaked pastry shell, Pricked
- 1 c (6 oz) semi-sweet chocolate Chips
- 1/3 c Half-and-half or Coffee Cream
- 1 cn (14 oz) sweetened condensed Milk (not evaporated milk)
- 1 c Peanut butter flavored chips
- 2 c Whipping Cream, stiffly Whipped
- 1/2 c Chopped peanuts

Preheat oven to 425 degrees F. Bake pastry shell 10 to 15 minutes or until lightly browned. In 1 quart glass measure with handle, combine chocolate chips with half-and-half; cook on 100% power (high) 1 to 2 minutes, in microwave, stirring until chips are melted and mixture is smooth. Spread evenly on bottom of prepared pastry shell. In 2-quart glass measure with handle, combine sweetened condensed milk and peanut butter chips; cook on 100% power (high) 2 to 3 minutes, stirring after each minute until chips are melted and mixture is smooth. Pour into large bowl; cool to room temperature, about 45 minutes. With mixer, beat until smooth. Fold in whipped cream and peanuts. Chill 30 minutes. Spoon into prepared pastry shell. Chill 4 hours. Garnish as desired. Refrigerate leftovers.

Favorite Banana Split Cake

---------------------------------CRUST #1------------------------
    2 c Graham cracker crumbs
  1/4 c Margarine

---------------------------------CRUST #2------------------------
    2 c Flour, all-purpose
  1/2 c Sugar
    1 c Margarine, softened
      1 Egg, slightly beaten
  1/2 t Vanilla

---------------------------------CRUST #3------------------------
    32 Oreo cookies
  2/3 c Margarine, melted

---------------------------------FILLING---------------------------
  1/2 c Margarine
2 1/2 c Sugar, powdered
     2 Eggs
     5 Bananas, sliced
        -lengthwise (or less)
 20 oz Pineapple (chunk),
        -drained
    4 c Strawberries, whole
    1 c Whipping cream
        Nuts, chopped

MAKE CRUST: Mix ingredients for first crust and press in bottom of a 9 x 13 pan. Bake 10 minutes at 350 degrees F. and cool.

  Blend all ingredients for second crust thoroughly; pat dough on bottom of a pan. Bake at 400 degrees F. for about 10 minutes or until golden brown.
  Cool. Crush cookies and mix them with the margarine. Press mixture in bottom of pan.

MAKE FILLING: Whip margarine/sugar/egg mixture with electric mixer and spread over cooled crust. Place bananas, cut side down, on top of above layer. Spread on the pineapple chunks, then the strawberries.

Whip the cream, cover the whole dish with whipped cream, and sprinkle with nuts. Refrigerate 4 hours before serving.

Ferris Wheel Peaches and Cream Pie

```
1   9 inch pie shell
4 lg Ripe peaches; peeled and halved
1 c  Light cream
1 ts Almond extract; or vanilla extract
2   Eggs
1/2 c  Sugar; divided
2 tb Unsalted butter
```

Arrange peach halves, pitted side up, in unbaked pie shell. Combine cream, extract, eggs, and 1/4 cup sugar. Pour over peaches. Dot tops of peaches with butter; sprinkle with remaining 1/4 cup sugar. Bake for one hour.

First Date Pie

   1   Unbake 9 inch pie shell
   1 c Granulated sugar
   1   Cub brown sugar
   2 T All purpose flour
1/2 t Ground cinnamon
    -
1/4 t Ground cloves
1/4 t Salt
   3   Eggs
   2 c Milk
   1 T Butter
   1 t Vanilla extract

Preheat oven to 350 F. Set out pie shell. In a large mixer bowl, combine the next 6 ingredients. In another mixer bowl, beat the eggs well. Add the remaining ingredients. Blend liquid mixture into flour mixture, then pour into the unbaked shell. Bake for 45 minutes. The filling will still be shaky when you remove it from the oven. The pie puffs up, but levels off as it cools. Serve at room temperature.

First Kiss Strawberry Pie

    1   Deep dish pie crust
1 qt Fresh strawberries
1 c Sugar
1/4 c Cornstarch
1 c Water
       Few drops red food coloring
       Whipped cream

Recipe by: arielle@bonkers.taronga.com (Stephanie da Silva) Preheat ove to 400F. Blind-bake pie shell. Cool. Chop one cup of strawberries. Combine sugar and cornstarch in a saucepan. Stir in water gradually until smooth.

Add chopped strawberries. Cook, over medium heat, stirring constantly, until mixture thickens. Remove from heat, stir in food coloring. Cool.

Pour 3/4 of the syrup mixture into prepared pie crust. Arrange remaining strawberries in crust, reserving 3 for garnish. Pour remaining syrup over strawberries. Chill until firm. Serve with whipped cream and slice of reserved strawberry.

Floating Orange-Almond Pastries - Lite

  1/2 c Orange marmalade
    3 dr Almond extract
     6   Phyllo dough; thawed
        Butter-flavored cooking
        -spray
  1/4 c Light cream cheese
    1 tb Powdered sugar; sifted
       Orange rind strip; for garnish

    Preheat oven to 375 degrees. Combine orange marmalade and almond extract; set aside. Coat phyllo sheets, working with one sheet at a time, lightly with cooking spray; fold each in half lengthwise. Lightly coat with cooking spray; cut crosswise into 4 rectangles (6 1/2 x 4 1/2-inches).
    Spread 1/2 teaspoon cream cheese on the short side of each phyllo strip; top with 1 teaspoon marmalade mixture. Fold long sides in about 1/2 inch.
    Beginning with the marmalade-filled end, roll up jelly roll fashion. Place each roll, seam side down, on a baking sheet. Lightly coat tops of rolls with cooking spray. Bake for 7 minutes. Remove from pans immediately; sprinkle with powdered sugar. Cool completely on a wire rack. Place on a serving tray and garnish with orange rind, if desired.

Fluffy & Crispy Peanut Butter Pie

6 Servings

----------------------------------BASE----------------------------
- 1/3 c Margarine
- 6 oz Chocolate baking chips
- 2 1/2 c Rice Krispies

---------------------------------FILLING--------------------------
- 8 oz Cream cheese
- 13 oz Condensed milk
- 3/4 c Peanut butter
- 3 T Lemon juice
- 1 ts Vanilla
- 1 c Whipping cream; whipped
-     Chocolate syrup

Melt margarine and chocolate chips; remove from heat and stir in rice cereal. Press into a greased 9-inch pie plate.

In mixing bowl, beat cream cheese until fluffy. Add sweetened condensed milk and peanut butter, combining well. Stir in lemon juice and vanilla.

Fold in beaten cream and turn into crust. Drizzle 1 or 2 tablespoons chocolate syrup over top. Chill at least 4 hours.

Fold'em Rum Pie

    Make two chocolate crumb
    Crusts using chocolate
    Wafers (8 or 9 inch crusts)
    Soak:
1 pk Gelatin
1/4 c Milk
    In a double boiler put:
1 c Milk
1/2 ts Nutmeg
  3   Egg yolks, beaten
1/2 c Sugar

  Cook in a double boiler, stirring constantly until consistency of thick cream. Add gelatin and stir until dissolved. Add 1 teaspoon of vanilla.
  Cool until nearly set. Add 3 tablespoons of rum. Whip 3 egg whites until fluffy, add 1/4 cup of sugar, beat until stiff and glossy. Fold into egg mixture. Chill. Cover with whipped cream. Chill.

Four Seasons Berry Pie

- 1 1/2 c Raspberries
- 1 1/2 c Strawberries -- sliced
- 1 c Blueberries
- 1 Pie crust (9 inch) -- baked And cooled
- 3/4 c Sugar
- 3 tb Cornstarch
- 1 1/2 c Water
- 1 pk Strawberry gelatin powder -- Jello, 4-serv. pkg
- 8 oz Cool Whip -- 1 tub

Mix berries and pour into pastry shell. Mix sugar and cornstarch in med. saucepan. Gradually stir in water until smooth. Stirring constantly, cook on medium heat until mixture comes to a boil; boil 1 min. Remove from heat. Stir in gelatin until dissolved. Cool to room temperature. Pour over berries in pastry shell. Refrigerate 3 hours. Spread whipped topping over pie before serving. Garnish with additional berries, if desired.

Fourth Of July Lemon Pie

   3 tb Margarine;
  10   Graham cracker squares;
 1/2 c Skimmed evaporated milk;
     -cold
   1 pk Dream Whip;
 27 pk Equal sweetener;
    2   Egg yolks;
   2 lg Lemons; 1/2 cup juice
    3   Egg whites;
   3 tb Sugar;

Melt margarine on medium to low heat. Roll graham crackers into crumbs with rolling pin. Mix crumbs and melted margarine. Pat to make crust on bottom and sides of pie pan. Chill.

Add cold evaporated milk to Dream Whip (do not add vanilla). Sprinkle in 24 pkg. Equal. Mix and beat according to directions. Beat egg yolks slightly, and gradually stir in lemon juice. Gradually fold in the whipped Dream Whip. Spread in pie crust. Turn on broiler so it will get hot. Beat 3 egg whites frothy (use clean beaters so whites will beat up as fluffy as possible). Add 1 tbs. sugar and beat until blended in. Add another tbs. sugar and 3 Equal pkg. and beat until soft peaks form. Spread meringue over top. Spread meringue to stick to the edges so it won't shrink when you broil it.

Put under broiler for 30-60 seconds until meringue is lightly browned. IT DOESN'T TAKE LONG AT ALL AND IS EASY TO BURN. The flavors will blend better if you chill for 5 hours.

Fresh Red Raspberry Pie

    1 c Powdered sugar
    4 tb Butter
1 1/2 pt Raspberries
  1/2 pt Whipping cream

Add butter to powdered sugar and put in a pie shell. Pat down with your hands until smooth. Add berries and top with whipping cream. Chill for 2 hours before serving.

Frozen Chocolate Peanut Butter Pie

  1 1/2 c Heavy cream
      4   1-oz semisweet chocolate squ
          Cocoa graham crust; (recipe
  1 pk Cream cheese; softened
  1 c Powdered sugar
  3/4 c Peanut butter
  1/4 c Peanuts; chopped

In a small glass bowl, combine 1/2 cup cream and chocolate.

Heat in microwave on High 1 to 1 1/2 mins, until melted and smooth when stirred. Let cool slightly. 2. Spread half of chocolate mixture over bottom of Cocoa Graham Crust. Freeze 1/2 hour, or until set. 3. Meanwhile prepare filling. In a medium bowl, beat cream cheese, powdered sugar, and peanut butter with an electric mixer on medium until well blended and fluffy, 1 to 2 mins. Whip remaining 1 cup cream until stiff; beat half of whipped cream into peanut butter mixture until well mixed, then fold in remaining whipped cream. 4. Spread filling evenly over chocolate mixture in crust. Freeze ½ hour. Then carefully spread remaining chocolate mixture over top and sprinkle peanuts over surface. Freeze 6 hours or overnight. Wrap tightly and store in freezer. Transfer pie to refrigerator 1 hour before serving. Cut into wedges to serve.

Frozen Tapioca Time Peach Pie

  9 lb Ripe peaches
  1 ts Ascorbic acid
  1 ga Water
3 1/2 c Sugar
  1/2 c Minute tapioca PLUS
  2 tb Minute Tapioca
  1/4 c Lemon juice
  1 ts Salt

PREPARE FILLING: Scald, peel and slice peaches. Measure 4 quarts.
Dissolve acid in water. Add peaches. Drain. Combine peaches with other ingredients.

FREEZE FILLING: Line four 8" pie pans with heavy-duty foil, letting it extend about 5" beyond rim. Divide filling among foil-lined pans. Fold foil over loosely; freeze until firm. Then cover tightly, remove from pan, and return to freezer. May be stored 6 months.

BAKE PIE: Remove foil from filling. Do not thaw. Place in pastry-lined 9" pie pans. Dot with butter. Add top crust. Seal & flute edges. Cut slits in top crust. Bake in hot oven (425 degrees) until syrup boils with heavy bubbles that do not burst - about one hour.

Fruit And Jello Pie

    3/4 c Sugar
3 1/2 T Jello
        -flavor of fruit.
        -Baked Pie Shell
2 1/2 T Cornstarch
     1 c Water
        -Whipped Creme
     4 c Fruit (frozen is alright)

Combine sugar, cornstarch and water in heavy saucepan. Cook at medium heat until thick and fairly clear. Remove from heat and add Jello Mix. Stir until dissolved. Stir in fruit, pour in shell and chill. Serve with whipped cream

** I don't cook the berries in the jello mix. I put them in the pie crust and pour the hot stuff over. It keeps everything fresher and more arranged.

**Use all of a small package of Jello with a little more juice or water and fill 2 small crusts.

Fruitful Fast Skillet Pie

Melt 1 stick of margarine
In a heavy skillet. Mix:
1 c Flour
1/2 c Milk
1 1/2 ts Baking powder
3/4 c Sugar

Pour batter on top of margarine. Pour in fruit mixed with 1 cup of sugar.
Bake at 350 degrees for 30 minutes or until brown.
Any fresh fruit may be used. If canned fruit is used, omit the cup of sugar.

Fudgey Chocolaty Pie

```
    3   Eggs
1 1/4 c  Sugar
  1/4 c  Flour
    1 ts Vanilla
    3 oz Unsweetened baking chocolate
        3 x 1 oz squares
  1/2 c  Butter
         Vanilla Ice Cream or
         Whipped Cream
```

Beat eggs until smooth. Add sugar, flour, and vanilla. Beat to mix. Melt chocolate squares and butter in small saucepan over low heat. Add to egg mixture and beat until mixed. Pour into greased 9 in plate. Bake at 350 for about 35 minutes. Center will be moist and soft when tasted with toothpick. Serve warm with ice cream or whipped cream.

Fun Mixed Oatmeal Fudge Cookies

    3 c Rolled oats
    1 t Vanilla extract
    1 c Nuts, chopped (optional)
    2 c Sugar, granulated
    1/2 c Cocoa powder
    1/2 c Evaporated milk
    1/4 lb Butter

Combine oats, vanilla and nuts in a bowl and set aside.

Combine sugar, cocoa and evaporated milk in a heavy, 2-quart sauce pan.
Bring to a full rolling boil over medium-high heat, STIRRING CONSTANTLY.
Let boil, while stirring, for 2 minutes.

Remove pan from heat and add the butter. Stir until butter is melted and incorporated. Quickly add oat mixture to pan and stir until well mixed.

Drop by the spoonful onto waxed paper. Let cool for 2 hours to set.

G-Force Rhubarb Pie

- 3 c Rhubarb, 1" slices
- 1/2 t Grated orange peel
- 1 x Dash salt
- 1 c Sugar
- 3 T Flour
- 2 T Butter or margarine

Combine all ingredients except butter or margarine. Line a 9" pie plate with Orange Pastry**. Fill with rhubarb mixture and dot with the butter or margarine. Top with lattice crust. Bake at 400 degrees 40 to 50 minutes.

Serve warm with vanilla ice cream. ** Substitute orange juice for the water in your favorite pastry recipe.

Gail's Great German Chocolate Pie

- 3 c Sugar
- 7 tb Baking Cocoa
- 13 oz Evaporated Milk
- 4 ea Eggs: Lg, Beaten
- 1/2 c Butter Or Regular Margarine
- 1 t Vanilla
- 2 c Coconut; Flaked
- 1 c Pecans; Chopped
- 2 ea Unbaked 9-inch Pie Shells

Melt the margarine and set aside. Combine the sugar and baking cocoa in a bowl. Stir in the evaporated milk, eggs, melted butter or margarine, and vanilla, blending well. Stir in the coconut and pecans and turn into two unbaked pie shells. Bake in a 350 degree F. oven for 40 minutes or until set around the edges. Cool on racks. Makes 2 pies of 6 servings each.

Get To The Party Pumpkin Pie

---------------------------------CRUST---------------------------
- 1/2 c Gingersnap crumbs;
- 1/2 c Graham cracker crumbs;
- 2 tb Liquid margarine;
- Vegetable cookin spray

---------------------------------FILLING---------------------------
- 1   Egg;
- 2   Egg whites;
- 16 oz (1 cn) pumpkin;
- 1/4 c Sugar;
- 2 tb Molasses; (blackstrap or
  -mild
- 1 ts Ground cinnamon;
- 1/2 ts Nutmeg;
- 12 oz Evaporated skim milk;

CRUST: Heat oven to 350 degrees. Mix the gingersnap and graham cracker crumbs together with the margarine. Light coat a nonstick 10" pie pan with with nonstick spray. Press crumb mixture into bottom of pie pan and bake for 7 minutes. (Crust will be partially baked.) Let cool on a wire rack.

Leave oven on. PIE: Whish together all pie ingredients until well blended.

Pour mixture into the partially baked pie crust. Bake for 40 to 50 minutes more, or until center of pie does not jiggle when you put on oven mitt and gently shake the pan. Let pie cool on a wire rack. Carefully cut 10 wedges and serve.

Glazed Fresh-Strawberry Pie

    1   Pie shell, 9"; baked
        -----glaze-----
    1 pt Strawberries
    1 c Sugar; granulated
    2 1/2 tb Cornstarch
    1 tb Butter; unsalted
        -----filling-----
    2 pt Strawberries
    2 tb Orange juice
    1 c Heavy cream; whipped
    2 tb Sugar; confectioners

Prepare and bake pie shell; let cool. GLAZE: Wash strawberries gently in cold water. Drain; hull. In medium saucepan, crush strawberries with potato masher. Combine sugar and cornstarch; stir into crushed strawberries. Add 1/2 cup w FILLING: Wash strawberries gently in cold water. Drain; hull.

Measure 3 cups; reserve rest for garnish. In medium bowl, gently toss strawberries with Cointreau; let stand about 30 Just before serving, whip cream until stiff; fold in confectioners' sugar. Variation – Strawberry Devonshire Glace Pie: Combine 1 package (3 oz) soft cream cheese with 1 tablespoon light cream.

Good Morning Fruity Frozen Yogurt

2/3 c Sugar (or vary based
    -on sweetness of fruit)
1/2 c Orange juice
  2 c Fruit, cut into pieces
  2 t Lemon juice
  1 c Yogurt, plain
  2   Egg whites

Combine sugar and orange juice in a saucepan. Heat and stir until sugar is dissolved. Set aside to cool.

Whirl fruit and lemon juice in blender until fruit is pulp. Add yogurt, blending well. With motor running, add cooled orange juice mixture.

Pour into a 9-inch square, flat pan and place in freezer for two hours or until mixture is frozen into a slush. Break up mixture and put in mixer bowl. Beat until smooth, adding eggs one at a time. Continue beating until light and fluffy.

Return to pan or freezer-proof dessert containers and freeze until firm, about one hour.

For very juicy fruit, such as raspberries or frozen fruit, the orange juice may be decreased in proportion to the amount of juice. Increase the lemon juice by 1 teaspoon for each 1/8 cup the orange juice is decreased.

Grandma Betty's Oatmeal Bars

    1 c Shortening
    1 c Brown sugar
    1 c Sugar, granulated
    4   Eggs, beaten well
    1 t Vanilla extract
1 1/2 c White flour, sifted
    1 t Salt
    1 t Baking soda
    2 c Oats, quick-cooking
  1/2 c Walnuts, chopped
      -(optional)

  Preheat oven to 350 degrees F. Cream shortening and sugars. Add eggs and vanilla. Beat well. Sift flour, salt and soda and add to creamed sugars.
  Add oatmeal and nuts and mix well. Spread evenly into a greased 13x9x2-inch baking pan. Bake at 350 degrees F. for 20 minutes. While still warm, cut into squares and remove from pan.

Grandma Bev's Best Carrot Cake

---------------------------------CAKE----------------------------
- 1 c Butter
- 2 c Sugar
- 3   Eggs
- 2 t Vanilla
- 2 c Flour, sifted
- 1 t Salt
- 2 t Cinnamon
- 2 t Soda
- 2 t Nutmeg
- 1/4 t Cardamom
- 1 c Walnuts, chopped
    -finely
- 1/2 c Raisins
- 1/2 c Pineapple (crushed),
    -well-drained
- 2 c Carrots, shredded
    -and packed

-------------------------------FROSTING------------------------
- 3 oz Cream cheese
- 1/2 c Butter
- 1 1/4 c Powdered sugar
- 1/4 c Walnuts, chopped
- 3 T Pineapple (crushed), chopped and well-drained
- 1/8 t Cardamom

MAKE CAKE: Cream butter until soft. Gradually add sugar and beat until fluffy, at least ten minutes. Beat in eggs one at a time until thoroughly blended. Add vanilla.

In a separate bowl sift flour, salt, cinnamon, soda, nutmeg and cardamom together several times and set aside. Add walnuts, pineapple, raisins and carrots to egg-sugar mixture. Stir in flour mixture and mix well. Pour into greased and floured pan and bake at 350 degrees F. for 1 hour. Cool completely. Apply frosting.

MAKE FROSTING: Mix cream cheese, butter and

powdered sugar until fluffy.
Add pineapple, walnuts and cardamom. Blend well.

Grandma's Thanksgiving Pecan Pie

- 3 Eggs, beaten
- 1 c Corn syrup (dark)
- 1 c Sugar
- 2 T Butter
- 1 t Vanilla extract
- 1 1/2 c Pecans
- 1 Pastry shell, unbaked

Preheat oven to 375 degrees F. Blend eggs, corn syrup, sugar, butter and vanilla together. Add pecans.

Bake at 375 degrees F. for 10 minutes, then lower the temperature to 350 degrees F. and bake for another 45 minutes or so (until a knife inserted halfway between the edge and the center comes out clean. Remove and let cool.

Grasshopper Pie

    1   Graham cracker crust
1 1/2 c Whipped cream
    3 tb White creme de cocoa
   33 lg Marshmallows
1/4 c Creme De Menthe
       Green food coloring

Heat in small sauce pan, Milk and marshmallows over low heat until marshmallows are melted. Refrigerate to cool mixture for approx. 20 minutes. Stir occasionally during cooling process until mixture mounds slightly. Stir liqueurs into mixture. Fold in whipped cream. Add food coloring until desired color is achieved. Pour mixture into graham cracker crust. Refrigerate at least 4 hours before serving.

Great Cream Cheese Pound Cake

3/4 lb Butter
3 c Sugar, granulated
1/2 lb Cream cheese
6 lg Eggs
3 c Cake flour, sifted
1/4 t Salt
1 1/2 t Almond extract
1 t Vanilla extract

Pre-heat oven to 325 degrees F. Cream the butter, sugar and cheese together until the mixture is light and fluffy. Add salt, vanilla and almond extract. Beat well. Add eggs, one at a time, blending well after each.

Stir in flour. Don't be vigorous; mix it just enough to incorporate the flour. Spoon into a greased tube pan. Bake in preheated oven for 1 ½ hours. Cool for 15-20 minutes, then invert the cake onto a serving dish and remove the tube pan. If you wait too long, it will stick.

NOTES:

* A pound cake made with cream cheese -- I got this recipe from Annette Hall at Computer System Resources, in Georgia (annette@gacsr.UUCP). She posted it to net.cooks, claiming that it's the best pound cake you'll ever taste. She's right! One large cake.

Great Thanksgiving Pie

- 1 Pie crust (deep dish), -unbaked
- 3 Eggs
- 1 c Corn syrup, dark
- 1 1/2 c Sugar
- 1/4 c Butter, melted -(or margarine)
- 1 c Pumpkin
- 1 t Vanilla
- 1 c Pecan halves

Preheat oven to 350 degrees F. Beat eggs. Add other ingredients except pecans and beat well. Put pecans in bottom of pie crust and slowly pour egg mixture over nuts. Bake 45 minutes, or until knife inserted one inch from edges comes out clean. Let pie cool (if cut warm, the pie will be runny). Serve with whipped cream.

Gumdrop Dream Cake

    4 c Flour
    2   Eggs
    1 t Baking soda
1 1/2 c Applesauce
  1/4 t Salt
    1 t Vanilla
    1 t Cinnamon
    1 lb Raisins, white
  1/4 t Cloves, ground
    8 oz Gumdrops (no black ones; 2 standard bags)
  1/4 t Nutmeg
    12 oz Coconut, shredded
      (1 standard bag)
    1 c Butter
      Walnuts, to taste
    2 c Sugar

Cream together butter, sugar and eggs in one bowl. In another bowl, mix the dry ingredients together (flour, salt, soda and seasonings). Add the flour mixture to the butter mixture half at a time, alternating it with the applesauce. Pick all the black gumdrops out and eat them or throw them away. Add the nuts, raisins, coconut and remaining gumdrops; blend well.

Line 2 large loaf pans or 5 small loaf pans with wax paper! (Grease won't work). Fill pans about 2/3 full. Bake at 300 degrees F. for about 2 hours. Let cool for about 15 minutes before you try to remove the loaves from the pan. They should just fall right out when turned upside down, then peel off the wax paper.

H2O Crust

1 1/2 c Flour
1/4 c Boiling water
1/2 c Of cooking oil or fat
1/2 ts Salt

Pour the water into the oil and stir well. To this add the flour and salt, which makes a soft rich dough. Use plenty of flour on the rolling board and pin and do not roll too thin. This makes crust for two pies.

Hammock Banana Custard Pudding

```
2 1/2 c  Sugar
  1/2 c  All-purpose flour
  1/4 c  Cornstarch
    7 c  Milk
    4 ea Egg yolks, beaten
  1/4 c  Butter, softened
    1 t  Vanilla extract
    1 pk (12-oz) vanilla wafers
    9 ea Med bananas, peeled & sliced
```

Combine sugar, flour, and cornstarch in a medium mixing bowl. Mix well, and set aside. Pour milk into a large saucepan; cook over medium heat until candy thermometer registers 160 deg F. Gradually stir one-fourth of hot milk into yolks; stir into reserved dry ingredients, and add to remaining hot milk. Cook, stirring constantly, until mixture thickens and coats the spoon. Remove from heat, and stir in butter and vanilla. Let cool to room temperature. Line bottom of a 13 x 9 x 2-inch baking dish with one-third of the vanilla wafers. Arrange half of banana slices over wafers; top with half of cooled custard. Repeat layers, reserving one-third of wafers to crumble and sprinkle over custard. Chill thoroughly. 20 to 25 servings.

Handpicked Raspberry Pie

1 Servings

3 oz Raspberry Jello
3/4 c Sugar
2 1/2 tb Cornstarch
1 3/4 c Boiling water
1 qt Raspberries
2 tb Margarine
1 ea Pastry for 10" pie

Place pastry crust into 10 inch pie plate, bake 15 minutes until browned at 375 degrees. Mix jello, sugar and cornstarch, add to boiling water and cook until thick, approx. 10 minutes, add margarine. Cool, add Berries. Pour into prebaked pie shell, chill.

Harvest Time Pumpkin Pie

    2 lg Eggs, lightly beaten
    1 t Vanilla
    1   16-oz can pumpkin
    1/4 c Golden or dark brown sugar
2 1/2 t Special Seasoning (recipe follows)
    1 c Evaporated milk
    1/2 c Half-and-half
    1/2 c Granulated sugar
    1   9-inch unbaked pie shell

Mix together the eggs, vanilla, pumpkin, sugar and seasoning mix. In a saucepan, mix the evaporated milk, half-and-half and sugar; cook over low heat until sugar dissolves. Add to the pumpkin mixture. Pour into unbaked shell and bake at 425 degrees for 15 minutes; lower heat to 350 and cook 25 minutes. Store in frig.

Special Seasoning 4 T. ground cinnamon 2 T. ground allspice 2 T. black pepper 2 T. salt 1 T. ground nutmeg 1 T. ground cloves 1 T. ground ginger

Mix all and store in an air-tight container. Makes about 3/4 cup.

Heartthrob Cherry-Cream Pie

    8 oz Philadelphia cream cheese; softened
    14 oz Can sweetened condensed milk -- borden eagle brand
      1 ts Vanilla
    1/3 c Lemon juice
    48 oz Comstock canned cherries
     2   8 inch graham cracker
        Pie crusts

Blend Cream Cheese, Vanilla, Lemon Juice and Condensed Milk well. No lumps

Pour half mixture into each pie crust. Refrigerate for 1 hour, until firm

Fill top half of pie crusts with cherries. Refrigerate 1 hour.

Serve cold.

Heaven on Earth Pie

  1 c   Crushed pineapple
  1 c   Cold water
3/4 c   Sugar
2 1/2 T   Cornstarch

Mix above ingredients and cook until thick; cool, beat 3 egg whites until stiff and fold two together. Pour into baked pie shell, top with whipped cream.

One of Grandma's recipes we all enjoyed.

Heroic Grape Pie

INGREDIENTS:
1 recipe pastry for a 9 inch double crust pie
5 cups Concord grapes
1 1/4 cups white sugar
1/4 cup all-purpose flour
1 pinch salt
3/4 teaspoon lemon juice
1 1/2 tablespoons butter

DIRECTIONS:
Wash grapes, and remove the skins. Save the skins. Place grape pulp in a large saucepan; mash a few at the bottom to release their juice. Cook over medium low heat until grapes come to a full boil. Remove pulp from heat, and press through a food mill to remove seeds. Combine pulp and skins in a large bowl. Stir in lemon juice.
In a separate bowl, mix sugar, flour, and salt. Stir into grape mixture. Pour filling into pastry crust, and dot with butter or margarine. Cover with second pastry shell. Flute edges, and cut little slits in the top crust for steam to escape.
Bake at 400 degrees F (205 degrees C) for 45 to 50 minutes, or until crust is brown and juice begins to bubble through slits in top crust. Cool.

Hide and Seek Pumpkin Pie

- 1 (9") unbaked pastry shell
- 1 (16-oz) cn pumpkin (about 2 c)
- 1 (14-oz cn Eagle Brand Sweetened milk (not evapo-Rated milk)
- 2 Eggs
- 1 ts Gound cinnamon
- 1/2 ts Ground ginger
- 1/2 ts Nutmeg
- 1/2 ts Salt

Preheat oven to 425 degrees. In mixer bowl, combine all ingredients except pastry shell. Mix well. Pour into pastry shell. Bake 15 min. Reduce oven temp. to 350 degrees; bake 35 to 40 min. longer or until center is set. Cool. Garnish as desired. Refrigerate leftovers.

His And Hers Vegetarian Mince Pies

1 Recipe

4 oz Currants

------------------------------MINCEMEAT----------------------
4 oz Raisins
4 oz Sultanas
2 oz Cooking dates
2 oz Candied peel
2 oz Glace cherries
2 oz Flaked almonds
1 ea Ripe banana, peeled
4 tb Brandy or whisky
1/2 ts Ground ginger
1/2 ts Grated nutmeg
1/2 ts Mixed spice

--------------------------------PASTRY--------------------------
8 oz Flour
4 oz Shortening
6 tb Cold water

MINCEMEAT: Mix everything together either by hand or, if you desire a smoother texture, in a food processor.

PASTRY: Rub shortening into the flour until the mixture resembles fine breadcrumbs. Add enough flour to enable the pastry to hold together. Roll out pastry & cut into 12 cm circles. Press circles into the bottom of lightly oiled baking tins. Fill with mincemeat & cover with another pastry circle. Press down at the edges & make a small steam hole in the top. Bake for 10 minutes at 400F, 200C Gas 6.

These pies can be frozen before baking either in the tin or remove from tin once they are solid.

Mincemeat will keep for 1 week covered in the fridge.

Hobo Apple Pie

---------------------------FOR THE PIE-------------------
- 1 1/2 c All-Purpose Flour
- 1/2 ts Salt
- 1/2 c Shortening
- 5 tb ICE Water
- 8 c Apples [peeled & sliced]
- 1/4 c Granulated Sugar
- 2 tb All-Purpose Flour
- 1/2 ts Nutmeg, Ground
- 2 tb Lemon Juice
- 1 ts Cinnamon, Ground

-----------------------------FOR THE TOPPING------------------
- 1/2 c Granulated Sugar
- 1/2 c All-Purpose Flour
- 1/3 c Butter
- 1 lg Paper Bag
- Vanilla Ice Cream

Preheat the oven to 400 degrees.

To make the pie: 1) Combine the first measure of flour, salt and shortening using a pastry blender until the mixture resembles coarse crumbs, then stir in the water a little at a time, using a fork, and form the dough into a ball.

2) Roll out the pastry dough on a lightly floured board. Roll to an 11" or 12" diameter and fit into a 9" pie pan fluting the edges.

3) Combine the sugar, the second measure of flour, the cinnamon, the nutmeg and the lemon juice in a large bowl then toss the apple slices in the mixture and arrange them in the pie crust.

To make the topping:
4) Combine the sugar and flour in a bowl and cut in the butter using a pastry cutter then sprinkle the topping over the apple filling.

5) Place the pie in the LARGE paper bag and place the paper bag on a baking sheet and loosely fold the open end of the bag under. Bake until the apples are tender (50-60 minutes).

6) Carefully remove the pie from the bag ~ CAUTION: WATCH OUT FOR THE STEAM COMING OUT OF THE BAG!

7) Serve warm with generous portions of vanilla ice cream.

Holiday Christmas Stars

----------------------------------COOKIES--------------------------
   1 c Solid shortening
      -(NOT butter)
 2/3 c Granulated sugar
   2   Eggs
   1 t Salt
   1 t Vanilla
   1 t Almond flavoring
2 3/4 c Flour

---------------------------------FROSTING-------------------------
1 1/2 c Powdered sugar
   2 T Cream or milk
 1 1/2 t Vanilla (not Mexican, unless you like tan frosting)
      Food coloring

Cream together the shortening and sugar. Beat in the eggs, salt and flavorings. Stir in the flour until blended. Chill in the refrigerator for an hour or two.

Preheat oven to 375 degrees F. Roll out on a floured surface to a thickness of about 1/8 to 1/4 inch. Cut with the cookie cutters of your choice (this was always a cause for argument in our family). Bake on ungreased cookie sheets until tan around the edges, about 8-10 minutes.
Allow to cool.

Make the frosting by beating together the sugar, milk and vanilla until smooth. Divide and color each portion. Frost the cookies.

NOTES:

* Frosted cookie-cutter cookies -- My mom got this recipe many years ago in a cookbook that came in installments, so it didn't have a name on the binder and I don't know what it was called. She had us (the kids) make these cookies every year. 2-4 dozen.

* These cookies are about the only ones I know that

taste better cooked and cold than as raw dough.

* Cinnamon red hots make good eyes for animals or Santas.

Holiday Party Coconut Meringue Drops

    3   Egg whites
    1 c Sugar
    1 t Vanilla
    1 c Coconut, shredded
        Almonds, whole,
        unblanched (optional)

Preheat oven to 300 degrees F. In large bowl use an electric mixer to beat the egg whites until stiff peaks form. Gradually beat in sugar. Add vanilla. With a rubber spatula gently fold in coconut.

Drop by rounded teaspoonfuls onto greased, floured cookie sheets. Press an almond in center of each cookie. Bake at 300 degrees F. for 20 to 25 minutes. Remove to racks to cool.

NOTES:

* Holiday cookies -- Coconut and almonds give this cookie a distinctive flavor. For me the almonds are required.

* It is a lot of work to beat the egg whites enough without an electric mixer.

* This cookie must be handled a little more carefully than most as it forms a white shell which causes it to be slightly delicate.

Homemade Sweet Potato Pie

- 4 Sweet potatoes (med)
- 1 c Light brown sugar
- 1/2 ts Cinnamon
- 1/8 ts Nutmeg
- 1/2 ts Ginger
- 1/4 ts Salt
- 6 tb Butter or margarine
- 1/2 c Heavy cream

Pastry for 2-crust pie. Boil sweet potatoes until half-cooked, 15-20 minutes. Peel and slice thinly. Mix sugar, spices and salt. Place a layer of sweet potatoes in pastry-lined 9" pie pan, sprinkle with some of the sugar-spice mixture and dot with a little butter. Continue until all ingredients are used, dotting top with butter. Add cream. Adjust top crust: flute edges and cut vents. Bake in hot oven (425 degrees) 30-40 minutes. If potatoes are still not tender reduce temperture to 350 F. and continue baking until done. Note: I tried the above baking directions and got a rather brown crust. When I tried baking it at an initial temp. of 425 F. for 15 minutes and reducing it to 325 F. afterwards for 45 minutes more, I got a better crust and the filling was always cooked...

Hot Hot Hot Butternut Rhubarb Pie

150 g Butternut cookies
1 c (100g) plain cake crumbs
60 g Butter, melted
1/3 c (25g) flaked almonds

----------------------------------FILLING-----------------------------
750 g Bunch rhubarb, trimmed and
- chopped
2 lg (400g) green apples, peeled
- and grated
1/2 c (110g) caster sugar
1 ts Grated orange rind
1/4 c (35g) cornflour
1/4 c (60ml) water
3/4 c (75g) plain cake crumbs

----------------------------------CRUMBLE--------------------------
1/3 c (50g) self-raising flour
50 g Cold butter, chopped
1/4 c (15g) shredded coconut
1/4 c (50g) brown sugar

Grease a 23cm pie dish. Process cookies until finely crushed. Combine cookie crumbs, cake crumbs and butter in bowl; mix well. Press over base and side of prepared dish; refrigerate 30 mins.

Spread rhubarb filling into prepared dish, top with crumble, sprinkle with almonds. Bake in a moderate oven about 30 mins or until pie is browned.
Serve hot with cream.

Filling: Combine rhubarb, apples, sugar and rind in the pan, simmer, covered, about 5 mins, stirring occasionally, or until rhubarb is soft.
Simmer, stirring, for a further 10 mins or until the mixture thickens. Stir in blended cornflour and water, and continue stirring until mixture boils.
Remove from the heat, stir in crumbs; cool.

Crumble: Sift flour into medium-sized bowl, rub in butter; stir in coconut and sugar.

I'm In Love Cherry Cream Cheese Pie

1 Pie shell
  -(graham cracker)
8 oz Cream cheese
1/2 c Sour cream
1/3 c Granulated sugar
1/2 t Vanilla (or to taste)
4 oz Whipped cream
14 oz Cherry pie filling
  -(1 can)

Cream together the cheese and sour cream. Fold in sugar gradually. Add vanilla and mix well. Fold in whipped cream. Pour into pie shell and chill for at least 3 hours.

Pour excess syrup from the can of cherry pie filling. Leave some, but you certainly don't need all of it. The sauce should cover the cream cheese mix, but the cherries shouldn't be drowning in it. Pour pie filling on top.
Serve cold.

NOTES:

* A simple cherry cream cheese pie -- My wife makes this for me periodically, and it is always delicious. No baking is required, and it is very easy to make. Makes one pie.

* If you don't have the time to sit around for 3 hours waiting for the pie to chill, make the cream cheese filling the night before and let the pie chill overnight.

* We prefer to use non-dairy whipped cream substitute. We usually use the same brand name ingredients for best results: Philadelphia cream cheese, Breakstone's sour cream, Cool-whip and Comstock cherry pie filling.

Ice Cream Pumpkin Pie

----------------------------------CRUST----------------------------
    1 c Ground pecans
  1/2 c Ground ginger snaps
  1/4 c Sugar
  1/4 c Butter or margarine,
      -softened

----------------------------------FILLING---------------------------
    1 c Cooked or canned pumpkin
  1/2 c Packed brown sugar
 1/2 ts Salt
 1/2 ts Ground cinnamon
 1/2 ts Ground ginger
 1/4 ts Ground nutmeg
   1 qt Vanilla ice cream,
      -softened slightly

In a bowl, combine the pecans, gingersnaps, sugar, and butter; mix well.

Press into a 9-inch pie pan; bake at 450 for 5 minutes. Cool completely.

In a mixing bowl, beat first six filling ingredients. Stir in ice cream and mix until well blended. Spoon into crust. Freeze until firm, at least 2-3 hours. Store in freezer.

Makes 8 servings.

If The Shoe Fits Cake

    1 1/2 c Flour
    1/4 c Lard
    1/4 c Butter
    1/2 c Water, hot
      1 x *pastry
      1 c Brown sugar
      1 x *or:
    1/2 c Molasses
    1/2 t Soda

  Make crumbs by combining the flour, sugar and shortening. Line a pie pan with pastry. Dissolve the soda in the hot water and combine with the molasses. Pour into the pastry-lined pan, top with the crumbs and bake at 350-F until firm.

Island Chocolate Coconut Crunch Pie

-----chocolate coconut -crust-----
Nonstick cooking spray
14 oz Semisweet chocolate;
-coarsely chopped
2 tb Unsalted butter
1 1/2 c Rice Krispies
1/2 c Sweetened coconut; shredded
-----filling-----
8 oz Bittersweet chocolate;
-coarsely chopped
2 tb Water
1 tb Unsalted butter
1/8 ts Salt
1 1/4 c Heavy cream
1/2 c Cream of coconut; (fx. coco
-lopez)
2 ts Vanilla extract

Make the chocolate coconut crust:

1. Spray the bottom and side of a 9-inch pie pan well with nonstick cooking spray. Melt the chocolate with the butter according to the directions in the Chocolate Key.

2. In a large bowl combine the melted chocolate mixture with the cereal and the coconut. Scrape the mixture into the prepared pan.
 Using a small offset metal cake spatula, spread the mixture evenly onto the bottom and side of the pan, covering it completely.
 Refrigerate the crust while preparing the filling.

Make the filling:

1. Melt the chocolate with the water and butter according to the directions in the Chocolate Key. Stir in the salt. Allow the chocolate mixture to cool for 15 minutes.

2. In a large, chilled bowl combine the cream, cream of

coconut andvvanilla. Using a hand-held electric mixer, beat the mixture until soft peaks begin to form.

3. Using a large rubber spatula, fold one third of the whipped cream mixture into the chocolate mixture to lighten it. Fold in the remaining cream mixture.

4. Scrape the filling into the prepared crust, smoothing the top with a cake spatula. Refrigerate the pie for at least 2 hours, until the filling is set. Allow the cake to stand at room temperature for at least 30 minutes before serving (the pie is very difficult to slice otherwise).

8   Servings.

. Allow the pie to stand at room temperature for 30 minutes before serving.

It's a Deal! Blueberry & Walnut Pie

-----sweet pastry dough-----
- 1 c Unbleached all-purpose flour
- 1/4 c Sugar
- 1 pn Salt
- 1/4 ts Baking powder
- 4 tb Butter
- 1 lg Egg

-----blueberry filling-----
- 2 pt Blueberries
- 3/4 c Sugar
- 3 tb Cornstarch
- 3 tb Water
- 1 tb Grated lemon zest
- 3/4 c Walnut pieces; toasted & coarsely c

-----walnut crumb topping-----
- 4 tb Butter
- 1/4 c Sugar
- 1/2 ts Cinnamon
- 3/4 c Unbleached all-purpose flour
- 1/2 c Walnuts; coarsely chopped

MIXING THE PASTRY DOUGH: Stir together the dry ingredients in a bowl. Cut up and add the butter; toss gently to coat. Rub in the butter until the mixture looks sandy. Beat the egg and toss into the flour and butter mixture. Press the dough together, wrap and chill it.
FORMING THE PIE SHELL: Lightly flour the work surface and dough. Roll the dough to a 14-inch diameter disk, 1/8-inch thick. Fit the dough into a 9-inch oven-proof glass pie pan and trim away all but 1/4-inch of the excess dough. Turn the excess dough under and flute the edge of the pie. Chill while preparing the filling.
MIXING THE FILLING: Rinse and pick over the blueberries and drain them on a paper-towel-lined pan. Combine one third of the berries and the sugar in a saucepan and bring to a simmer over medium heat, stirring occasionally. Simmer the berries in the juices that accumulate about 5 minutes. Strain the juices into another pan. Pour the water into a small bowl and stir in the cornstarch to dissolve it. Return the blueberry juices

to a boil and beat about one quarter of it into the dissolved cornstarch. Return the remaining juices to a boil and beat the cornstarch mixture into it. Return the juices to a boil, beating constantly, and allow to boil about 1 to 2 minutes, beating constantly.

Stir in the remaining blueberries, the cooked berries, lemon zest and walnuts, and cool. MIXING THE CRUMB TOPPING: Cream the butter until soft, add the sugar and cream until soft and light. Beat in the cinnamon. Mix in the flour, then the walnuts. The mixture should fall into large, soft crumbs. Pour the filling into the prepared pan and smooth. Scatter over the crumbs and bake at 350F until the filling is set, the crumbs have colored and the crust is baked through, about 40 minutes. Cool on a rack. Makes one 9-inch pie.

It's Possible Banana Cream Pie 2

```
    1 c  Milk
  1/3 c  Butter
    1 ts Vanilla
    3    Eggs
1 1/2 c  Sugar; granulated
  1/2 c  Bisquick baking mix
    2    Bananas; medium, sliced
    1 c  Whipping cream; chilled
    2 tb Sugar; powdered
```

Preheat to 350F. Grease pie plate, 9x 1 1/4". Beat milk, butter, vanilla, eggs, granulated sugar and Bisquick till smooth, 30 seconds in blender on High or 1 minute with hand beater. Pour into plate. Bake till knife inserted in centre comes out clean, about 30 minutes. Cool completely.

Arrange bananas slices on pie. Beat whipping cream and powdered sugar in chilled bowl till stiff; spread over top.

Jack O's Pumpkin Cheese Pie (Low Cal)

- 1 Recipe unbaked pie shell (recipe follows)
- 8 oz Cream cheese softened
- 2 tb Granulated sugar replacement
- 1 ts Vanilla extract
- 1 Egg
- 2 1 1/2 c Unsweetened pumpkin puree
- 1 c Evaporated skim milk
- 2 Eggs
- 2 tb Granulated suagr replacement
- 1 ts Cinnamon
- 1/4 ts Ea ground nutmeg & ginger

Combine the softened cream cheese,2 T replacement(I use granulated fructose) vanilla and 1 egg in a bowl. stir well. Spread into bottom of the pie shell.

Combine the pumpkin,milk and remaining ingredients in a mixing bowl or workbowl of processor. Beat or process until well blended. Careful pour mixture over prepared shell. Bake in a 350^ oven for 65-70 minute or until a tester comes out clean.

Jacqueline's Meringue Crust

   3 lg Egg whites; at room
       -temperature
 1/4 ts Cream of tartar
 1/4 ts Salt
 3/4 c Sugar; superfine
 1/2 ts Vanilla

Spray 9" pie plate with vegetable oil spray. Combine whites, cream of tart and salt in large bowl. Beat to soft peaks. Gradually beat in sugar. Add vanilla. Beat till stiff and shiny. Spread in pie pl
  Using the back of a spoon form a decorative rim. Bake 1 hour, 15 min. at 275F till firm and crisp. Cool on a rack.

Jay's Venison Mincemeat

- 4 lb Venison
- 2 lb Beef suet
- -Tart apples
- 3 lb Brown sugar
- 2 c Maple Syrup OR
- 2 c Dark molasses
- 2 qt Cider
- 3 lb Currants
- 4 lb Seeded raisins
- 1/2 lb Citron, cut fine
- 1 Ot
- 1 qt Brandy OR
- 1 qt Wine
- 1 T Cinnamon
- 1 T Ground clove
- 1 t Allspice
- 1 t Mace
- 1 t Nutmeg
- -Salt to taste
- -Apple jack OR

Cover and cook the venison and suet with boiling water until tender; let it cool in the liquid. When it is cold and the fat has solidified, remove meat and chop the cake fat (suet). Reboil the liquid until it has been reduced to 1 1/2 cups. Chop the venison and add it to twice as much peeled, cored and finely chopped apple. Add the sugar and maple syrup or molasses. Add the dried fruit, suet, cider and the reduced boiling liquid. Boil slowly for 2 hours, stirring to prevent burning. Add the apple jack or brandy or wine and the spices. Mix thoroughly and store in crocks or jars. May also be frozen, but doesn't freeze hard. 15 pies, recipe can be cut in half.

Jazzy Smooth Velvet Cream Pies

3/4 c C and H Granulated Sugar
1/3 c All-purpose flour
1/4 ts Milk
  2   Eggs; or...
  3   Egg yolks
  1 tb butter or margarine
  1 ts vanilla
  1   9" pastry shell
       (baked and cooled)

In a saucepan mix sugar, flour and salt. Add milk and eggs. Beat with a whisk until smooth. Bring to boil over medium heat stirring constantly.

Continue cooking and stirring until smooth and thickened. Remove from heat, stir in butter and vanilla. Cool 5 minutes. Pour into pastry shell. Chill until set.

BANANA CREAM PIE: Make a base filling; cool. Slice 2 or 3 large bananas in bottom of baked pie shell; add cooled filling and chill. Serve with Whipped Cream Topping.

BUTTERSCOTCH CREAM PIE: Use 3/4 cup firmly packed C and H Golden or Darn Brown Sugar instead of granulated sugar in basic filling recipe; increase butter to 3 tablespoons. Top with Tall 'N' Tender meringue (see separate recipe) or chill and serve with Whipped Cream Topping.

COCONUT CREAM PIE: Stir 1 cup flaked coconut into basic filling before pouring into baked pie shell. Top with Tall 'N' Tender meringue or chill and serve with Whipped Cream Topping. Garnish with toasted coconut, if desired.

CHOCOLATE CREAM PIE: Make basic filling; add 1/2 cup semi-sweet chocolate pieces to hot, cooked filling in saucepan. Stir until completely melted.

Pour into baked shell; chill. Spread with Whipped Cream Topping; garnish with shaved chocolate.

MICROWAVE DIRECTIONS: Combine sugar, flour and salt in deep 2 quart glass mixing bowl. Add eggs and milk. Beat with whisk until smooth. Microwave at full power 8 minutes, stirring 3 times. Precede {sic} as recipe directs.

Jess's Pumpkin Cheese Pie

    -Cheese layer.....
  8 oz Softened cream cheese
  1   Egg
    -Pie layer...............
1 1/2 c Canned pumpkin
  2   Eggs
1 1/2   Pumpkin pie spice
    -Prepare pie shell but do
    -not bake.
  2 tb Granulated sugar replacement
  1 ts Vanilla
  1 c Evaporated milk
  2 tb Granulated sugar replacement

For cheese layer, combine cream cheese, sugar replacement, vanilla and 1 egg in mixing bowl. Stir to mix well, spread in bottom of unbaked pie shell. For pie layer, combine pumpkin, milk, 2 eggs sugar replacement and spices in a mixing bowl, beating to blend thoroughly. Carefully pour over cheese layer. Bake at 350 degree for 65 to 70 min or until knife inserted comes out clean.

Jessica's Coffee Cake

----------------------------------CAKE-----------------------------
- 1 1/2 c Flour (unbleached),
    -sifted
- 1 c Sugar, granulated
- 2 t Baking powder
- 1/2 t Baking soda
- 1/4 t Salt
- 2 Eggs
- 1 c Sour cream
- 1/2 t Vanilla
- 1/4 c Blueberries, fresh,
    optional (or other fruit, or nuts such as walnuts)
- Vegetable oil

---------------------------------TOPPING--------------------------
- 5 T Sugar, granulated
- 2 T Butter
- 1/2 t Cinnamon, ground

Preheat oven to 350 degrees F. In a large mixing bowl, resift sift flour with baking power, baking soda, salt and about 1 cup of sugar.

In a separate bowl, beat together the eggs, sour cream and vanilla. Add egg mixture to flour mixture and beat until smooth.

Oil a 9-inch square baking pan (you can also use an 8 inch square pan, or anything of similar surface area, if you increase the baking time by about 5 minutes).

Spread the batter in the pan. If you are using fruit or nuts, scatter them over the batter and stir a little bit so that they stay in the top layer.

In a small bowl, mix about 5 T sugar with the butter and cinnamon with a sturdy fork, until they are blended and resemble cornmeal (i.e., you should have a mixture of fine crumbs, not a smooth mixture). Sprinkle topping over batter. Bake for 20-25 minutes, until a clean toothpick inserted in the center of the cake comes out dry. Cool slightly; serve warm or at room temperature.

Joanne's Chocolate Chip Pie

INGREDIENTS:
2 eggs
1/2 cup white sugar
1/2 cup all-purpose flour
1/2 cup packed brown sugar
1 cup butter, melted and cooled
1 cup semisweet chocolate chips
1 cup chopped walnuts
1 recipe pastry for a 9 inch single crust pie

DIRECTIONS:
Preheat oven to 325 degrees F (165 degrees C).
In a large bowl, beat the eggs until foamy. Add the flour, white sugar and brown sugar; beat until well blended. Blend in the melted butter. Stir in the chocolate chips and walnuts. Pour batter into one unbaked 9 inch pie shell.
Bake at 325 degrees F (165 degrees C) for 1 hour.
Serve warm with whipped cream or ice cream, if desired.

JBP's Chocolate Malted-Milk Pie

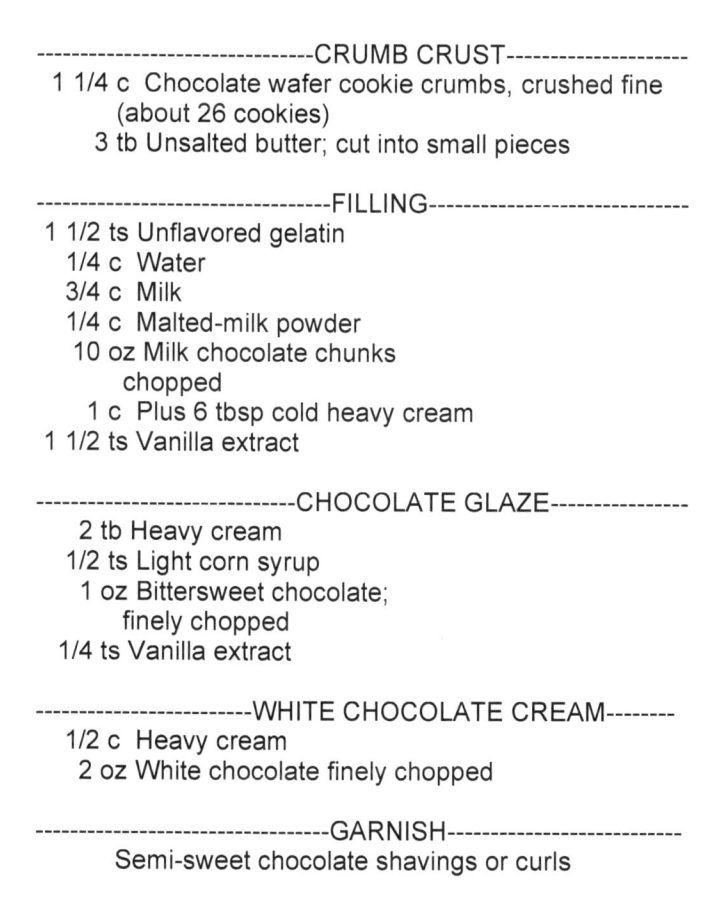

----------------------------------CRUMB CRUST--------------------
1 1/4 c Chocolate wafer cookie crumbs, crushed fine
         (about 26 cookies)
      3 tb Unsalted butter; cut into small pieces

----------------------------------FILLING----------------------------
1 1/2 ts Unflavored gelatin
    1/4 c Water
    3/4 c Milk
    1/4 c Malted-milk powder
     10 oz Milk chocolate chunks
           chopped
      1 c Plus 6 tbsp cold heavy cream
1 1/2 ts Vanilla extract

------------------------------CHOCOLATE GLAZE----------------
      2 tb Heavy cream
    1/2 ts Light corn syrup
      1 oz Bittersweet chocolate;
           finely chopped
    1/4 ts Vanilla extract

-------------------------WHITE CHOCOLATE CREAM--------
    1/2 c Heavy cream
      2 oz White chocolate finely chopped

----------------------------------GARNISH--------------------------
Semi-sweet chocolate shavings or curls

Prepare crust: Preheat oven to 350 F. In food processor, mix crumbs and butter until moist and crumbly. Press over bottom and sides of 9-inch pie plate. Bake 5 minutes, until crust is set. Cool on wire rack.

Filling: In a small saucepan, soften gelatin in the water for 2 minutes.
Heat gently over low heat, stirring until dissolved. Stir in milk, then malted-milk powder until dissolved. Stir in chocolate over low heat to melt. Scrape into medium sized metal bowl. Set bowl into a larger bowl filled with

ice water; stir chocolate mixture 10 minutes or until it begins to mound slightly, resembling the consistency of unbeaten egg whites. In another large bowl, with mixer, beat all cream until soft, billowy peaks form. Stir one-third of cream into chocolate mixture; fold into chocolate mixture; fold in remainder until no streaks appear. Pour into crust and refrigerate.

Glaze: In a glass measure, microwave cream and syrup on high until boiling, 20 seconds, or heat to boiling in a saucepan. Add chocolate and vanilla, let stand 1 minute, then stir until melted and smooth. Refrigerate 30 minutes. Pipe the glaze over the pie. Refrigerate until filling is soft set, 6 hours or overnight (after the first 2 hours cover loosely with plastic.

Cream: In a 2-cup glass measure, microwave cream on high until boiling, or heat to boiling in a saucepan. Add white chocolate; let stand 1 minute. Stir until melted. Chill, about 2 hours. At high speed, beat until soft peaks form. Dollop mixture in center of pie. Garnish with chocolate gratings or curls. Refrigerate until ready to serve.

Joyful Nesselrode Pie

INGREDIENTS:
1 (3.5 ounce) package instant vanilla pudding mix
1 1/2 cups milk
1/2 teaspoon rum flavored extract
8 maraschino cherries, chopped
8 ounces heavy cream
1 (9 inch) prepared graham cracker crust
1/8 cup grated semisweet chocolate

DIRECTIONS:
In a saucepan, combine pudding mix with 1 1/2 cup milk. Cook until thick. Add rum flavoring and chopped cherries. Remove from heat. Let cool to room temperature.
In a large bowl, whip the cream. Add 1/2 of the cream to the pudding mixture and fold in. Pour pudding mixture into graham cracker crust.
Decorate with remaining whipped cream and then grated chocolate.

Jump For Joy Popovers

   2   Eggs
1/4 ts Salt
   1 c Milk
   2 tb Unsalted butter; melted
   1 c All-purpose flour

Butter a 6-cup popover or Texas-sized muffin pan.

In a medium bowl lightly whisk together the eggs and salt. Stir in the milk and butter and beat in the flour until just blended. DO NOT OVERBEAT! Fil each cup about half full using all the batter.

Place popovers in a cold oven, set the temperature to 425 degrees F and bake for 20 minutes. Popovers should rise considerably during this time. Reduce oven to 375 F and continue baking 10-15 minutes longer until popovers are golden and crisp on the outside. Quickly pierce each popover with a thin metal skewer or the tip of a small knife to release the steam. Turn the oven off and leave in for 5-10 minutes more for further crisping. Remove and serve at once.

Makes 6 popovers

Justin's Secret Sweet Potato Pie

- 1 1/2 lb Sweet potatoes
- 1 c Sugar, granulated
- 12 T Butter, unsalted
  (or use corn-oil margarine)
- 2 Eggs
- 1 t Vanilla
- 1/2 t Nutmeg
- 1 Pie crust, unbaked

Boil potatoes until tender (20-30 minutes). Drain and peel.

In a blender, put the potatoes, sugar and butter. Mix up a little, then add eggs, vanilla and nutmeg. Blend ingredients together well, until mixture is very smooth. Pour into unbaked pie shell and bake at 375 degrees F. for 45-55 minutes until filling is set.

NOTES:

* This is an extremely simple and extremely good pie recipe. You can even cheat and use store-bought pie crusts, in which case the whole thing takes about 5 minutes to put together. Serves 3-8.

* If you don't want to make your own pie shell, I find that the Pet Ritz factory pie shells work well.

Keep A Secret Sugar Cookies

    1 c Butter, softened
    1 c Salad oil
    1 c Sugar, powdered
       -(sifted if it is lumpy)
    1 c Sugar
    2   Eggs
    1 t Vanilla
    4 c Flour
    1 t Baking soda
    2 t Cream of tartar
 1/2 t Salt
       Extra sugar
       -(for dipping)

Cream the butter and sugars, then add oil and mix well. Add the eggs and vanilla and mix well.

Sift the flour, baking soda, cream of tartar and salt together, then add to above and mix well. Refrigerate overnight, or until dough is firm. If you want to speed this up, put the dough in the freezer, but keep an eye on it.

Preheat oven to 350 degrees F. Drop dough in 1/2 t amounts on an ungreased cookie sheet. Dip a glass in dough and wipe excess off. Then dip the glass in sugar and flatten a cookie. Repeat the dip-in-sugar flatten-cookie sequence until all are done. The cookies won't spread in baking, so you can easily judge how far apart to put them (you want room to cook, but not to grow). If you find that the dough is getting too soft to flatten easily, put it in the refrigerator between batches.

Bake for about 5-6 minutes, until the edges are JUST beginning to turn golden brown. Take off the cookie sheet and put on waxed paper or foil to cool.

Key Lime Pie (Nutrasweet)

    1 c Graham cracker crumbs
    3 tb Melted Margarine
    2 tb NutraSweet (r) Spoonful (tm)
1 1/4 oz Envelope Unflavored gelatin
1 3/4 c Skim milk
    8 oz (1) Pk Reduced Fat Cream Cheese, Softened
    1/3 c To 1/2 c fresh lime juice
    1/2 c NutraSweet(r)Spoonfull(tm)
        Lime Slices
        Mint Sprigs

Combine Graham Cracker Crumbs, Margarine and 2 Tbl NutraSweet (r) Spoonfull (tm) in bottom of 7-inch springform pan; Pat evenly on bottom and 1/2 inch up the side of the pan.

Sprinkle Gelatin over 1/2 cup of the milk in a small saucepan; Let stand 2 to 3 minutes. Cook over low heat, stirring constantly, until gelatin is dissolved. Beat cream cheese until fluffy in small bown; beat in remaining 1 1/4 cups milk and the gelatin mixture. Mix in lime juice and 1/2 cup NutraSweet (r) Spoonful (tm). Refrigerate pie until set, about 2 hours.

To serve: Loosen side of pie for pan with small spatula and remove side of pan. Place pie on serving plate; Garnish with lime slices and mint.

Makes 8 servings

Kids Muddy Pie

    1 pk Jello chocolate instant
        pudding (4 serve size)
    1 c   Milk, cold
    1 pk Cool whip
    20   Choc sandwich cookies
        chopped
1 1/2 c   Kraft min marshmallows
      1   Prep Graham Crumb Crust
        * - 9 inch
    1 pk Gummy worms for decoration

  Prepare pudding according to package directions reducing milk to 1 cup.

  Fold in whipped topping. Stir in 2/3 of the cookies and all the marshmallows. Spoon this into the crust. Sprinkle top with the remaining cookies. Decorate with gummy worms. Freeze until firm, about 4 hours.

  Remove from freezer 10 minutes before serving for easy slicing.

Lake Superior Whipping Cream

   1/2 c Whipping cream
    2 t Vanilla sugar
       (or use white sugar and about 1/2 t vanilla extract)

Shake the carton of whipping cream well and pour it into the blender or food processor. Add the vanilla sugar (see below if you don't know what vanilla sugar is.)

Whip the cream in the machine. If it's a food processor, leave the pushing device out; if a blender, remove the center of the lid, or just cover the top of the jar with your hand. The trick is to allow lots of air into the cream. Run the machine for no more than five seconds at a time, to avoid making butter. The cream is done when it holds a peak.

Lakeview Strawberry-Rhubarb Pie

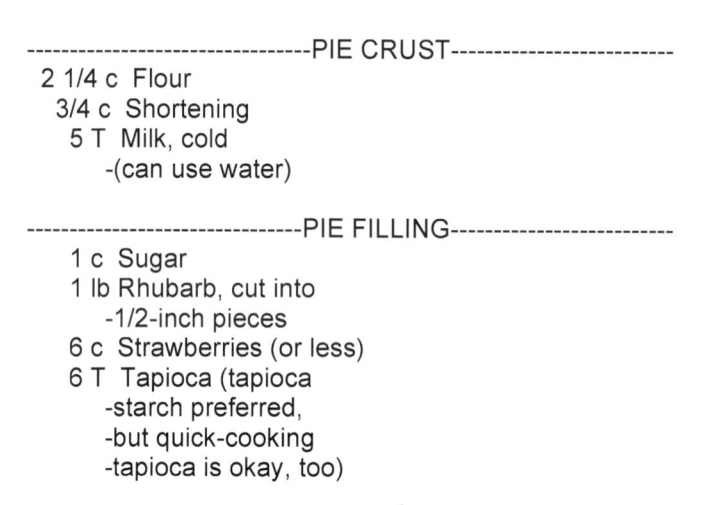

---------------------------------PIE CRUST-------------------------
- 2 1/4 c Flour
- 3/4 c Shortening
- 5 T Milk, cold
  - -(can use water)

---------------------------------PIE FILLING------------------------
- 1 c Sugar
- 1 lb Rhubarb, cut into
  - -1/2-inch pieces
- 6 c Strawberries (or less)
- 6 T Tapioca (tapioca
  - -starch preferred,
  - -but quick-cooking
  - -tapioca is okay, too)

Cut the strawberries in half. Place in a bowl with the rhubarb and add the sugar and tapioca. Mix and let sit for at least 15 minutes. Make the pie crust: Cut the shortening and flour together. This can be done with two knives, with a pastry cutter, or with some electric mixers. (I do mine in a Kitchen Aid food processor/mixer.) When the mixture has an even consistency (it should resemble coarse sand), add in the milk (or water).Take about 5/8ths of the dough and roll out on a floured board until it is a little bit larger than a 10-inch pie pan. Put this in the pie pan. (The rest of the dough is for the top of the pie.)

Pour the strawberries and rhubarb mixture into the pie crust. Roll out the remainder of the pie crust. Place on top of the pie, crimping the edges of the top and bottom crusts together. Make one or two slits in the top of the crust for steam to escape. Bake 45 to 50 minutes at 400 degrees F. or until Ayrup boils with heavy bubbles that do not burst.

Lazy River Pie

- 1 c Flour
- 1   Stick of butter
- 1 c Cut pecans
- 8 oz Philadelphia cream cheese
- 1 c Powdered sugar
- 1 c Cool Whip
- 1 sm Instant vanilla pudding
- 1 sm Instant chocolate pudding
- 2 c Milk
- 1 ts Vanilla
-    Cool Whip
-    Hershey Bar

In a 13 x 9 inch dish, mix flour, butter, and pecans. Bake and let cool--making the crust. Mix together cream cheese, powdered sugar, 1 cup of Cool Whip; spread over the crust. The mix instant puddings, milk and vanilla; spread over cheese layer. Next, spread Cool Whip over the pudding layer. Grate candy bar over the Cool Whip. Chill until ready to serve.

Lemon Cream Cheese Pie

1 Servings

1/4 c Squeezed lemon juice
1   8 oz pk cream cheese
2   Eggs; beaten
3/4 c Sugar
1   9 inch vanilla wafer crust
      Topping:
1 tb Grated lemon peel
1 tb Sugar
1 c Sour cream

Blend lemon juice, cream cheese together. Add beaten eggs, sugar together. Add this to cream cheese and beat until fluffy. Bake in 350 degree oven about 25 minutes. Cool for 5 minutes. Prepare topping of sour cream, lemon rind and sugar mixed together. Spread over cool pie. Return to oven and bake 10 minutes longer. Cool; chill about 5 hours before serving.

Lemon Lips Pie

1 servings

-----crust-----
1 1/2 c Cookie crumbs; lemon
1/2 c Almonds; finely chopped
6 tb Butter
1/4 c Sugar
1/4 c Heavy cream
-----filling-----
1 c Powdered sugar
6 oz Cream cheese; softened
1/2 c Sour cream
1/2 c Whipped topping
3 1/2 oz Lemon pie filling
1 3/4 c Milk
1 ts Lemon juice
1 ts Lemon rind; grated
-----topping-----
2 c Whipped topping
1/4 c Lemon drop hard candies; finely crushed

For crust: Mix cookie crumbs, ground almonds, butter, sugar and heavy cream together. Pat in bottom and up sides of a nine-inch pie pan. Bake at 300 for 15 minutes. Set aside to cool.

For filling: Mix powdered sugar, softened cream cheese, sour cream and whipped topping until smooth and creamy. Spread in bottom of cooled crust lemon pudding and pie mix (according to package directions), milk, lemon juice and grated lemon rind. Spread over cream cheese layer in crust. Refrigerate one hour.

For topping: Spread whipped topping over top of pie and sprinkle with crush lemon candies. Refrigerate.

Let's Party Margarita Pie

INGREDIENTS:
1 1/4 cups crushed pretzels
1/2 cup butter, melted
1/4 cup white sugar
2 limes, zested and juiced
1/4 cup orange juice
1 (14 ounce) can sweetened condensed milk
1 (8 ounce) container frozen whipped topping, thawed

DIRECTIONS:
In a medium bowl, combine crushed pretzels, melted butter, and sugar. Press mixture into a pie pan.
In a large bowl, mix together lime juice, lime zest, orange juice, and sweetened condensed milk. Fold in whipped topping. Spoon filling into pretzel crust. Chill pie for 25 to 30 minutes.

Lingering Blueberry Torte

    1/2 c Butter or margarine, softened
      2 ts Grated lemon peel
       1   Egg
1 1/2 c Pillsbury's BEST all Purpose
         Flour or unbleached
         Flour
     2 tb Poppyseed
  1/2 ts Baking soda
  1/4 ts Salt
  1/2 c Dairy sour cream

1. Cake Mix: 2/3 cup sugar

2. Filling: 2 cups fresh or frozen blueberries, thawed, drained on papertowels 1/3 cup sugar 2 tsp. flour 1/4 tsp. nutmeg

3. Glaze: 1/3 cup powdered sugar 1 to 2 tsp. milk

Heat oven to 350 degrees. Grease and flour bottom and sides of 9-10 inch springform pan. In a large bowl, beat 2/3 cup sugar and butter until light and fluffy. Add lemon peel and egg; beat 2 minutes at medium speed. Lightly spoon flour into measuring cup; level off. In a medium bowl, com- bine 1 1/2 cups flour, poppyseed, baking soda and salt; add to butter mix- ture alternately with sour cream. Spread batter over bottom and 1 inch up sides of greased and floured pan, MAKING SURE BATTER ON SIDES IS 1/4 INCH THICK. In a medium bowl, combine all filling ingredients; spoon over batter. Bake at 350 degrees for 45-55 minutes or until crust is golden brown. Cool slightly. Remove sides of pan. In a small bowl, combine powdered sugar and enough milk until glaze is of desired drizzling consistency; blend until smooth. Drizzle over warm cake. Serve warm or cool; makes 8 servings.

Little Chapel Butterscotch Oat Squares

    2 c Oats, quick or instant
    1 c Brown sugar (packed)
  1/2 c Butter, melted
  1/2 t Vanilla extract

Mix oats and brown sugar, mix in butter and vanilla. Divide mixture evenly in 2 ungreased 8-inch square pans, spread evenly. Bake at 375 degrees F. for about 10 minutes or until it looks golden-brown. Squares will be soft, but will harden when cool.

Allow to cool for 5 minutes, then mark in squares with a sharp knife.
Loosen edges and allow to cool before removing from pans.

NOTES:

* Easy butterscotch oatmeal pan cookies -- The easiest cookies (actually cookie-like objects) to make. My mother makes these, I don't know where the recipe is from. makes 30-40.

Little Elf's Coconut Cream Pie

Ingredients

```
----------------------------PIE-----------------------------------
    3   egg yolks; well beaten
    2 c milk, whole
  3/4 c sugar, granulated
  1/3 c flour, all-purpose
  1/4 ts salt
    2 ts butter, unsalted
    1 ts vanilla
1 1/3 c coconut
    1   pie shell, 9, baked

--------------------------MERINGUE--------------------------
    3   egg whites
  1/2 ts vanilla
  1/4 ts cream of tartar
    6 tb sugar, granulated
```

Instructions

Preheat oven to 350~. In a med. saucepan, combine egg yolks and milk; mix well. Add sugar, flour, and salt. Cook over med. Heat until thick; stirring constantly. Remove from heat. Add butter, vanilla, and 1 cup of coconut. Pour into baked pie shell.
Spread meringue over filling, sealing edges to crust, and sprinkle with 1/3 cup remaining coconut. Bake for 12 to 15 mins. Makes 6 to 8 servings.
Meringue: Beat egg whites with vanilla and cream of tartar until soft peaks form. Gradually add sugar, beating until stiff.

Little Jenna's Sweet Potato Pie

-Filling:
- 3 Sweet potatoes
- 1/2 Lemon
- 1 Stick butter
- 3 T Flour
- 1 c Sugar
- 1 t Vanilla

Pie shell: 3 oz cream cheese 1 stick butter 1 cup flour

Mix cream cheese, butter and flour by hand and roll out on floured board.
Place in pie pan.

Peel and cut up sweet potatoes. Place in pot with 1/4 of lemon with 1" of boiling water; cook until tender. Mash sweet potatoes, measure 2 cups and mix with other ingredients. Add juice of 1/4 lemon, mix and pour into pie shell. Bake in a 350F oven for 1 hour.

Loveable Peaches and Cream Pie

- 3 1/2 c Sliced peaches, well drained
- 1 ts Ground cinnamon
- 1/4 ts Ground nutmeg
- 1 c Whipping cream
- 2 Eggs
- 3/4 c Sugar
- 2/3 c Bisquick
- Streusel (below)
- Sweetened whipped cream

Heat oven to 375F. Grease pie pan 10 x 1/2". Pat peach slices dry; place in plate. Sprinkle with cinnamon and nutmeg; toss. Spread evenly in plate.

Beat remaining ingredients except streusel and sweetened whipped cream until smooth, 15 seconds in blender on high or 1 minute with electric mixer on high. Pour into plate. Sprinkle with Streusel.

Bake until knife inserted in center comes out clean, 40-45 minutes. Top each serving with seetened whipped cream.

Streusel: 1 T. firm margarine, 1/4 c. bisquick, 2 T. sugar, 1/3 c. slivered almonds.

Lunch Pail Apple Squares

- 2 c White flour, unbleached
- 2 c Brown sugar, firmly packed
- 1/2 c Butter (or margarine)
- 1 c Chopped nuts (optional)
- 2 t Cinnamon (or less)
- 1 t Soda
- 1/2 t Salt
- 1 c Sour cream (or yogurt)
- 1 t Vanilla extract
- 1 Egg
- 2 c Apples, peeled and finely chopped (about 2 apples)

Preheat oven to 350 degrees F. In a large bowl, combine the flour, brown sugar and margarine. Blend at low speed, until the mixture forms fine crumbs. If you want to include them, stir in the nuts now. Place about 2 ¾ cups of the crumb mixture into an ungreased pan, about 13 x 9 inches.
Press down firmly.

Add the remaining ingredients (except for the apples) to the remaining crumb mixture. Blend well. Stir the chopped apples into the batter. Spoon the batter evenly over the crumb base in the pan. Bake at 350 degrees F. for 30-40 minutes. If you use the larger pan, bake for 25-30 minutes. Cool before cutting. Better yet, let it wait 24 hours before cutting. Store loosely covered.

NOTES:

* Sugary, moist apple squares -- Try to avoid eating very many of these squares on the day you make them, as they improve immeasurably on the second and third day! This recipe originally came from a Pillsbury bake-off. Makes 12-15 squares.

Magical Black Bottom Pie

    Vanilla wafers or graham
    - crackers
15 oz Can sweetened condensed milk
1/2 c Lemon juice
  2   Eggs; seperated, yolks not
    - beaten
1 ts Grated orange rind
4 tb Sugar

Line a pie plate with fine crumbs of vanilla wafers or graham crackers. Dot
all over with tart berry jam. Over the jam pour the filling made by mixing
the milk, lemon juice, 2 egg yolks, and lemon rind together in a seperate
bowl. This mixture becomes a smooth custard as it is stirred together; it
requires no cooking. Cover with a meringue made by beating the 2 egg
whites stiff and beating in the sugar gradually. Bake in a slow oven (325ø)
for 15 to 20 minutes, or until meringue is delicately browned. Serve cold.

Make Mice

      Angelica (Cut two pieces of crystalized (candied) angelica, each about 1/8 inch by 2 inches)
- 2 Almonds (blanched)
- 2 Pear halves, preferably canned (for authenticity), but cooked, fresh pear would do

Carefully halve the almonds along the natural split in the nut. (This is easiest after they are still wet from blanching.) Place the pear halves, round side up, in the serving dish.

At the narrow end of each half, add two almond halves to make mouse ears.

At the other end, insert the angelica to make a tail.

Mama Bear's Lime Bars

- 2 c   Flour
- 1/2 c   Confectioner's sugar
- 1 c   Butter
- 4   Eggs
- 2 c   Sugar
- 1 ds   Salt
- 1/3 c   Lime juice
-         Confectioner's sugar

  Preheat oven to 350 degrees F. Combine flour and powdered sugar; cut in the butter. Press mixture into a 13x9-inch baking pan. Bake at 350 degrees F. for 20-25 minutes, or until golden.

  Beat eggs at high speed with electric mixer until light and pale yellow.
  Gradually add sugar, salt, then lime juice, continuing to beat at high speed. Pour lime mixture over hot crust and return to 350 degree F. oven for 20-25 minutes or until golden. Sprinkle at once with powdered sugar. Cool. Cut into bars.

Managers Special Walnut Crumb Crust

    1 c Fine graham cracker crumbs
         OR gingersnap wafer crumbs
  1/2 c Chopped walnuts
  1/4 ts Salt
  1/4 c Soft butter
    1 T Honey

Mix all the ingredients and press into 9" pie pan. Bake in moderate over about 6 minutes. Cool before adding the pie filling.

Delicious base for cream pies or pumpkin pie.

Mardi Gras Pecan Pie

3 Servings

---------------------------------THE CRUST------------------------
- 1 1/4 c Flour;all purpose
- 1 ts Salt
- 4 tb Butter;sweet,cold&cut up
- 3 tb Shortening; cold
- 3 tb Water; ice

---------------------------------THE FILLING-----------------------
- 3 Eggs; beaten
- 1 c Sugar
- 1/2 c Light corn syrup
- 1/2 c Dark corn syrup
- 1/3 c Butter; melted unsalted
- 2 tb Bourbon
- 1/2 ts Salt
- 1 c Pecans; chopped

1. Crust - Place flour, sugar and salt in bowl of food processor. Pulse just to combine. Add butter and shortening. Pulse until mixture resembles coarse meal. With machine running, slowly pour in water. Process just until mixture begins to come together. Gently press dough into a ball. Wrap in plastic and refrigerate for 30 minutes.
2. On a lighly floured surface, roll out dough to fit a 9 in. plate. Place dough in plate and trim, crimp edges.
3. Preheat oven 375 degrees.
4. FILLING Whisk together the eggs, sugar, corn syrups, butter, bourbon and salt. Place the pecans in the bottom of the pie plate. Pour the filling over the pecans. Bake until set, about 35-40 minutes.

Marshawna's Hot Toddy Pie

1 1/2 c Canned eggnog
1/2 c Sugar
1/2 c Bisquick
4 Eggs
2 T Rum OR
1 ts Rum flavoring
Ground nutmeg

Heat oven to 350 F. Grease pie plate, 9 x 1 1/4". Place all ingredients except nutmeg in blender container. Cover and blend on high 15 seconds. Pour into plate; Sprinkle with nutmeg.

Bake until knife inserted in center comes out clean, about 40 minutes. Cool 5 minutes. Serve with spiced whipped cream if desired.

Spiced Whipped Cream: Beat 1/2 c. chilled whipping cream, 1 T. sugar and 1/4 ts. ground nutmeg in chilled bowl until stiff.

Megan's Chocolate Mousse Pie

1 1/2 ts Unflavored gelatin
1 1/2 tb Cold water
   3 tb Boiling water
3/4 c Sugar
1/4 c Cocoa powder; (plus 2 tbsp.)
1 1/2 c Heavy cream
1 1/2 ts Vanilla

Sprinkle gelatin over cold water in small bowl and let stand 1 minute to soften. Add boiling water; stir until gelatin is dissolved (mixture must be clear). Stir together sugar and cocoa in small cold mixer bowl; add cream and vanilla. Beat at medium speed until stiff peaks form. Pour in gelatin mixture and beat until well blended. Spoon into serving dishes OR in graham cracker pie crust.

Megan's Chocolate Mousse Pie - 2

```
-----crust-----
1 1/4 c  Chocolate wafer crumbs
  1/2 c  Melted butter; or margarine
-----mousse-----
   8 oz Semisweet chocolate; finely
        -ground
   1 oz Unsweetened chocolate;
        -finely ground
   4 oz Heavy whipping cream
   6 tb Unsalted butter
   2    Eggs; separated
        Bailey's irish cream;
        -optional
```

Add butter to crumbs just until it will hold its shape when pressed into a pan I'm sorry but I've never bothered to measure the butter!

MOUSSE:

Beat the egg whites until stiff peaks forms. Set aside. Heat the cream and medium heat. When the butter is well-incorporated into the cream, add the chocolates. Stir off the heat until melted and well-blended. Add the egg yolks.

Quickly fold 1/4 of the chocolate mixture into the beaten whites, then fold the whites into the chocolate.

Fill the crust with the filling and refrigerate several hours. If you like may add Bailey's Irish Cream to the filling to flavour and whip cream with a tiny bit of sugar and some Frangelico liqueur. Amaretto for the whipping cream is also nice. It's just a decadent final touch to an already-decadent dessert.

Memories Of Mincemeat

- 3/4 c   Suet; minced (or butter/ma
- 2 c   Seedless raisins
- 2 1/2 c Currants
- 1 3/4 c Brown sugar
- 1 1/2 ts Cinnamon
- 1 1/2 ts Mace or cloves
- 1 1/2 ts Nutmeg
- 3/4 ts Salt
- 4   Apples, peeled; grated
- 1 c   Candied citron
- 1   Lemon (rind and juice only)
- 1   Orange (rind and juice only)

Makes 8 cups (not 8 servings) Combine all ingredients in a large saucepan.

Bring to a boil and simmer 5 minutes. Note: Processing mincemeat is recommended for long term storage 1-2 years

Meringue Cream Peanut Butter Pie

```
     9 inch pie shell; baked
2 1/2 c  Milk; scalded
   1/2 c  Sugar
   1/2 c  Flour, all-purpose
   1/8 ts Ground ginger
      2   Egg yolks; beaten
      1 ts Vanilla
   1/2 c  Peanut butter
         Meringue:
     3 lg Egg whites; room temp
   1/2 ts Vanilla extract
   1/4 ts Cream of tartar
     6 tb Superfine sugar
```

Prepare the prebaked pie shell; cool completely. In the top of a double boiler set over simmering water, combine 1/2 cup of the hot milk with the sugar and flour. Add 1 1/2 cups of hot milk to the mixture in the double boiler and cook, stirring frequently, for 20 minutes or until thickened.

Stir a small amount of the hot custard into the egg yolks. Combine the egg yolk mixture with the mixture in the double boiler. Cook for 2 minutes more. Remove the pan from the heat. Add the vanilla. Beat the peanut butter with the remaining milk. Add the peanut butter mixture to the hot custard. Turn the filling into the pie shell. Preheat the oven to 350 degrees. While the filling is still hot, prepare the meringue. Beat the egg whites, vanilla, and cream of tartar until the mixture holds stiff peaks.

Gradually add the sugar, 1 tablespoon at a time, beating until very stiff and glossy. All the sugar must be dissolved. Spread the meringue over the hot filling, sealing it to the edge of the crust. Bake 12 to 15 minutes or until golden brown. Cool, and chill until serving.

One 9-inch single-crust pie

Merry Mincemeat

    2 lb Lean beef round stew meat
    8 c Water
    1 lb Suet, cut up
    12 md Cooking apples, pared and
        Cored
    3 lb Seedless raisins
    3 c Dried currents
    1 c Candied orange peel, finely
        Diced
    4 t Salt
    4 t Cinnamon
    1 t Powdered allspice
    1 t Ground cloves
    2 c Sugar
    2 c Brown sugar
    1 c Molasses
    8 t Lemon juice
    2 c Apple cider

  Boil beef in water. Cover and simmer 2 hours. Remove meat and reserve 4 cups of stock. Put meat, suet, apples through a food chopped. Put in large, 7-8 quart, pan. Add remaining ingredients, except lemon juice and cider. Add reserved stock and simmer uncovered 1 hour, stirring occasionally. Add juices during last 5 minutes of cooking. Pack while hot into sterilized jars. 1 quart will make a 9-inch pie (3 cups) with 1 cup left over for cookies or tarts.

Miss Pretty Persimmon Pie

    1   Unbaked 9-inch pie crust
    2 c Persimmon puree
    1 tb Flour
  1/3 c Honey
    1 tb Sorghum
    1 ts Cinnamon
  1/2 ts Nutmeg
  1/8 ts Allspice
    3 ea Eggs
    1 c Evaporated milk

  Brush crust with egg white from one of the eggs; set aside. Mix persimmon with flour, honey, sorghum and spices. Beat in eggs and milk. Pour into prepared pie crust. Bake at 400F 40-50 minutes until pie doesn't jiggle when shaken. Cover edges with circle of foil if crust begins to brown too much.
  Native persimmons are so sweet that they have also been called wild figs or sugar plums. The English word persimmon is said to have come from the Algonquin word pessemin. Like apricots, persimmons contain ample amounts of vitamins A and C. The easiest way to get persimmon pulp is to puree fully ripe persimmons using a food mill or a Chinaman sieve. Aluminum or plastic sieves are best since iron or tin will turn the rosey orange pulp dark. Freeze any you don't use now for use later in winter and spring.
  When ripe, persimmons are very soft and take on a dusty pale lavender cast.
  Persimmon pulp can be used in any pumpkin recipe with similar results. It marries well with cinnamon, nutmeg and orange. Since it is not as think as pumpkin, adding a little flour to pie fillings is a good idea.

Mission Possible Banana Cream Pie 1

```
        Ingredients
     1 c  Milk
   1/3 c  Margarine, melted
     1 ts Vanilla
     3    Eggs
 1 1/2 c  Sugar
   1/2 c  Bisquick
     2    Bananas, sliced
     1 c  Whipping cream, chilled
     2 tb Sugar, confectionary
```

Heat oven to 350 deg. Grease 9 in. pie plate. Place milk, margarine, vanilla, eggs, sugar and Bisquick in blender and blend for 30 seconds. Pour into plate.

Bake about 30 min. Arrange bananas on pie. Beat whipping cream and powdered sugar until stiff. Spread over top of pie, covering bananas. Suggestion:
Slice bananas after pie is baked and just before covering with whipped cream.)

Modern Mincemeat

3/4 lb Unsalted butter or margarine
   -OR beef suet
3/4 lb Raisins
3/4 lb Currants,
3/4 lb Sultanas
3/4 lb Chopped apples
 3 oz Citron
 3 oz Candied lemon peel
 3 oz Candied orange peel
1/2 lb Almonds
1/8 ts Cinnamon
1/8 ts Mace
1/8 ts Allspice
1/8 ts White pepper
3/4 c Brandy

PREHEAT OVEN TO 325F. Combine all ingredients and grind twice through the finest blade of your meat grinder. Place in a lidded oven-proof pot and place in the oven. Bake for 40 minutes. Remove from oven and stir in brandy. Store the mincemeat in a cool place for at least 1 week before using, or up to 6 months.

Mom's Manageable Peanut Brittle Pie

1 Pie

- 1 T Gelatine
- 1/4 c Cold water
- 1 pk Butterscotch pudding mix
- 2 c Milk
- 2 Eggs, separated
- 2 T Butter
- 2 T Sugar
- 1 c Whipping cream
- 3/4 c Crushed peanut brittle
- 1 Baked pie shell

Soften gelatine in water. Combine pudding mix and milk. Cook to directions on package. Beat egg yolks. Gradually add to pudding and cook 2 minutes, stirring constantly. Blend in gelatine. Remove from heat.

Add butter. Cool. Beat egg whites until soft peaks form. Gradually add sugar and beat until stiff. Whip the cream; put aside 1/2 and fold egg whites into other 1/2, then fold in peanut brittle and pudding mixture.

Pour into crust. Spread the cream put aside on top. Chill.

Monkey Business Peanut Butter Pie

6 Servings

```
  1 c  Karo, dark
  1 c  Sugar
1/2 ts Vanilla
    3  Egg; slightly beaten
1/2 c  Peanut butter, creamy
    1  Pie shell, 9"; unbaked
```

Blend the corn syrup, sugar, vanilla, eggs, and peanut butter and pour into the unbaked crust. Bake in a 400 degree oven 15 minutes, then lower the temperature to 350 degrees and continue baking 30 to 35 minutes more. The
center should look "wobbly"; it will set as the pie cools.

Moonshine Sour Cream Raisin Pie

    1   9" baked pie shell
1 1/2 tb Cornstarch
    1 c Sugar; (plus 2 tbsp.)
  3/4 ts Ground nutmeg
  1/4 ts Salt
1 1/2 c Sour cream
1 1/2 c Raisins
    1 tb Lemon juice
    3   Egg yolks
     -----brown sugar meringue-----
    3   Egg whites
  1/4 ts Cream of tartar
    6 tb Packed brown sugar
  1/2 ts Vanilla

Mix corn starch, sugar, nutmeg, and salt in a 2 quart sauce sour cream. Stir in raisins, lemon juice, and egg yolks. Cook over medium heat, stirring constantly, until mixture thickens and boils. Boil and stir 1 minute. Pour into baked pie shell.

Meringe: Beat egg whites and cream of tartar in a 2 1/2 quart bowl until foamy. Beat in sugar, 1 Tbsp. at a time; continue beating until stiff and glossy. Do not underbeat. Beat in vanilla.

Spread meringue over filling, carefully sealing meringue to edge of crust to prevent shrinkage or weeping. Bake at 400 degrees until delicate brown, about 10 minutes. Refrigerate any remaining pie immediately.

8 servings.

Morning Blend Sour Cream Coffee Cake

1/2 c Shortening
3/4 c Sugar
1 t Vanilla
3 lg Eggs
2 c Flour, sifted
1 t Baking powder
1 t Baking soda
1/2 pt Sour cream
6 T Butter, softened
1 c Light brown sugar, firmly packed
2 t Cinnamon
1 c Nuts, chopped
   (walnuts or pecans)

Prepare a 10-inch tube pan. I use one with a removable center. Grease the pan and cut a circle of waxed paper to cover the bottom. Preheat oven to 350 degrees.

Cream shortening, sugar and vanilla, thoroughly. Add eggs, singly, beating well after each addition.

Sift flour, baking powder and baking soda together. Add flour mixture and sour cream to creamed mixture. Alternate a little of each, blending after each addition.

In separate bowl, cream butter, brown sugar and cinnamon together. Add nuts and mix well.

Spread 1/2 of the batter in the tube pan. Sprinkle 1/2 of the nut mixture evenly over batter in pan. Cover with remaining batter. Sprinkle with remaining nut mixture. Bake in preheated oven for about 50 minutes.

When the cake cools, run a knife around the side of the pan and remove the inner section. Carefully remove the cake from the base of the pan and remove the waxed paper.

Morning Maple Custard Pie

   3 c Milk
   3   Eggs, separated
   1 c Maple syrup
1/4 c Sugar
   1 T Flour
1/4 t Salt
   1 t Vanilla

  Scald milk and add it to the well beaten yolks of eggs mixed with the maple syrup, sugar, flour and salt. Continue cooking, stirring constantly, until it begins to thicken slightly. Then fold in stiffly beaten egg whites and vanilla. Pour into uncooked 10 inch pie shell and bake in moderate oven, 325 degrees, until firm.

Mr. Mississippi Mud Pie 1

- 1/2 c Roasted Pecans, chopped
- 1/2 c Roasted walnuts, chopped
- 2 Pie crusts, Prepared 9"
- 16 oz Cream cheese
- 1 Sour cream 1 carton (8 oz)
- 8 oz Confectioners powdered sugar
- 1 ts Vanilla extract
- 1/4 c Sugar, granulated
- 2 tb Cornstarch
- 1 tb Flour
- 1/4 c Cocoa, powdered
- 1/4 ts Salt
- 1/4 c Milk
- 3 Egg yokes, beaten
- 2 c Milk
- 3/4 c Sugar, granulated
- 1 tb Butter
- 1 ts Vanilla extract
- 1 ts Almond extract

CRUST: Mix pecans and walnuts and add to your favorite pie crust recipe, or, if desired, use 2 frozen pie crusts, baked according to package instructions, with nuts divided evenly over bottom of crusts. Set aside to cool FILLING: Mix cream cheese, sour cream, confectioner's sugar and 1 tsp vanilla with electric mixer or food processor until well blended. Divide evenly between pie crusts. Refrigerate for 2 hours or longer. TOPPING: In a bowl, blend 1/4 cup sugar, cornstarch,flour,cocoa,salt,1/4 cup milk and egg yokes; set mixture aside. Place 2 cups milk and 3/4 cup sugar in a saucepan and bring to a boil over high heat, whisking constantly, to bowl ingredients. Transfer bowl ingredients back into saucepan and bring to boil, stirring constantly, over medium heat. Continue to cook for 5 minutes. Stir in 1 Tbsp butter and 1 tsp vanilla and almond extracts. Cool and spoon over Pies. Refrigerate Pies.

Mrs. Mississippi Mud Cake

```
    1 c   Margarine
  1/2 c   Cocoa
    2 c   Sugar
    4     Eggs, slightly beaten
    1 t   Vanilla
1 1/2 c   Flour
  1/8 t   Salt
1 1/2 c   Peanuts, chopped
    2 c   Miniature marshmallows
```

Preheat oven to 350 F. Melt the margarine in a saucepan. Add the cocoa and stir until blended. Remove the saucepan from the heat, add the sugar, eggs, vanilla, and mix them all together.

Combine the flour, salt and the nuts in a bowl, and stir so that the nuts are coated with the flour. Add this gradually to the mixture in the saucepan.

Spoon this into a greased 13 x 9 x 2 pan and bake for 35-40 minutes in the preheated oven. Spread the marshmallows on the warm cake.

When the cake cools, you will notice the reasoning behind its name. It may not look like much, but it sure tastes great.

Ms. Love's Butterscotch Custard Pie

    1 c Brown sugar
    3   Eggs
    3 c Milk
1/2 ts Salt
1/4 ts Nutmeg
    1   Unbaked pie shell

    Beat eggs well, add sugar and milk, salt and nutmeg. Pour into unbaked pie shell. Bake at 450 for 10 minutes to set pastry, then reduce heat to 325 degrees for about 30 minutes, or until custard is done.

Never Ending German Friendship Cake

    1 c Cake starter

------------------------------STARTER FOOD-------------------
    1 c Milk
    1 c Flour, self-raising
    1 c Sugar

----------------------------------CAKE-----------------------------
    2 c Flour, self-raising
    1 c Sugar
  2/3 c Oil
    2 t Cinnamon
    2 t Vanilla extract
    2   Eggs
  1/2 c Raisins
  1/2 c Nuts (or other fruits)
  15 oz Pineapple chunks, drained (one can)

PREPARE STARTER:

Day 1: Blend the starter feed together, and then hand mix in the starter.
  I find it easiest to mix the flour and sugar together dry, add the milk to the starter, and then slowly add the flour and sugar to the liquid. The starter should never be beaten with a blender or refrigerated. Pour the mixture into a large bowl, cover with cling-film or a damp towel, and leave to brew.

Day 2: Thoroughly mix the sourdough, then leave to brew again.

Day 5: As day 1

Day 6: As day 2

Day 10: Print off three copies of this recipe. Here now is why this is called a friendship cake. Take 3 cups of Sourdough mixture, and gi

MAKING THE CAKE: Blend all ingredients thoroughly with remaining starter.
Pre-heat oven to 350 degrees F. Pour mixture into a well-greased baking tin. Bake for 1 3/4 hours (less in a fan oven), cool.

During preparation put the starter into a very large bowl (it foams up), and cover with a lid or with cling film. Starter and one cake.

* If you don't get cake starter from a friend, you can probably buy it in a baking supply store.

Nice Little Fruit Tarts

1 (3-ounce) package cream cheese, softened
1/4 cup LAND O LAKES® Sour Cream
1 tablespoon orange juice
1/2 teaspoon vanilla
1 (2.1-ounce) package (15) frozen mini filo dough shells, thawed
Chopped assorted fruit* and/or finely chopped nuts
1/4 cup seedless strawberry jam, melted
Fresh mint leaves (if desired)
Combine cream cheese, sour cream, orange juice and vanilla in medium bowl until well mixed.
Spoon about 1 teaspoon cream cheese filling into each filo shell; top with fruit. Drizzle jam over fruit. Garnish with mint leaves, if desired.
Makes 15 tarts.

* Fruit suggestions include strawberries, raspberries, blueberries, kiwifruit, nectarines and/or drained crushed pineapple.

TIP: To melt strawberry jam, spoon into microwave-safe bowl. Microwave on HIGH 30 seconds or until melted.

TIP: Frozen mini filo dough shells can be found in the frozen dessert section of your supermarket.

TIP: Filled tarts may be covered and refrigerated up to 3 hours before serving.

Nitty-Gritty Pie

Ingredients
3 egg whites, beaten stiff
1 tsp baking powder
1 cup sugar
1 tsp vanilla
20 soda crackers
1 (coarsley broken)
1/2 cup pecans, chopped

Directions

Beat egg whites until stiff; add baking powder and beat more. Add sugar and vanilla; beat again. Fold in crackers and pecans. Put in buttered pie plate and bake at 300 degrees for 30 minutes. Let cool and top with Cool Whip and chopped pecans.

No Sweat Peanut Brittle Crust

1 Pie

1 1/2 c Graham cracker crumbs
 1/2 c Crushed peanut brittle
 1/2 c Coconut
 1/3 c Melted butter
 1/2 c Choppee peanuts

Mix all ingredients well. Press firmly into pie tin. Chill.

Note: May be used for topping, too.

Now Serving Boysenberry Syrup Pie

- 1 c Knotts Berry Farm -Boysenberry Syrup
- 1 c Water
- 3 tb Cornstarch
- 2   Egg yolks
- 1 ts Butter
- 1   Nilla Wafer pie crust
- 2   Egg whites
- 1 tb Knotts Berry Farm -Boysenberry Syrup

Combine syrup, water, and cornstarch and bring to a boil, stirring until thick. Remove from heat. Beat egg yolks, add a bit of the hot syrup mixture to the yolks, whisking constantly. Add the yolk mixture to the hot syrup and reheat until pudding consistency. Add the butter, and stir until melted. Cool slightly. Pour into pie crust. Beat egg whites stiff, adding slowly the tablespoon of syrup. If soft peaks do not form, add a little more syrup. Pile on pie and place in 400 F oven until peaks have browned.

Nutty Buddy Macadamia Cream Pie

```
1 1/3 c  Milk
  3/4 c  Sugar
  1/2 c  Chopped macadamia nuts
    ds Salt
   1 ts Vanilla
    1    Egg
   5 ts Cornstarch
    2    Egg whites
    1    9 inch baking pie shell
    1 c  Heavy cream, whipped
```

In a saucepan, combine 1 cup of the milk, 1/4 cup of the sugar, 1/4 cup of the nuts, the salt and the vanilla; scald. Mix the remaining 1/3 cup milk with egg and cornstarch. Thoroughly stir some of hot mixture into egg mixture; return all to saucepan. Cook 5 more minutes, stirring constantly, until mixture thickens. Cool 1 hour. Beat egg whites until soft peaks form; fold carefully into cooled mixture. Pour into pie shell; chill.

Before serving, top with sweetened whipped cream and remaining 1/4 cup nuts. Makes 8 servings.

Nutty Caramel Pie

1 servings

    Pie shell
2   Egg whites
1 qt Coffee ice cream
1/4 ts Salt
1 qt Chocolate ice cream
1/4 c Sugar
1 1/2 c Almonds, finely chopped; or pecans
-----caramel sauce-----
2 tb Butter
1/2 ts Vanilla
1/2 c Brown sugar, packed
2 tb Nuts
1/4 c Half and half

Beat whites to soft peaks. Gradually add sugar, 1 tablespoon at a time, beating 1 minute after each addition to form a stiff meringue. Fold in nuts. Spread into well-buttered 9-inch pie pan w/ sides extending over the rim. Bake 10 minutes or untill lightly browned. Remove & cool. Fill w/ ice cream; cover tightly; freeze.

In saucepan, melt butter; stir in sugar and cook until dissolved. Slowly mix in half & half and cook one minute, stirring constantly. Stir in vanilla & nuts; cool slightly. When ready to serve, pour over the frozen pie.

Oh Honey Meringue

1 Pie

1 c Honey
2   Egg whites
1/2 ts Vanilla
1 ts Baking powder
1/8 ts Salt (or less)

Boil honey to 250 about 10 minutes. Pour slowly over beaten egg whites, beating constantly. Add vanilla and beat until cool.

This mixture may be used on pies, baked apples, or puddings.

One Of A Kind No Bake Blueberry Pie

  1   Baked pie crust
     -----filling-----
  3 c Fresh or frozen blueberries
1/3 c Sugar
  1 tb Cornstarch; (plus 2 tsp.)
1/4 ts Salt
1/4 ts Ground cinnamon
2/3 c Water
1/4 c Medium sherry
  2 ts Lemon juice

Spread the berries in the pie shell.

Mix sugar, cornstarch, salt and cinnamon in a 4 cup glass measure. Stir in the water. Microwave uncovered on high stirring every minute until thicken and clear, 3 to 4 minutes.

Stir in the sherry and lemon juice. Pon on the fruit in the pie shell.
Refrigerate at least 2 hours.

Serve with sour cream topping: Mix 1 cup sour cream, 2 tablespoons sugar and 1 teaspoon vanilla.

Original Mint Cream Pie

```
   6 c  Mini marshmallows
 1/4 c  Milk
 1/3 c  Creme de menthe
   1 ts vanilla extract
   3 dr Green food color <3 or 4>
   8 oz Whipped cream
   1    Choc. ready pie crust
```

  Combine marshmallows and milk. Cook and stir over low heat until melted.
  Remove from heat, cool, stirring every few minutes until partially set.

  Stir in liquer, vanilla and food coloring. Fold in whipped cream and pour into crust.

  Freeze until firm.

  Before serving, let stand for 10 mins at room temp and garnish with grated chocolate.

Out Of World No-Bake Strawberry Pie

---------------------------NUTTY DATE PIE CRUST-----------

- 1/2 c Walnuts
- 1/2 c Almonds
- 1 3/4 c Dates, pitted

----------------------------------FILLING----------------------------

- 5 c Strawberries, sliced
- 1 tb Maple syrup

CRUST: Grind nuts finely in a food processor & set aside. Place the dates in a food processor or blender & grind to form a paste. With the motor still running, add the ground nuts & blend until the mixture forms a ball.

Press this mixture evenly on the bottom of a lightly oiled 8" pie pan.

Refrigerate until ready to fill.

FILLING: Toss the strawberries with the maple syrup. Spoon into the pie crust. Cover with waxed paper & refrigerate for 1 hour before serving.

Papa's Up High Papaya Pie

- 1 c Pineapple juice
- 3/4 c Sugar
- 3 c Chopped papaya
- 1/3 c Cornstarch
- 1/3 c Water
- 1 T Margarine
- Pastry from 2 crust pie

Combine juice and sugar; bring to a boil and add papaya. Cook until papaya is tender. Strain fruit out carefully and set aside. Combine cornstarch and water; stir into juice. Cook until mixture thickens, stirring constantly. Return fruit to syrup; add butter and cool. Preheat oven to 425, line a 9inch pie plate with pastry; pour in filling. Roll out remaining dough and cut strips 1/2 inch wide and about 11 inches long.

Weave strips on waxed paper, slip hand underneath, and quickly invert on pie. Trim lattice ends at edge of pan, seal with water, and crimp with edge of lower crust. Bake for 25 minutes.

Park Peanut Pie with Shortbread

- 8 oz Shortbread cookies; broken-up
- 4 tb Peanut butter
- 3/4 c Light brown sugar
- 2/3 c Dark corn syrup
- 2 tb All-purpose flour
- 3 lg Eggs; slightly beaten
- 2 ts Vanilla extract
- 8 oz Peanut butter cookies; coarsely chopped
- 1 c Dry-roasted peanuts

Preheat oven to 375 degrees.

Grind the shortbread cookies in a food processor until finely ground. Add the peanut butter and continue to process until all of the cookie crumbs are moistened with peanut butter. Press the mixture into a 9-inch pie pan, forming a thicker edge near the rim. Bake in the preheated oven for 6 minutes. Remove pie shell and reduce oven temperature to 350 degrees.

Meanwhile mix the brown sugar, corn syrup, flour, eggs and vanilla in a bowl just until blended. Stir in the chopped peanut butter cookies and the peanuts. Pour into the partially baked pie shell and return to the oven to bake for about 45 minutes, until the top is browned but the filling is still gooey in the center. Cool on a rack for at least an hour before serving.

Parkside Pineapple Cream Cheese Pie

1 Pie

1/3 c Sugar
 1 tb Cornstarch
 1 cn (9 oz) Crushed Pineapple
   - do not drain
1/2 lb Cream cheese
1/2 c Sugar; additional
1/2 ts Salt
 2   Eggs
1/2 c Milk
1/2 ts Vanilla

Blend 1/3 cup sugar with the cornstarch. Add pineapple; cook, stirring constantly, until thick and clear. Blend cream cheese (softened to room temperature) with 1/2 cup sugar and the salt. Add eggs, one at a time, stirring well. Blend in milk and vanilla. Spread pineapple mixture over the bottom of a 9-inch unbaked pie shell. Pour in cream cheese mixture.

Bake in 400 F oven for 10 minutes; reduce heat to 325 F for 50 minutes.

Cool before serving.

Paul's Surprise Coconut Cream Pie

        2 1/2 c Water
          1/2 c Grits, regular
            1 c Sugar
           2 tb Butter or margarine
           2 lg Eggs, beaten
          1/2 c Coconut, flaked
          1/2 c Sour cream
              1 6 oz chocolate-graham
                 Cracker crust, prepared
                 Whipping cream, whipped
                 And sweetened (for garnish)
                 Maraschino cherries (for Garnish)

In a medium saucepan, bring the water to a boil; stir in the grits.
Cover, reduce heat, and simmer for 15 minutes, stirring occasionally.
Remove from the heat, and stir in the sugar and butter/margarine.
Gradually add to the bowl containing the beaten eggs, about 1/4th of the hot mixture; add the egg mixture to the remaining hot mixture, stirring constantly. Cook over low heat until the mixture thickens and reaches 160 degree F (about 8 minutes). Remove from heat, and stir in the flaked coconut and sour cream. Spoon mixture into the prepared pie crust; cover and chill. Garnish, if desired. Makes one 9-inch pie.

Peach Beach Streusel Pie

- 2 c flour
- 3/4 ts Salt
- 10 tb butter; chilled
- 2 tb Shortening; chilled
- 1 c Brown sugar
- 3/4 ts Nutmeg
- 1/2 c Almonds; sliced
- 1   Lemon
- 9   Peaches; about 3 pounds
- 3 tb Cornstarch
- 1/4 ts Almond extract
- 2 tb Dry bread crumbs

Combine 1 cup flour and 1/2 ts. salt. Cut in 4 tb. of butter and the shortening until mixture resembles coarse meal with a few pea-sized pieces remaining. Sprinkle in 3 to 4 tb ice water, a tablespoon at a time, until dough just comes together. Gather into a disk. Wrap and chill at least 30 minutes. Combine remaining cup of flour, 1/3 cup brown sugar, 1/4 ts. salt, and 1/4 ts. nutmeg. Cut in remaining 6 tb. Of butter until crumbly. Stir in almonds. Chill. On a lightly floured work surface, roll out chilled pie pastry to fit a 9" pie pan. Fit pastry into pan. Trim and flute edges. Chill. Heat oven to 475. Grate 1 ts. of lemon zest from the lemon and squeeze 1 tb. Of juice. Peel peaches and slice. Combine with remaining 2/3 cup brown sugar, remaining 1/2 ts nutmeg, lemon zest and juice, cornstarch and almond extract. Sprinkle bread crumbs over bottom of pie shell and fill with peach mixture. Sprinkle almond crumb mixture on top. Bake 15 minutes. Reduce temperature to 350. Continue baking until top is browned and fruit juices are bubbling, 50 to 55 minutes. Cool completely before cutting.

Peach Pie Awakenings

1 Servings

5 c Sliced fresh peaches
1   Unbaked pie shell
1/3 c Butter, melted
1 c Sugar
1/3 c Flour
1   Egg

Place peaches in a pie shell. Combine remaining ingredients and pour over peaches. Bake at 350 degrees for 1 hour and 10 minutes.

Peanut Butter-Chocolate Mini Cutie Pies

 1 1/4 c Graham cracker crumbs
     5 tb Unsalted butter; melted
   1/2 c Plus 2 t sour cream
 2 1/2 tb Powdered sugar
     2 tb Whipping cream
   1/2 c Plus 2 t creamy peanut; butter..do not use o
          Fashioned style or freshly ground!
   1/2 c Whipping cream (in addition to above)
     4 oz Simisweet chocolate; chopped

  Mix graham cracker crumbs and butter in a small bowl. Press crumb mixture o

  Whisk sour cream, powdered sugar and 2 T whipping cream in bowl to blend.

  Bring 1/2 C cream to simmer in heavy saucepan. Reduce heat to low. Add chocolate; stir until melted. Cool completely, stirring occasionally.

  Spoon 2 teaspoons chocolate mixture over each peanut- butter pie. Place in freezer until set. (can be prepared 1 week ahead. Keep frozen.) Using tip of small sharp knife as an aid, gently pry pies from tins. Let stand at room temperature for 10 minutes before serving.

Pear Pie In A Deep-Dish

2 lb Pears; peeled, halved and
-cored (about 4 medium)
1 tb Lemon juice
3 tb Flour, all-purpose
1 c Sugar
ds Salt
1/2 ts Cinnamon, ground
1/2 ts Nutmeg, ground
1 tb Butter Whipped cream; opt.

--------------CHEDDAR CHEESE PASTRY---------------
1 c Flour, all-purpose
1/2 ts Salt
1/3 c Shortening
1/4 c Cheese, cheddar; shredded
2 tb Water; cold (to 3 tb.)

Place pear halves in a 1-1/2 qt. casserole or deep-dish 9" pieplate.
Sprinkle with lemon juice. Combine flour, sugar, salt, cinnamon, and nutmeg; sprinkle over pears. Dot with butter. Cover with Cheddar Cheese Pastry, crimping pastry to sides of dish. Cut slits in top of pastry for steam to escape. Bake at 350 degrees for 30 to 40 minutes. Serve with whipped cream, if desired.

Cheddar Cheese Pastry: Combine flour and salt; cut in shortening with pastry blender until mixture resembles coarse meal. Stir in cheese.
Sprinkle cold water evenly over surface; stir with a fork until all dry ingredients are moistened. Shape dough into a ball.

Roll out dough on a floured surface; cut dough to cover top of a deep-dish 9" pieplate pastry for one 9-inch pie.

Peter's Low-Calorie Pumpkin

Pie

  16 oz Can solid-pack pumpkin;
  13 oz Can evaporated skim milk;*
    1 Egg;
    2 Egg whites;
  1/2 c Biscuit mix like Bisquick;
    2 tb Sugar;
    8 pk Sugar substitute;(16 ts-1/3c
    2 ts Pumpkin pie spice;
    2 ts Vanilla;

Heat oven to 350 F. Lightly grease or spray 9 inch pie pan with vegetable pan spray. Place all ingredients in blender, food processor or mixing bowl. Blend 1 minute or beat 2 minutes with mixer.

Pour into pie pan and bake for 50 minutes or until center is puffed up.

Pick Me Up Linzer Tart

- 1/4 c Butter; softened
- 2 Egg yolks
- 2 tb Juice, apple, conc.
- 2 ts Extract, vanilla
- 1 c Flour
- 1/2 ts Baking powder
- 1/4 ts Salt
- 1/4 ts Cinnamon, ground
- 1/8 ts Allspice, ground
- 1 1/2 c Almonds, ground
- 10 oz Fruit spread, raspberry

Use blanched almonds or hazelnuts.

Beat butter in large bowl until light and fluffy. Blend in egg yolks, juice concentrate, and vanilla. Combine flour, baking powder, salt, cinnamon, and allspice; mix well. Stir in almonds. Gradually add to butter mixture, mixing until well-blended. Spread 1-1/2 c batter evenly onto bottom of 10" tart pan with removable bottom or 10" springform pan. Spread fruit evenly over batter, leaving 1" border around edge. Spoon remaining batter into pastry bag fitted with 1/2" plain or star tip. Pipe batter in lattice design over fruit spread. Chill 30 minutes.

Preheat oven to 350. Bake tart 35 minutes, until crust is golden brown and fruit spread is bubbly. Cool completely on wire rack. Serve at room temperature.

Piece In The Dark Fruitcake

- 16 oz Citron, candied
  - -(or candied fruit
  - -and peels)
- 8 oz Cherries, candied
- 1 c Raisins, dark
- 1 c Raisins, golden
- 1 1/3 c Calmyra figs, cut
  - -into pieces
- 1 1/3 c Dates (pitted), cut
  - -into small slices
- 1 1/2 c Pecan halves
  - -(or walnut halves
  - -if necessary)
- 1/2 c Brandy
- 3 c Flour (white)
- 2 t Baking powder
- 2 t Salt
- 1 T Cinnamon, ground
- 1 t Nutmeg, ground
- 1 t Allspice, ground
- 1 t Cloves, ground
- 4 Eggs
- 1 3/4 c Brown sugar, packed
- 1 c Orange juice
- 3/4 c Butter, melted
  - -(cooled)
- 1/4 c Molasses, light
  - -(treacle)

Mix fruits together in a bowl. Pour brandy over fruits. Turn fruit mixture over every 20 minutes. Soaking time is a matter of taste, but two hours is typical. Preheat oven to 300 degrees F. Prepare tube pan: grease sides and bottom. Line bottom and sides with greased brown paper.

In a very large bowl, mix flour, spices, baking powder and salt. Stir until spices are evenly blended throughout.

In a third bowl beat eggs until fluffy. Add brown sugar, orange juice, molasses and butter. Mix, making sure that all the sugar dissolves.

Pour off any liquid from fruit mixture and add the fruit and the nuts to the dry ingredients. Mix until all fruit pieces are coated. Then pour in the liquids and mix gently until you have an evenly-mixed batter.

Pour batter into pan and bake at 300 degrees F. for 1 hour. Cover pan with foil and bake for 1 hour more or until toothpick inserted in center comes out clean. Cool for 30 minutes before removing from pan. Peel off paper very carefully.

Put cake in cake tin lined with foil. For the next 3 to 4 weeks, sprinkle a little brandy over cake twice a week. Keep cake covered and store the tin in the refrigerator. If you prefer to omit the brandy, cover top of cake with very thin slices of apple instead.

Pipsqueak's Double Layer Pumpkin Pie

    4 oz Philly Cream Cheese [softened]
    1 tb Milk
    1 tb Sugar
1 1/2 c CoolWhip [thawed]
    1 Graham cracker pie crust [prepared]
    1 c Milk [cold]
    1 cn (16oz) pumpkin
    2 pk Vanilla flavored Jell-o Pudding & Pie filling
    4 ts Pumpkin pie spice

1) Mix the cream cheese, 1 tb milk, and the sugar in a large bowl with a wire whisk `til smooth, then gently stir in the whipped topping and « of the pumpkin pie spice. Spread on the bottom of the prepared pie crust...

2) Pour 1 c cold milk into a bowl and add the pumpkin, pudding mixes, and the remainder of the spices beating with wire whisk `til well mixed (it will be thick). Then spread over the cream cheese layer in the prepared pie crust...

3) Refrigerate for at least 4 hrs. `til set then garnish with additional whipped topping before serving...

Plain Jane's Pastry Pie

   3 c Flour
   1 c Shortening
   1 ts Salt
   1 ts Baking powder
   2/3 c Water (iced)

   Sift flour, salt and baking powder into a bowl and cut in shortening with a pastry blender. Add ice water and mix lightly until dough forms a solid mass. Chill. Roll out and line pie shell. Trim edges and bake at 450 degrees for 15-20 minutes.

Please Chocolate Banana Pudding Pie

```
  4   Semisweet chocolate; baker's
2 tb Milk
2 tb Butter or margarine
  1   Graham cracker pie crust, 9 inch -- prepared
  2 md Banana; dole, sliced
2 3/4 c  Milk; cold
  2 pk Banana pudding mix; jello
1 1/2 c  Cool whip lite®
```

Microwave chocolate, milk, and maragrine in medium microwaveable bowl on HI Pour milk into large bowl. Add pudding mixes. Beat with wire whick 1 min.

Refrigerate 4 hours or until set. Store leftover pie in refrigerator.

Please Hold-The-Sugar Apple Pie

                12 oz Frozen apple juice
                    -concentrate, thawed
                3 tb Cornstarch
                1 ts Cinnamon
                1/4 ts Allspice
                1/4 ts Nutmeg
                6 lg Baking apples, peeled cored,
                    Thinly sliced
                    (Pippin, Rome or Gr Smith)
                2 tb Butter or margarine
                1   9-inch pie shell, baked
                    Flavored whipped cream
                    (optional--recipe below)
                    Nuts (optional)
                    FLAVORED WHIPPED CREAM
                1 c Whipping cream; whipped
                2 tb Frozen lemonade concentrate
                    Thawed
                    OR
            1/4 c Peanut brittle; crushed
                    AND
            1/2 ts Ground orange peel

Measure about 1/4 cup concentrate into small bowl; stir in cornstarch and spices. Place the remainder of the concentrate into a large skillet with the apples. Simmer gently until apples are just tender. Lightly stir in cornstarch mixture until quite thick. Stir in butter. Pour into pie shell; top with whipped cream and nuts.

Flavored Whipped Cream: Into whipping cream, fold 2 frozen lemonade concentrate, thawed, crushed peanut brittle and ground orange peel. (Tart shells may be substituted for the baked pie shell).

Please Pass The Butter Cookies

    1/2 lb Butter
      1 c Sugar
2 1/2 c Flour, all-purpose
      1   Egg yolk
  4 oz Cream cheese
        Raspberry jam

Preheat oven to 350 degrees F. Cream together the butter and sugar. Add the flour and egg yolk and mix well. Add the cream cheese and mix well.

Roll into balls about 5/8 inch diameter. Place them on an ungreased cookie sheet (the cookies don't grow when baked, so they can be somewhat close together). Then press your thumb into each to flatten it and make an indentation to hold some jam. Fill it with jam. Bake at 350 degrees F for 15 to 20 minutes.

You can use any flavor jam you like. The jam is the only part of the cookie that has any texture, so I prefer using it to jelly.

Don't eat the cookies straight from the oven, or you'll probably burn your tongue. The jam stays hotter much longer than the cookie.

Poker Room Rum Cream Pie

INGREDIENTS:
2 (9 inch) prepared graham cracker crust
6 egg yolks
1 cup white sugar
1 (.25 ounce) package unflavored gelatin
1/2 cup cold water
2 cups heavy cream
1/2 cup rum
1/8 cup grated semisweet chocolate

DIRECTIONS:
Beat the egg yolks with the sugar until light and fluffy.
In a saucepan, soak gelatin in water. Bring to a boil. Stir slowly into egg mixture.
Whip the cream to peaks, and add rum. Fold into egg mixture. Pour filling into cooled pie shells. Sprinkle with shredded chocolate. Serve after chilling for several hours.

Presidential Suite Pudding Pies

```
 16   Pastry shells, 2"
1/2 c Butter; softened
3/4 c Sugar
3/4 c Sugar, dark brown; firmly
      -packed
  2   Eggs
1/2 c Half-and-half
1/2 ts Vanilla extract
      Nutmeg, ground
      Cream, whipped
```

Bake pastry shells at 350 degrees for 4 to 5 minutes; set aside.

Combine butter and sugar, creaming until light and fluffy. Add eggs, half-and-half, and vanilla; beat well. Spoon filling into pastry shells, and sprinkle lightly with nutmeg.

Bake at 350 degrees for 15 to 20 minutes or until set (filling will settle while cooling).

At serving time, top with whipped cream and sprinkle lighty with nutmeg.

Pretty Super Open-Faced Peach Pie

     14   Peach halves; * see note
    3/4 c Sugar
    1/4 c Flour
    1/4 c Water; or peach juice
     2 tb Butter
     2 tb Lemon juice
          9 inch pie crust; thawe * or canned, enough for one pie

  Combine sugar, butter and flour to make crumbs. Sprinkle half this mixture in the bottom of an unbaked pie crust. Place peach halves with cut side up in pie shell. Cover with remaining crumb mixture. Add fruit juices or water if needed. Bake at 375 degrees for 40-45 minutes. May be served with whipped cream. Makes 1 (9 inch) pie.

Pristine Praline Pumpkin Pie

-PRALINE (OPTIONAL)
2 T (1/4 stick) butte, softened
1/3 c Chopped pecans
1/3 c Brown sugar
  2 Unbaked 8 inch pie shells, or one
    Unbaked 10 inch pie shell
2 T (1/4 stick) butter
1 29 oz. can pumpkin puree
1/2 c Granulated sugar
1/2 c Brown sugar
1 T All purpose flour
1 T Bitters (optional)
1 t Ground cinnamon
1/2 t Ground ginger
1/2 t Salt
1/4 t Grated nutmeg
1/4 t Ground cloves
1 Egg, beaten
1 12 oz. can evaporated milk
1/4 c Milk
1 c Water

Prepare the praline filling, if desired. Preheat oven to 450 F. In a small bowl, creme together the butter and brown sugar. Blend in the pecans. Press firmly into the bottom of the unbaked pie shells. Bake for 10 minutes, watching carefully so crusts do not puff up or slip down. Prick puffs with a fork if you see this happening, and pat the slipping crusts back up in place with the back of a fork. (This may not happen, but if it does, that is what you should do.) Let cool before filling. Preheat oven to 400 F. Melt the butter in a large skillet; add the pumpkin puree. Simmer for 10 minutes, stirring now and then with a wooden spoon. In a large mixer bowl, mix together the next 9 ingredients. Add the egg, and mix again. Add the hot pumpkin gradually, then blend in the milks and water. Pour into pie shells and bake for 1 hour. Let cool completely before cutting. NOTE: The filling can be made a day in advance and refrigerated. If you've used the praline, you may have extra pumpkin filling; bake it in individual custard cups.

Proud Pumpkin Pudding

```
1 1/2 c  Browned, strained pumpkin
   2 tb All purpose flour
   1 c  Brown sugar
   2 c  Milk
   1 c  Carnation 2% canned milk
   1 ts Cinnamon
1/2 ts Ginger
1/2 ts Nutmeg
   2    Eggs, beaten
```

This recipe calls for browned pumpkin which is accomplished by buttering a heavy cast iron frying pan and cooking the 2 cups pumpkin over medium heat, stirring and turning so all parts dry properly. Keep this up til it is reduced to 1 1/2 cups. It will be slightly browned.

Place the browned pumpkin in a bowl, sprinkle with flour and brown sugar and stir til thoroughly mixed. Add spices and eggs and beat well. Scald milk. Add the canned milk to scalded milk. Add milks to pumpkin mixture
Beat together til well mixed.

Place mixture in a greased casserole and place it in a larger casserole with hot water that comes half way up the outside of inner casserole. Place in a 325 F oven and oven poach til a knife comes out clean when tested.
Serve hot or cold.

This is actually my pumpkin pie filling, but I prefer it without the pastry and it is better for me. No great amount of fat in this one.

Proud Shortbread

2 c Butter
1 c Brown sugar
5 c Flour

Preheat oven to 300 degrees F. Cream the butter and sugar. Gradually add the flour. Roll out dough until it is about 1/4 inch thick. Cut into squares, or any other shape you desire. Bake on greased cookie sheet for 20-30 minutes at 300 degrees F. The cookies are done just before they start turning brown.

Pumpkin Pie Perfection

    1 c Pumpkin
1/4 c Molasses
    1 ts Cinnamon
1/2 ts Cloves
    1 c Brown sugar
    1 c Sweet milk
    1 ts Allspice
1/4 ts Ginger
    3   Eggs, separated

Mix the pumpkin (either freshly stewed or canned), the sugar, molasses and the spices thoroughly; add the milk. Beat the egg yolks and whites separately, adding first the yolks and lastly the stiffly whipped whites, folding in gently.

This makes one very large to two small pies. It (or they) should be put into a hot oven for 10 minutes at 450 degrees. Then reduce heat to 325 degrees and bake forty minutes. For superior flavor add 2 T. of thick sour cream.

Quick Chocolate Cheese Pie

    4 oz Unsweetened baking chocolate -- broken into pie
    1/4 c Butter or margarine; softened
    3/4 c Sugar
    3 oz Cream cheese; softened
    1 ts Milk
    2 c Frozen non-dairy whipped topping -- thawed cool whi
    1   8-inch packaged crumb crust
    (6 oz.)
    Additional whipped topping
    (optional)

In small microwave-safe bowl, place chocolate. Microwave at HIGH (100%) 1 to 1 1/2 minutes or until chocolate is melted and smooth when stirred; set aside. In small mixer bowl, beat butter, sugar, cream cheese and milk until well blended and smooth. Blend in chocolate. Gradually blend in whipped topping. Spoon into prepared crust. Refrigerate until firm. Serve with additional whipped topping, if desired. 6 to 8 servings.

Rags To Riches Banana Pie

    6 c Sliced bananas
  3/4 c Pineapple juice
       Pastry for 2 crust pie
  3/4 c Sugar
    1 tb Flour
1 1/2 ts Cinnamon
    1 tb Butter or margarine

Soak bananas in pineapple juice for 20 minutes. Preheat oven to 400 degrees F. Line a 9 inch pie plate with pastry. Drain bananas, saving 3 tablespoons of the juice. Place bananas in pie shell. Combine sugar, flour and cinnamon; sprinkle over bananas. Sprinkle with the 3 tablespoons of pineapple junice. Dot with butter, cover with top crust. Bake for 30 to 45 minutes or until crust is browned. Makes 8 servings.

Railroad Cross Sweet Green Tomato Pie

- 1 Premade pie crust recipe for 9" pie, chilled
- 8 Medium-size green tomatoes
- 1/2 c Golden raisins
- 2 ts Grated lemon peel
- 2 tb Lemon juice
- 1 tb Cider vinegar
- 1 1/2 c Sugar
- 1/3 c Toasted chopped pecans
- 1/4 c All-purpose flour
- 1/4 ts Salt
- 1 ts Ground cinnamon
- 1/2 ts Ground ginger
- 2 tb Butter, chilled & cut into small pieces
- Powdered sugar

  Preheat oven to 400. On lightly floured board, roll out pie dough into a circle about 12 inches in diameter. Edges will be ragged, this is okay.

  Just leave like this as edges will get folded in later. Center dough in 9 inch pie plate. Cover & chill. Cut tomatoes into thin slices. Put into large mixing bowl & add raisins, lemon peel, juice & vinegar. Stir & set aside. Mix together sugar, pecans, flour, salt, cinnamon, & ginger. Blend well. Sprinkle 2 tablespoon over chilled pie crust. Add remaining sugar-pecan mixture to tomato slices. Toss to coat well. Scrape tomato filling into pie crust. Dot with pieces of chilled butter. Fold overhang of pastry into center over filling. Bake 15 minutes. Turn heat down to 325 & bake for 45 minutes or until bubbly & crust is golden brown. Let pie cool on wire rack before cutting. Dust top with powdered sugar for decoration.

Raspberries & Cream Snowflake Pie

Pillsbury pie crust (15 oz)
21 Ounces raspberry fruit pie filling
8 Ounces cream cheese, softened
14 Ounces sweetened condensed milk
1/3 Cup lemon juice
1/2 Teaspoon almond extract
1/2 Teaspoon powdered sugar, (to 1 ts)

Allow both crust pouches to stand at room temperature for 15-20 minutes. Heat oven to 450-degrees. Prepare 1 crust according to package directions for unfilled one-crust pie using 9-inch pie pan. Bake at 450-degrees for 9-11 minutes or until lightly browned; cool. To make snowflake crust, unfold remaining crust onto ungreased cookie sheet; remove plastic sheets. Cut crust into 7-1/2-inch-diameter circle; discard scraps. Refold circle into fourths on cookie sheet. With knife, cut designs from folded and curved edges; discard scraps. Unfold. Bake at 450-degrees for 6-8 minutes or until lightly browned; cool completely. Reserve 1/2 cup raspberry filling; spoon remaining filling into cooled crust in pan. In large bowl, beat cream cheese until light and fluffy. Add milk; blend well. Add lemon juice and almond extract; stir until thickened. Spoon over raspberry filling in crust. Refrigerate 1 hour. Spoon reserved raspberry filling around edge of pie; place snowflake crust on top. Refrigerate several hours. Just before serving, sprinkle with powdered sugar. Store in refrigerator.

Ready In A Jiffy Butter Pie Crust

2 c All-purpose flour
  3/4 ts Salt
  2/3 c Butter,chilled,cut into 8 pi
   1 ea Yolk of large egg

This rich,all-butter recipe makes two single piecrusts or one double crust pie; margarine may be substituted for butter,if desired.

In a large bowl,combine flour and salt.With pastry blender or two knives,cut in butter until mixture resembles coarse crumbs.In small bowl,beat egg yolk with 3 tablespoons ice water;sprinkle mixture,1 tablespoon at a time,over flour mixture;toss with fork to blend lightly but evenly.Add up to 1 tablespoon water,if necessary,until dough begins to form a ball.Knead dough gently 2 or 3 times;flatten into disk shape.

TO MAKE SINGLE CRUST:On lightly floured surface,roll out half dough to 11 to 12" circle(see note);fit into 9" pie plate;trim, leaving 1" overhang.Dampen underside of hangover with water; turn under;flute edges or make decorative edging as described below.Place in freezer 10 minutes.Note:Depending on depth of edge or type of edging used for crust,you may need up to full recipe dough.Any unused dough can be frozen,tightly wrapped, for up to 2 months.

TO MAKE DOUBLE CRUST:Roll out dough as for single crust pie; fit into pie plate;trim.Roll out remaining dough to 11 to 12" circle;fit over top of pie;trim,leaving 1"overhang.Dampen edges of pastry with water;press together or turn under; flute edge. Cut vents for steam in center of top crust.

PREBAKED PIE SHELL:Prepare jiffy Butte r crust,recipe above, or one 10 or 11 ounce package piecrust mix according to package directions.Roll out half dough;fit into 9" pie plate; prepare single crust as directed.After fluting,place in freezer 10 minutes.Heat oven to 425 degrees.Line crust with foil;fill foil with dried beans or rice.Bake 6 minutes.Remove foil and beans;bake 8 to 10 minutes longer until pie shell is lightly browned. Cool completely on wire rack before filling.Makes one 9"pie shell.

EDGINGS:

ROPE: Fit and shape pastry crust as in Jiffy Butter Crust recipe; trim to leave 1 1/2" overhang. Dampen overhang with water; roll under to make high standing edge.Press right thumb into pastry edge at an angle;press and squeeze pastry between thumb and knuckle of forefinger.Repeat,keeping same angle to make ropelike edging.

LEAF: Fit and shape pastry crust as in Jiffy Butter Crust recipe, turning edge under.Press flat to rim of pie plate.With sharp paring knife,cut out 1" oval-shaped leaves from leftover pastry scraps. Lightly mark veins on leaves.Dampen rim of pastry crust with water;place leaves in slightly overlapping pattern around edge;press gently but firmly to adhere.

SCALLOPED: Fit and shape crust as in Jiffy Butter Crust recipe,turning edge under.Place forefinger of left hand inside crust edge. Using thumb and forefinger of right hand,pinch around left forefinger to make wide scallops.Repeat around border,making sure scallops are same size.

BRAIDED: Fit and shape pastry crust as in Jiffy Butter Crust recipe, turning edge under.Press edge flat to rim of pie plate.Roll leftover pastry into long thin rectangle;cut into long strips,1/4"wide.Weave strips into one long continuous braid to fit around rim of piecrust.Brush rim with water;set braid in place;press gently to adhere.

SUNBURST: Fit and shape pastry crust as in Jiffy Butter Crust;trim edge exactly to fit pie plate rim.Cut pastry edge at 1/4" intervals, making each cut 3/4" long.Dampen cut edge with water;fold over each pastry section into triangle,pressing to seal.

Real Spanish Cream

```
2 1/2 c  Milk
         -(one Imperial pint)
    4 t  Gelatine
    2    Eggs
  1/2 t  Vanilla essence
  1/3 c  Sugar
```

Save a small amount of the milk; put the rest in a saucepan, together with the sugar and vanilla and heat.

Separate the egg whites and save for later. Beat the egg yolks with the remainder of the milk and add to the heating mixture.

Stir to ensure the sugar is dissolved and bring to near boiling point to thoroughly cook the eggs. Do not actually boil. Take the saucepan off the heat. Dissolve the gelatine in about 1/4 cup of boiling water and stir into hot custard. Pour into serving dish and put into refrigerator to cool.

When mixture has cooled and almost set (it should be shivery at this point) thoroughly beat the egg whites until stiff and fold them in using a metal spoon. Return mixture to refrigerator to properly set.

Red Carpet Pie Crust

Put in large mixing bowl:
4 c Unsifted Gold Medal flour
1 tb Sugar
1 ts Salt
Add:
1 3/4 c Crisco
Blend with a pastry blender
Or fork.
Add all at one time:
1/2 c Cold water
1   Egg
1 tb Vinegar

Mix gently into a soft ball. This recipe makes 5 pie shells.

Rhubarb Custard Pie

　　2 ea Eggs, slightly beaten
　　2 c Sugar
　　1 t Vanilla
　　2 T Milk
　1/2 c Flour
　　4 c Rhubarb

 Combine ingredients; pour into 9" pastry-lined pan or pie plate. Bake @ 400 degrees 10 minutes. Then bake @ 300 degrees 50 to 60 minutes. Cool. Top with whipped cream.

Rhubarb Streusel Perfect Pie

        Streusel topping (below)
2 1/2 c Thawed, well drained rhubarb
   3/4 c Milk
      2   Eggs
     1 c Sugar
   1/2 c Bisquick
     2 T Margarine, softened
   1 ts Ground cinnamon
 1/4 ts Ground nutmeg

Heat oven to 375 F. Grease pie plate, 9 x 1 1/4 ". Prepare Strusel topping; reserve.

Arrange rhubarb evenly in plate. Beat remaining ingredients until smooth, 15 seconds in blender on high, or 1 minute with hand beater. Pour into plate. Sprinkle evenly with Streusel topping.

Bake until knife inserted in center comes out clean, about 40 minutes.
Serve with sweetened whipped cream if desired.

Streusel Topping: 2 T. firm margarine, 1/2 c. Bisquick, 1/4 c packed brown sugar, 1/4 c. chopped nuts.

Cut margarine into baking mix and brown sugar until crumbly; stir in nuts.

Rich Taste Poor Man's Pie

  2   Eggs
1 c Sugar
1 tb Flour, heaping
1 pn Salt
1/2   Stick of margarine, melted
1/3 c Buttermilk
 1 ts Vanilla

Mix in a small bowl in the order given with a fork. Pour into a 8 or 9 inch shallow pie crust and bake at 350 degrees for 30 to 35 minutes

Riverside Pear-On-Pear Tart

```
1 1/4 c  All-purpose flour
   1/8 ts Salt
         Sugar
   1/2 c  Unsalted butter
      1   Egg yolk
2 1/2 tb  Ice water (approximately)
      8   Ripe pears (comice/anjou)
         (about 3 pounds)
     1 ts Ground ginger
   1/3 c  Apricot preserves
```

   Preheat oven to 425 degrees. To make the pastry: Combine the flour with the salt and 2 tablespoons of sugar in a large bowl. Cut in the butter with a knife. Blend with a pastry blender until the flour has the texture of coarse crumbs. Combine the egg yolk with the ice water and work into the flour mixture to form a soft dough. Add more water if necessary. Knead briefly and press the dough over the bottom and sides of a buttered loose bottomed 10-inch quiche pan. Trim the edges. Line the pastry with aluminum foil and weight with rice or beans. Bake 10 minutes. Remove foil and rice or beans; bake until the pastry is golden, 5 to 10 minutes. Cool on a rack.

   To make the caramel: Combine 1/3 cup of sugar with 2 tablespoons water in a medium skillet. Heat to boiling and boil until the mixture turns a light caramel color. Carefully, but quickly, brush the caramel over the bottom and sides of the pastry shell.

   To make filling: Peel 6 of the pears, cut in half, and remove the cores.
   Cut each half into 4 slices. Place the pears in a large heavy skillet or saucepan. Combine 2/3 cup sugar, the ginger, and 1 cup water and pour over the pears. Heat to boiling; reduce the heat. Simmer, covered, until pears are soft but not mushy, 6-8 minutes, depending on ripeness of pears. Cool.

   Drain the pears, reserving the liquid. Arrange the pears over the bottom of the pastry shell.

Peel the remaining pears, cut into quarters, and remove the cores. Cut each quarter into thin slices. Arange symmetrically over the cooked pears.

Combine the apricot preserves with 4 tablespoons of the pear liquid in a small saucepan. Heat to boiling; strain.

Brush the tart with half the apricot mixture. Bake 30 minutes. Remove from oven and brush with the remaining apricot mixture. Serve slightly warmed with whipped cream if desired.

Rock The Banana Guava Pie

    1 1/2 c Sliced bananas
    1 1/4 c Guava nectar
       1/2 c Sugar
         1 tb Lemon juice
      1/4 ts Salt
         3 tb Cornstarch
         3 tb Cold water
              Baked pie shell

  Combine guava nectar, lemon juice, sugar and salt. Bring to boil over low heat. Mix cornstarch and water to a smooth paste and stir into mixture.
  Stir until thickened and clear. Cool. Combine with bananas and pour into baked pie shell. Serve with whipped cream.

Ronaldo's Passion Fruit Pie

 4   Eggs, separated
 1/4 t Salt
 1/4 t Cream of tarter
 1 c Sugar
 3 T Sugar
 1/4 c Frozen passion fruit juice
 1 t Grated orange rind
 1 c Heavy cream, whipped

Preheat oven to 275, grease a 9 inch pie place. In small bowl beat egg whites with salt and cream of tarter until soft peaks form. Gradually add the 1 cup sugar, beating until stiff peaks form and all sugar is dissolved.
Spread on bottom and sides of prepared pie plate. Bake for 1 hour. Turn off oven and allow meringue shell to cool in oven with door ajar. Beat egg yolks until thick and lemon colored. Gradually beat in the 3 T sugar. Stir in undiluted passion fruit juice and orange rind. Cook over low heat, stirring constantly, until thickened. Cool. Spread half of whipped cream in merinque shell. Top with passion fruit filling; spread remaing whipped cream on top. Chill 8-12 hours before serving.

Rosy Cheeks Cherry Almond Mouse Pie

14 oz Milk, sweetened condensed -divided
1 oz Chocolate, unsweetened
1/2 ts Extract, almond; divided
1 x Pastry shell, 9"; baked
10 oz Cherries, maraschino; drain
8 oz Cheese, cream; softened
1 c water, cold
1 pk Pudding mix, vanilla, 3.4 oz
1 c Cream, whipping; whipped
1/2 c Almonds, toasted
Chocolate curls; optional

  In a saucepan over low heat, cook and stir 1/2 cup milk and chocolate until the chocolate is melted and mixture is thickened, about 4-5 minutes. Stir in 1/4 teaspoon extract. Pour into pastry shell, set aside. Reserve eight whole cherries for garnish. Chop the remaining cherries; set aside. In a mixing bowl, beat the cream cheese until light. Gradually beat in water and remaining milk. Add pudding mix and remaining extract; mix well. Fold in whipped cream. Stir in chopped cherries and almonds. Pour over the pie.
  Chill 4 hours or until set. Garnish with whole cherries and chocolate curls if desired.

Rosy Rhubarb Pie

- 2 ea Eggs
- 1/4 c Flour
- 1 ea Pie shell
- 1 x -----stuuessel topping------
- 1/4 c Shortening
- 1 ea Pinch of salt
- 3/4 c Flour
- 1/2 c Sugar
- 2 c Frozen strawberries
- 2 c Frozen rhubarb
- 1/2 c Sugar
- 1/4 c Butter
- 3 T Liquid honey

Pre heat oven 425 degrees f Wisk eggs in large bowl. Wisk sugar, flour until smooth. Set aside. Cut rhubarb, fold into egg mixture. Put in pie shell. Bake 15 minutes, remove and reduce heat to 350 degrees. Apply topping and bake for 40 minutes.

Runnin' Rich Coconut Pie

- 1 Pie crust
- 1/4 c Butter, softened
- 1 c Superfine sugar
- 2 Eggs
- 2 T Flour
- 1/2 c Milk
- 1/4 t Almond extract
- 2 c Finely grated coconut

Preheat oven to 350 degrees. Make a pastry as directed and fit into a 9" piepan, making a high fluted edge; do not bake. Cream butter and sugar until light, beat in eggs, one at a time. Sprinkle in flour and blend until smooth. Mix in remaining ingredients and spoon into pastry shell.

Bake 45 minutes until browned and springy to the touch. Cool on wire rack and serve at room temperature.

Ryan & Nora's Baked Apples

    4 md Green apples
       (crispy, tart; Granny Smiths are good)
        Cinnamon stick (3-inch),
       broken and ground
       OR use 1 1/4 t powdered
   14   Allspice berries, ground
       OR about 1/2 t allspice
  1/8 t Nutmeg, grated
  1/2 c Brown sugar
   3 T Butter (grate if cold)
      Lemon juice (from 1/2 medium lemon)
  3/4 c Golden raisins
  1/4 c Prunes, dried, pitted
  3/4 c Walnuts, chopped
      (or other nuts)

Preheat oven to 400 degrees F. Butter a deep baking dish that has a lid.

Core the apples but do not peel them. Arrange them in the dish. Cut apples to fit, if necessary.

Combine all remaining ingredients in bowl. Mix well (this is where grating the butter comes in handy). Stuff this mixture into the holes and spaces in and between the apples.

Bake covered at 400 degrees F. for about 30 minutes. Serve hot with vanilla ice cream (spoon extra sauce over ice cream).

NOTES:

* A quick substitute for apple pie.

* Grind the cinnamon stick and allspice berries with a coffee grinder; makes interesting coffee afterwards. Alternative: Use about 1 1/4 t powdered cinnamon and 1/2 t allspice.

Ryan's Nutty Cocoa-Peanut-Butter Pie

----------------------------------CRUST----------------------------
   14   Nutter Butter peanut butter sandwich cookies, crushed
   3 tb Butter, melted

---------------------------------FILLING---------------------------
   1/3 c Chocolate chips; semi-sweet
   4 tb Corn syrup, light; divided
   4 tb Water, divided
   1/3 c Peanut butter, creamy
   1/3 c Sugar; + 2 Tbsp
   1/4 c Peanuts; chopped
   2   Egg whites
   1 ts Vanilla
   1 c   Heavy cream; whipped

Prepare the crust by combining cookies and butter. Press into bottom and up sides of a 9" pie plate. CHILL UNTIL SET.

Combine the chocolate chips, 1 Tbsp corn syrup and 1 Tbsp water in the top of a double boiler. Cook over simmering water until the chocolate melts and the mixture is smooth. Remove from heat and COOL WELL.

Meanwhile combine the peanut butter, 1/3 cup sugar, 3 Tbsp corn syrup, and 3 Tbsp water in a 2 quart saucepan. Cook over medium heat, stirring constantly until the sugar is dissolved and the mixture is well blended.
Pour into a bowl and stir in the peanuts; COOL.

Beat the egg whites until foamy, using an electric mixer at high speed.
Gradually add 2 Tbsp sugar, 1 Tbsp at a time, beating well after each addition. Beat in the vanilla and continue beating until stiff, glossy peaks form when the beaters are slowly lifted. Fold the egg white mixture into the whipped cream. Then fold in the peanut butter mixture.

Pour half of the peanut butter mixture into the crust. Drizzle half of the chocolate mixture over the filling. Top with the remaining filling.

Drizzle the remaining chocolate in parallel lines over the filling. Pull a knife across the lines at 1 inch intervals. FREEZE UNTIL FIRM. Wrap securely in aluminum foil. Return to the freezer and CONTINUE FREEZING 8 HOURS OR OVERNIGHT. Remove from the freezer 10 minutes before serving.

Sail Away Chocolate Brandy Cream

1 1/2 tb Cocoa powder
1 tb Confectioners sugar
1 c Heavy whipping cream
1 tb Brandy
1 1/2 ts Vanilla

Sift together the cocoa and confectioners sugar and set aside. In a chilled bowl with chilled beaters, combine all ingredients and beat the cream until stiff peaks begin to form. With a spoon or pastry bag fitted with a star tip, use cream to garnish slices of Double Chocolate Ice Box Pie.

Sally's Best Darn Turtle Pie

   1   Unflavored gelatin
1/4 c Cold water
  1 pt Whipping cream; divided
  6 oz Chocolate chips
  2   Eggs
  1 ts Vanilla
  1   Kraft caramels
  2 tb Butter
    Crust
  2 c Chocolate wafer cookie
    crumbs
3/4 c Pecans
1/2 c Melted butter

Combine crust ingredients. Press in pie plate. Bake at 350 degrees 10 minutes. Cool. Sprinkle gelatin over cold water. Let stand 1 minute. Put in saucepan, stir over low heat until dissolved. Add 1 cup of cream and bring to boil. Put chocolate chips in food processor. Pour milk mixture into processor and blend until chocolate is melted. Add 1/2 cup cream, eggs and vanilla. Beat unti smooth. Chill until thick. In bowl mix unwrapped caramels and 1/4 cup cream. Heat in microwave until melted. Stir until smooth. Pour into crust. Cool. Add chocolate mixture on top. Chill. Top with whipped cream.

Santa's Helper Eggnog Pie

- 2 pk 4 Serving size Vanilla Pudding and Piefilling
- 2 c Eggnog
- 1 1/4 c Milk
- 1/8 ts Ground nutmeg
- 1 9 inch Baked Pieshell
- Coolwhip to taste
- 1 tb Rum is desired

Combine puddingmix, eggnog, milk and nutmeg in pan. Cook and stir over medium heat until mixture comes to a full boil; remove from heat; add rum if desired and cool 5 minutes, stirring twice. Pour into pieshell. Cover surface with plastic wrap. Chill at least 3 hours. Garnish with coolwhip and pecans or other nuts or just a little nutmeg sprinkled on coolwhip.

Satisfying Baklava

3	c	Almonds, ground (1 lb)
4	c	Walnuts or pecans, -ground (1 lb)
3/4	c	Sugar
3/4	c	Water
1		Cinnamon stick
1 1/2	c	Honey
1/2	c	Sugar
2	t	Lemon peel, grated
2	t	Cinnamon, ground
1 1/2	c	Butter, melted
1	lb	Filo, thawed

Spread nuts in a shallow baking pan and toast at 300 degrees F. for 10 minutes or until lightly browned. Cool.

Combine 3/4 C sugar, water and cinnamon stick in a saucepan. Boil until clear. Add honey and heat until well-blended. Cool and remove cinnamon stick.

Combine 1/2 C sugar, lemon peel, and ground cinnamon in a large mixing bowl. Mash together with back of a spoon to blend citrus oil with sugar.
Add cooled toasted nuts and mix well.

Butter a 9x13 inch pan. Line it with 3 sheets of filo, each of which has been brushed with melted butter. Let filo overlap sides of pan. Sprinkle with 1/2 cup of nut mixture. Repeat, alternating 2 sheets of buttered filo and nut mixture, ending with filo. (After the second set of sheets overlap the edges of the pan, start folding the sheets in half after they are buttered. They will fit almost perfectly in the pan.)

After you put in the final sheet of filo, fold the filo that has been hanging off the pan back onto the top sheet of filo so you have a neat, sealed package. Using a razor blade or very sharp knife, cut through the top layer of filo, making lengthwise strips 1 1/2 inches wide. Cut diagonally, making diamonds.

Bake at 325 degrees F. for 1 hour or until golden brown. Remove from oven, place pan on rack, and quickly cut pieces through completely. Immediately pour cooled honey syrup over the baklava. Stop when you run out of syrup or when the baklava stops sizzling when the syrup hits it. This will help keep it crispy and keep it from becoming soggy. Cool and serve. Makes about 4 dozen pieces.

Saturday Night Vanilla Almond Puff

  2 c Flour
1/2 ts Salt
  1 c Unsalted butter
  2 tb Ice water
  1 ts Almond extract
  3   Eggs
1/2 c Confectioner's sugar
  4 tb Cream
  1 tb Unsalted butter
  1 ts Vanilla
      Almonds; sliced

Combine 1 cup of flour and salt in processor. Add 1/2 cup butter and process until mixture resembles fine crumbs. Add ice water and process until mixture forms ball. Chill until puff mixture is ready.

Puff: Combine remaining 1/2 cup butter with 1 cup water in a large saucepan and bring to a boil. Remove from the heat and add almond extract. With a wooden spoon, add 1 cup of flour and stir until well blended. Then add eggs, one a a time, stirring well after each until mixture is glossy.

Divide pastry into 2 parts. Roll each out to a 12 x 3 inch strip and place on an ungreased cookie sheet. Spread puff on pastry and bake for one hour.
Glaze when cool and sprinkle almond slices on top..

Glaze: Combine confectioners sugar, cream, softened butter and vanilla and blend until smooth.

Scary Larry's Berry Pie

 1 c   Sugar
 1/4 c Cornstarch
 1 c   Blueberries
 3/4 c Blackberries
 1/2 c Water
 2 tb Butter or margarine
 1 ds Salt
 1/2 ts Ground cinnamon, optional
 1 c   Strawberries
 3/4 c Red raspberries
 2 tb Lemon juice
       Pastry for 9" double crust

In a saucepan, combine sugar, salt, cornstarch, and cinnamon if desired.
  Stir in berries. Add water and lemon juice. Cook over medium heat just to the boiling point. Pour into pie shell; bake until crust is golden brown.

Scrumptious Cranberry-Apple Cookies

- 1/2 c Butter
- 1 c Brown sugar
- 3/4 c Sugar
- 1 Egg
- 1/4 c Milk
- 2 c Flour
- 1 t Baking powder
- 1 t Cinnamon
- 1/2 t Salt
- 1 t Orange rind, grated
- 1 1/2 c Apples, pared, chopped
- 1 c Cranberries, chopped

Preheat oven to 375 degrees F. Cream butter and sugars; beat in egg and milk. Sift together flour, baking powder, cinnamon and salt. Stir into butter mixture until well-blended. Stir in orange rind, apple and cranberries. drop onto baking sheets. Bake for 12-15 minutes at 375 degrees F.

* Don't store these in a cookie jar, they will get too mushy.

Senorita Amanda Chocolate Sponge Pie

- 1 c   Sugar
- 1/3 c   Flour
- 1/4 ts Salt
- 1/2 c   Ground chocolate
- 3   Eggs; seperated
- 1 c   Milk
- 9   Inch unbaked pastry shell

Sift together sugar, flour, salt, and chocolate. Beat egg yolks well and mix with milk; combine with dry ingredients. Beat egg whites stiff and fold into chocolate mixture, mixing well. Pour into pie shell. Bake in a hot oven (450ø) for 10 minutes, then reduce the heat to moderate (350ø) and bake until firm. Test by inserting a knife blade; when it comes out clean, the chocolate sponge is done. Serve cold with whipped cream or ice cream.

Sherry Fruit Tickle

```
-------------------------------FRUIT----------------------------
   3    Pears
   8 oz Raspberries
        (tinned or fresh)
   1    Passion fruit
        Dry sherry
        (1 bottle)

----------------------------SPONGE CAKE--------------------
   1/2 c  Butter
   10 T   Sugar, castor
   1 1/4 c Flour, self-raising
   2      Eggs (slightly whisked)

-----------------------------CUSTARD-------------------------
   2     Eggs
   1 pn  Salt
   1 pn  Nutmeg
   10 oz Double cream
         (or use whipping cream)

-----------------------------TOPPING--------------------------
   10 oz Double cream
         Roast almonds
```

Peel and slice pears, drain raspberries if tinned, and scoop out passion fruit. Place fruit in large trifle bowl and add an ample quantity of sherry. Leave for twenty-four hours to soak in the refrigerator.

Preheat oven to 350 degrees F. Cream butter and sugar until light and fluffy. Add eggs and about 2 T of flour and beat. Fold in rest of flour.

Bake in 7-inch square tin for 25-30 mins until brown. Let cool. Slice into fingers and arrange on top of fruit. More sherry may be added at this point.

Pour one large glass of sherry. Mix eggs and add all ingredients to smallbowl. Place bowl in pan of simmering water. Stir continuously with wooden spoon, sipping sherry, until custard thickens. This takes about ten minutes. Pour custard on top of sponge. Chill in fridge. Whip cream until stiff and smooth over top of custard. Arrange almonds decoratively.

Shoo-Fly Don't Botha Me Molasses Cake

   1 x *pastry
 1/2 c Molasses
 1/2 T Soda
 3/4 c Water, boiling
 3/4 c Flour
   2 T Shortening
 1/8 t Ginger
 1/2 t Cinnamon
   1 x *liquid:
   1 ea Egg yolk, well beaten
   1 x *dissolved in:
   1 x *crumbs:
 1/2 c Brown sugar
 1/8 t Nutmeg
 1/8 t Cloves
 1/4 t Salt

Combine the ingredients for the liquid part mixing well. Combine the dry ingredients for the crumbs, working in the shortening. Line a pie pan with pastry. Make alternate layers of crumbs and liquid. Top with crumbs and bake at 450-F until crust edges start to brown. Reduce heat to 350-F and bake until firm (about 20 minutes).

Shooting Star Sour Cream Apple Pie

- 6 c Apples, pared, cored; sliced
- 1/2 c Sugar
- 1 tb Flour
- 1/4 ts Salt
- 1/4 ts Cinnamon
- 1/4 ts Nutmeg
- 1 Unbaked pie-shell
- 1 c Dairy sour cream
- 1/4 c Brown sugar
- 1/3 c Graham cracker crumbs
- 1/4 c Sugar
- 1/2 ts Cinnamon
- 1/4 ts Nutmeg
- 3 tb Butter; melted
- 1/4 c Chopped walnuts or pecans

Combine sugar, flour, salt, cinnamon and nutmeg. Toss with apples and arrange in unbaked pie-shell. Cover loosely with foil. Bake in hot oven (400'F) 50 to 55 minutes. Remove foil. Combine sour cream and 1/4 cup brown sugar. Pour evenly over apples. Combine graham cracker crumbs, sugar, cinnamon, nutmeg, and melted butter. Sprinkle over sour cream mixture.

Sprinkle nuts atop crumbs and return to oven. Bake 5 - 7 minutes longer or till nuts and crumb topping are lightly toasted.

Shoreline Rhubarb and Banana

    1 lb Rhubarb
  1/4 c Brown sugar, soft
1 1/4 t Ginger, preserved
     2 lg Bananas, thinly sliced
     2   Egg whites
    1 T Sugar, castor
   8 oz Quark (soft cheese)

Cook and puree the rhubarb, and allow to cool. Add the sugar, ginger and most of the banana (leave some for decorating). Mix well.

Gradually beat the mixture into the quark. Fold in the egg whites.

Transfer into individual dishes and chill. Top with the rest of the banana and serve. Enjoy.

Show Me The Poppyseed Bundt Cake

- 1 c Butter (or margarine)
- 1 1/2 c Sugar
- 2 1/2 c Flour (sift before measuring)
- 1 t Baking soda
- 2 t Baking powder
- 1 c Buttermilk
- 2 oz Poppy seeds (about 1/4 cup)
- 1 t Almond extract (or vanilla extract)
- 4 Eggs (separated)
- 1/4 c Brown sugar
- 1 t Cinnamon

Soak poppyseed in the buttermilk for 15 minutes.

Cream together butter and sugar. Add yolks to creamed mixture. Add almond extract or vanilla. Add dry ingredients alternately with buttermilk mixture, a little at a time.

Beat egg whites very stiff as for angel food. Fold egg whites into mixture. Pour half of this batter mixture into well-greased Bundt pan.

Sprinkle with a mixture of about 1/4 cup brown sugar and about 1 t cinnamon. Pour in remaining batter. Bake at 350 degrees F. for 1 hour.

Cool and invert onto serving dish, then remove Bundt pan.

Simple Delight Butterscotch Cookies

---------------------------------COOKIES--------------------------
- 1 c   Brown sugar
- 1/2 t Salt
- 1/2 c Butter, softened
- 1   Egg
- 1/2 t Vanilla
- 1 3/4 c Flour, sifted
- 1/2 t Baking powder
- 1/4 t Baking soda
- 1/4 t Cinnamon

----------------------------------GLAZE----------------------------
- 1 1/2 c Confectioner's sugar
- 1   Egg white, slightly beaten
- 1 T   Butter, melted
- 1/8 t Salt
- 1/2 t Vanilla
- Food coloring (optional)

Mix sugar, salt and butter thoroughly. Add egg and vanilla and beat till fluffy.

Sift flour, baking powder, soda and cinnamon and add to mixture. Chill well, several hours, or overnight.

MAKE THE GLAZE: Mix the glaze ingredients together until smooth.

Roll the dough out until it is about 1/8 inch thick. Cut into fancy shapes and bake on ungreased cookie sheet for 8-10 minutes at 350 degrees F. Let cool and glaze.

NOTES:

* It helps to keep most of the dough in the refrigerator while you are cutting shapes. It cuts much better when it is cold.

Simply Maple Syrup Pie

1/2 c Butter; melted
1 c Heavy maple syrup
1/2 c Brown sugar, firmly packed
1/8 ts Salt
4   Eggs; lightly beaten
1 1/4 c Pecan halves
1   9-inch pie shell, unbaked
     Sweetened whipped cream

Preheat oven to 350 degrees F.

Blend together butter, maple syrup, brown sugar, and salt. Stir in eggs, mixing until well blended. Add pecans and pour into unbaked pie shell.

Bake for 40 to 45 minutes until firm.

Serve with sweetened whipped cream.

NOTE: For a less rich pie, use only half the amount of butter.

Simply Tasty Rhubarb Cream Pie

  1 1/2 c Sugar
    3/4 t Nutmeg
      4 c Rhubarb in 1" slices (1 lb)
    2 T Butter or margarine
  1/4 c Enriched flour
    3 ea Egg; slightly beaten
    1 ea Pastry for 9" lattice crust

  Blend sugar, flour, nutmeg. Beat into eggs. Add rhubarb. Line 9" pie plate with pastry; fill; dot with butter. Top with lattice crust.
  Bake at 400 degrees 50 to 60 minutes. Cool.

Sinful Cherry Pie

  1 c Milk
  2 T Margarine, softened
  1/4 ts Almond extract
    2   Eggs
  1/2 c Bisqick
  1/4 c Sugar
    1   Can (21 oz.) cherry pie
       Filling.
       Streusel (below)

Heat oven to 400 F. Grease pie plate, 10 x 1 1/2". Beat all ingredients except pie filling and streusel until smooth, 15 seconds in blender on high or 1 minutes with hand beater. Pour into plate. Spoon pie filling evenly over top. Bake 25 minutes. Top with Streusel. Bake until Streusel is brown, about 10 minutes longer; cool.

Streusel: Cut 2 T. firm margarine into 1/2 c. Bisquick mix, 1/2 c. packed brown sugar and 1/2 ts. ground cinnamon until crumbly.

Six Item Frozen Peanut Butter Pie

   3 oz Cream cheese, softened
   1 c Confectioners sugar
   1/2 c Peanut butter
   1/2 c Milk
   8 oz Whipped topping
     1   9" graham cracker shell

Beat cream cheese until fluffy; beat in confectioners sugar, peanut butter, milk and topping. blend well. Turn into baked graham cracker shell.
  Sprinkle graham cracker crumbs on top, if desired. Freeze until ready to serve.

Skinny Lemon Lips Pie (Lowfat Version)

```
  1    Nonfat yogurt; (8 oz)
  6    Graham crackers
  1 tb Canola oil
1/2 c  Honey
1/4 c  Cornstarch
  2    Lowfat vanilla yogurt; (8 oz. each)
1/2 c  Egg beaters® 99% egg substitute
1/2 c  Lemon juice
1/2 ts Lemon extract
1/2 ts Almond extract
  3    Egg whites
1/2 ts Cream of tartar
  1 tb Honey
  1 ts Vanilla extract
```

Place a coffee filter in a medium strainer. Spoon the plain yogurt into the filter and set the strainer over a deep bowl. Cover, refrigerate and allow to drain for 8 hours or overnight. Discard the drained-off whey.
Refrigerate yogurt until needed.

Crumble the graham crackers into the work bowl of a foodprocessor. Process with on/off turns to make crumbs. Add the canola oil and process to combine

Coat a 10-inch pie plate with nostick spray. Press the crumbs into the pan to make a crust. Chill.

In a 2-quart saucepan, whisk together 1/2 cup honey and the cornstarch.
Whisk in the vanilla yogurt and drained plain yogurt. Cook over medium heat, stirring constantly until the mixture thickens and boils.

Remove from heat. Pour some of the hot mixture into the egg substitute.
Stir. Very slowly whisk that mixture back into the remaining hot mixture.
Reduce heat to low. Cook, stirring constantly, for 2 minutes. Remove from heat and whisk in lemon juice,

lemon extract and almond extract. Spoon into the prepared crust. In a medium bowl, beat egg whites and cream of tar foamy. Add 1 tablespoon honey and the vanilla. Beat at high speed until sti peaks form. Spread over pie filling, avoiding gaps where the meringue toppi meets the crust.

Bake at 325 degrees for 10 to 15 minutes, until meringue is golden. Chill.

Skip The Meeting Pie

8 inch baked pie shell

Filling:

1/2 cup butter

3/4 cup sugar

1 ounce unsweetened chocolate, melted

1 teaspoon vanilla

1 1/2 tablespoons instant coffee

2 eggs

1/2 cup cream, for whipping

Prepare 8-inch pastry shell. Cream butter in medium size bowl and gradually add sugar, creaming well after each addition. Cool melted chocolate; blend into butter-sugar mixture with instant coffee and vanilla. Add eggs, one at a time, beating VERY WELL after each addition. (Use an electric beater or mixer, for you'll need to beat in each egg 5 minutes to make mixture creamy, thick, and fluffy.) Turn into baked pastry shell; chill 1 - 2 hours. Just before serving, whip cream and garnish pie

Sky Rocket Plum Torte

>   1 c Sugar
>   1/2 c Butter
>   1 c Flour
>   1 ts Baking powder
>   2   Eggs
>   20   Plums; pit, halves

----------------------------------TOPPING--------------------------
>   Sugar
>   Lemon juice
>   Cinnamon

  Cream sugar and butter. Add flour, baking powder, eggs and beat well.
  Spoon batter into 9" springform pan. Place plum halves skin side up on top of batter. Sprinkle lightly with sugar and lemon juice. Sprinkle with aboout 1 tsp cinnamon and a small amount of nutmeg. Bake at 350 degrees for 1 hour.
  Batter will rise and cover plums. Remove and cool, refrigerate or freeze if desired. Or cool to lukewarm and serve with vanilla ixe cream or whipped cream.

  To serve frozen tortes, defrost and reheat briefly at 300F.

Sky's The Limit Vanilla Pie

AMISH VANILLA PIE

1/2 c. firmly packed brown sugar
1 tbsp. flour
1/4 c. dark corn syrup
1 1/2 tsp. vanilla
1 egg, beaten
1 c. water
1 c. flour
1/2 c. firmly packed brown sugar
1/2 tsp. cream of tartar
1/2 tsp. baking soda
1/8 tsp. salt
1/4 c. butter
1 unbaked 9" pie shell

Combine first 5 ingredients in 2 quart saucepan. Slowly stir in water. Cook over medium heat until mixture comes to a boil, stirring constantly. Let cool. Combine rest of ingredients (except pie shell) and mix until crumbly. Pour cooled mixture into pie shell and top with crumbs. Bake at 350 degrees for 40 minutes or until golden brown.

Slap-Happy Peanut Butter Cream Pie

```
3/4 c  Powdered sugar
1/2 c  Smooth peanut butter
  1 c  Sugar; divided
  3 c  Milk; divided
    3  Eggs; separated
 6 tb  Cornstarch; divided
 3 tb  Flour
1/4 ts Salt
 2 tb  Butter
 2 ts  Vanilla; divided
    1  Pie shell; baked
1/4 ts Cream of tartar
```

Beat together the powdered sugar and peanut butter until the mixture is crumbly; set aside. In a large, heavy saucepan, combine 2/3 c sugar and 2 cup milk; heat to scalding or until bubbles start to form on the bottom. Do not let it boil.

Meanwhile, in a medium bowl, beat the egg yolks to mix; blend in 3 T cornstarch, flour and salt. Stir to make a paste. Whisk in the remaining 1 cup cold milk, whisking until the mixture is smooth. Pour in some of the hot milk mixture, stirring to combine.

Add mixture in bowl to the milk in the saucepan. Cook over medium-low heat, stirring constantly, until the mixture bubbles up in the center. Add the butter and 1 t vanilla. Remove from heat and let custard cool. Preheat oven to 350 degrees. Sprinkle 2/3 of the crumbly peanut butter mixture in the bottom of the baked (and cooled) pastry shell. Pour the cooled custard mixture over the top.

In a large mixer bowl, place the egg whites, cream of tartar and remaining 1 teaspoon vanilla. Beat until stiff peaks form. Gradually, while beating, add the 4 tablespoons remaining sugar and 3 T remaining cornstarch.
Continue beating until whites are very think and glossy.

Spread on top of pie; sprinkle the remaining peanut butter mixture on top.

Bake for 10 to 15 minutes; watching carefully, or until the meringue is golden brown. Cool.

Smart & Flakey Pie Pastry

1 1/3 c All-purpose flour
  1/2 t Salt
  1/2 c Crisco
    3 tb Or 4, ice water

Blend flour and salt together in large mixing bowl. Blend Crisco into flour mixture using pastry blender until mixture resembles a combination of coarse meal and peas. Add ice water one tablespoon at a time, tossing mixture lightly with a fork to combine. When mixture can be compressed easily with a fork, enough ice water has been added. Form pastry mixture into a flat disk and wrap tightly in plastic wrap or waxed paper. Pastry may be refrigerated until ready for use. Roll between two sheets of waxed paper to 1/8-inch thickness. If pre-baking for non-baked filling, bake at 425 degrees F. for 12 minutes. Yields one 9-inch pie shell.

Smile For Coconut Pie

```
    2 c  Milk
  1/4 c  Butter
1 1/2 ts Vanilla
      4  Eggs
    1 c  Coconut; flaked or shredded
  3/4 c  Sugar
  1/2 c  Bisquick
```

Heat oven to 350F. Grease pie plate, 9x1 1/4" or 10x 1/2". Place all ingredients in blender container. Cover and blend on High 15 seconds. Pour into plate. Bake till knife inserted in centre comes out clean, 50 to 55 minutes; cool.

Smooth And Creamy Fruit Pie Filling

    2 c Milk
    1 c Sugar
    5 T Flour
    1   Baked 9" pie shell
    1 pt Any kind of fruit
    3   Egg yolks, slightly beaten
    2   Egg whites, unbeaten
  1/2 ts Salt
1 1/2 ts Vanilla
    1 c Coconut (optional)

  Sift 1/2 c. of the sugar, flour, salt, into top of a double boiler. Add milk and egg yholks beaten thoroughly together. Place over rapidly boiling water and boil 10 minutes, stirring constantly. Remove from boiling water and add 1/2 c. coconut and 1 ts. of the vanilla. Cool. Place half of the fruit in pie shell and then add cream filling.

  Place the egg whites, the other 1/2 c. sugar and 2 T of water in the top of the double boiler. Beat with a rotary beater until thoroughly mixed. Place over rapidly boiling water and beat one minute. Then remove from fire and continue beating until it peaks (stands in sharp points). Add the rest of (1/2 ts.) the vanilla. Pile lightly on filling. Arrange remaining fruit if fresh on top of meringue. If not, dot it here and there on top, but put most inside the pie. Sprinkle with other 1/2 c. coconut and brown.

Smooth Blackberry Custard Pie

1 Servings

```
    1   Unbaked 9 inch pie shell
    2 c Fresh blackberries
    4   Eggs
  2/3 c Sugar
1 1/3 c Milk
    1 ts Vanilla
```

Sprinkle blackberries in bottom of pie shell. Mix beaten eggs, milk and vanilla together and pour over blackberries. Bake at 400 degrees until custard tests done with a knife coming clean when stuck halfway between the rim and the middle.

Snow Angel Pie

    1 pk 9 in pie crust
  1/2 c Hershey's Cocoa
1 1/4 c Sugar
  1/2 c Cornstarch
  1/4 ts Salt
    3 c Milk
    3 tb Butter
1 1/2 ts Vanilla
      Sweetened whipped cream

Combine cocoa, sugar, salt and cornstarch in a medium saucepan. Gradually blend milk into dry ingredients, stirring until smooth. Cook over medium heat, stirring constantly, until filling boils; boil 1 minute. Remove from heat; blend in butter and vanilla. Pour into pie crust. Carefully press plastic wrap directly onto pie filling. Cool; chill 3 to 4 hours. Garnish with whipped cream in the shape of a ghost with snowflakes dotting the background.

So Easy Sugar Pie

- 1 c Brown sugar
- 3 T Flour
- 1 c Evaporated milk
- 1   9 inch pie shell, unbaked

Preheat oven to 400 degrees. In a medium bowl, mix sugar and flour well together. Add milk and mix with electric beater for 1 minute at medium speed, until mixture thickens slightly and lightens in color. Pour into pie shell. Bake 10 minutes, then lower temperature to 350 degrees and continue baking for 20 - 35 minutes or until filling is firm. Cool and serve with whipped cream.

Serves 5

So Good Banana Caramel Pie

INGREDIENTS:
1 (9 inch) prepared graham cracker crust
1 (14 ounce) can sweetened condensed milk
3 bananas
1 cup whipping cream
1/4 cup confectioners' sugar
2 (1.4 ounce) bars English toffee-flavored candy, crushed

DIRECTIONS:
Preheat oven to 325 degrees F (165 degrees C). Fill a large saucepan with water and bring to a boil. Pour sweetened condensed milk into a small baking dish. Cover with aluminum foil. Set dish in a larger baking pan. Place pan on oven rack and pour boiling water into larger pan, to at least 1 inch deep. Carefully slide rack back into oven. Bake 1 hour, until milk is thick and caramelized.
Slice bananas and arrange on bottom of graham cracker crust. Pour caramelized milk over bananas and allow to cool 30 minutes.
In a medium bowl, whip cream until soft peaks form. Add confectioners' sugar and continue to whip until stiff. Spread over cooled caramel. Sprinkle with crushed toffee. Chill 3 hours before serving.

So Good South Fried Pies

    3 c Dried apples *
1 1/2 c Water; boiling
    1/2 c Sugar
    1/4 ts Cinnamon; optional
    1/4 ts Allspice, ground; optional
        Shortening or lard
        -----pastry-----
    2 c Flour; all-purpose
    1 ts Baking soda
1/2 ts Salt
    1/2 c Lard or vegetable shortening
    3 tb Cold water

Instructions

First make the pastry: combine flour, baking soda, and salt; cut in lard with a pastry blender until mixture resembles course meal.
Sprinkle ice water over flour mixture by tablespoonsful, mixing lightly with a fork until enough has been added to allow dough to form a ball. Wrap ball, and chill at least 1 hour.

Cook fruit in boiling water, covered, for 30 minutes, or until very tender; cool and mash slightly. Stir in
1/2 cup of sugar and spices.

Divide chilled pastry in half; roll each half to [a] inch thickness and cut into 5 inch circles. Reroll scraps, and cut into circles. Place 2 to 3 tablespoons of fruit mixture on half of each pastry circle; moisten edges of pastry circles and fold over filling, make sure edges meet. Press edges together, using a fork dipped in flour. Fry in skillet (cast iron preferred) using lard or vegetable shorting until browned on both sides. Drain on paper towels. Serve hot, warm, or cold. * Peaches or Apricots may be substituted for Apples. Fresh fruit may used, increase to 4 cups and simmer, covered in a small amount of water, until tender. Mash coursely or chopped finely, and mix with sugar and spices.

** Betty Crocker Pie Crust Mix may be substituted. Use

(2) 11oz boxes per box instuctions.

Use a 5 inch saucer to cut circles.

May by sprinkled with powdered or granulated sugar while hot if desired.

Space Odyssy Reeses Peanut Butter Pie

INGREDIENTS
1 1/4 c Graham crackers, finely Crushed
6 tb Butter, melted
1/4 c SugarFILLING:
1 pk Chocolate pudding mix
2 c Skim or 1% milk
4 tb Peanut butter

Mix together well and spread into a 9-inch pie plate. Bake at 375 degrees for 6 to 9 minutes, or until edges are browned. Cook the chocolate pudding mix and the milk together over medium heat until boiling. Add the peanut butter and return to a boil. Remove from heat immediately. Pour into the 9-inch graham cracker crust and cool. Refrigerate after it has cooled approximately 1/2 hour at room temperature.

Sparkling Peach Pie with Crumb Topping

- 8 Peaches; peeled & sliced
- 1 T Lemon juice
- 1/4 t Vanilla
- 3 T Flour
- 1/2 c Sugar
- 1/4 c Brown sugar
- 1/2 t Cinnamon
- 1/4 t Salt
- 9 Inch unbaked pie shell

----------------------------------TOPPING--------------------------

- 3/4 c Sugar
- 1/2 c Flour
- 1/3 c Margarine; softened

In a large bowl, combine filling ingredients; toss well to distribute evenly. In another bowl, mix together topping ingredients until crumbly.

Turn filling into shell and sprinkle with topping. Bake in a preheated 375 oven for 1 to 1 1/4 hours or until brown and bubbly. Each serving contains 351 calories and 12 grams fat.

Specialty Persimmon Pie

    2 c Persimmon pulp
    1   Egg; beaten
    1 c Milk
 1/2 c Sugar
 1/8 ts Salt
   1 tb Cornstarch
   1   Pastry shell (9"); uncooked

Mix persimmon pulp, egg, and milk. Mix sugar, salt, and cornstarch and add to first mixture. Line 9-inch piepan with pastry and pour in filling. Bake at 450 degrees for 10 minutes. Then reduce temperature to 350 degrees and bake 50 to 60 minutes longer.

Spoonfull Blueberry Cream Pie

    Graham cracker pie crust, 9 -inch
  8 oz Cream cheese; softened
1/2 c Sugar
  1 ts Vanilla
3/4 c Heavy cream
  1 pt Blueberries
  3 tb Apple jelly

Combine the cream cheese, sugar and vanilla in a bowl, and mix well. Whip cream and fold into cream cheese mixture. Spoon filling into crust.

Arrange blueberries on top. Heat jelly in pan and using pastry brush, glaze top of pie with jelly. Chill 3-4 hours.

Springtime Nectarine Pie

- 1 9" unbaked pie shell
- 4 md Nectarines
- 2/3 c Sugar
- 4 tb Flour
- 1/2 ts Cinnamon
- 1/4 ts Almond extract
- 1 c Cream
- 1/4 ts Salt

Combine sugar, flour, salt, cinnamon, cream and almond extract.

Set aside. Preheat oven to 400F. Placenectarines in boiling water for 30 to 45 seconds. then plunge into cold water and remove skins. Cut in half and remove pits. Place halves flat side down in pie shell. Pour cream mixture around nectarines and bake 35 to 40 minutes.

Squeeky Peachy Peach Pie

Dehydrated peaches

----------------------------------COMBINE--------------------------
- 1 Egg or 2 egg yolks
- 2 T Flour
- 2/3 c Sugar
- 1/3 c Melted butter

Pour the mixture over peaches placed cut side up (if halves) in a 9" unbaked pie shell.

In a preheated 400 degree oven, bake 15 minutes, then reduce the heat to 300 degrees and bake an additonal 50 minues. Serve hot or cold. Garnish with whipped cream.

Starlight Eggnog Pie

```
    1 tb Gelatin
  1/4 c  Cold water
  1/2 c  Sugar
  1/4 ts Nutmeg
  1/4 ts Salt
  3/4 c  Milk
    4    Eggs, separated
  1/4 c  Sugar
         Bourbon to taste
    1 c  Whipping cream
    2    8 or 9 inch baked pie shells
```

  Soften gelatin in cold water fro 5 minutes. Combine egg yolks, lightly beaten, 1/4 cup of sugar, nutmeg, salt and milk. Cook in a double boiler until thick, stirring constantly, after mixture gets hot. Remove from heat; add softened gelatin and fold in egg whites that have been stiffly beaten with 1/4 cup of sugar. Add bourbon to taste. Fold into mixture the 1 cup of cream, whipped. Pour into 2 pie shells and store in the refrigerator until serving time.

Stellar Pineapple Cheese Pie (Low Calorie)

    1 lb Lowfat cottage cheese
    2   Egg whites
    1 ts Lemon juice
    6 pk Sweet 'n low® sweetener
    1 ts Vanilla
  1/4 c Pineapple juice
    1 pk Gelatin powder, unsweetened
  3/4 c Crushed pineapple in juice
        --- drained
        Cinnamon
  1/4 c Wheat germ; or crushed
        -cereal

Recipe by: My files Blend cheese, egg whites, Sweet and Low, lemon juice and vanilla in food processor. Dissolve geletin in pineapple juice, Blend into cheese mixture. Stir in pineapple and cinnamon.

Spray 9" pie plate with Pam. Sprinkler wheat germ over. Pour in cheese mixture, Bake 30 min. at 350. Let cool before cutting,

Step Ahead Sour Cream Pie

```
3/4 c      sugar
1 Tbsp (slightly rounded) flour
1 tsp      cinnamon
1 tsp      nutmeg
½ tsp      cloves
1          egg
1 c        sour cream
1 Tbsp cider vinegar
2/3 c      raisins
2/3 c      chopped walnuts
1          pie shell
```

Mix sugar, flour, cinnamon, nutmeg, cloves, egg, sour cream, vinegar, raisins, and nuts. If time permits, let sit about 45 minutes to allow raisins to absorb moisture. Preheat oven to 450 degrees. Put into unbaked pie shell. Cook 10 minutes, then turn down to 350 degrees. Cook about 30 minutes more.

Serve at room temperature with a dollop of whipped cream on top.

Straight To The Point Choco Hazel Tart

   3 T Cocoa powder
   4 T Butter
   4 oz Bittersweet or semisweet cho
   1 c Dark corn syrup
   3 ea Eggs
1/4 c Sugar
   1 ea Lg Egg
   4 T Butter
1/2 c Sugar
   2 T Dark rum (optional)

     Chocolate Dough

   1 c Unbleached all-purpose flour
Pinch salt
1/4 t baking soda

     Chocolate-Hazelnut Filling

   2 c whole Hazelnuts

The already buttery flavor of the hazelnuts pairs them naturally with the chocolate filling. Walnuts or pecans make good variations. Mixing the Dough. Sift the dry ingredients together three times. Rub in the butter and moisten with the egg as for Sweet Pastry Dough. Shape into a disk, wrap, and refrigerate. Cooking the Chocolate-Hazelnut Filling.

  Place the hazelnuts on a baking pan and toast at 350 degree F until the skins are loose and come off easily, about 10 minutes. Rub the hazelnuts in a towel to remove the skins. Chop the hazelnuts coarsely, by hand or with a food processor. Combine the chocolate with the butter in a small bowl. Bring a small pan of water to a simmer and turn off the heat. Place the bowl of chocolate and butter over the hot water and stir to melt.

  Combine the corn syrup and sugar in a small saucepan. Bring to a full rolling boil over medium heat. Remove from heat and stir in the chocolate mixture. Beat the eggs and salt with the optional rum. Beat in the chocolate mixture, taking care not to overbeat. Assembling. Lightly flour the work surface and dough. Roll the dough to a 14-inch diameter disk, 1/8 inch thick. Line a 10-inch tart pan with the dough, trimming away the excess. Stir the chipped hazelnuts into the filling and pour the filling into the pan. Baking. Bake at 350 degree F until the filling is set and the crust is baked through, about 40 minutes. Holding. Store the tart at room temperature up to 2 days.

Sugar Free Blueberry Blast Pie

- 1 Recipe pastry crust
- 4 c Blueberries, fresh or frozen, thawed
- 4 ts Sweet and Low
- 1/4 ts Cinnamon
- 1/8 ts Nutmeg
- 1 tb Lemon juice
- 2 tb Quick tapioca
- 8 10 drops liquid butter flavoring.

LIne 10" pie plate with crust Pick over, wash and drain berries mix next 6 ingredients together in small bowl toss with berries being careful to not crush the berries too much pour berries in crust, making sure all the "goodies" are scraped from the bowl. Cover with top crust, slit for steam to escape. Bake at 425 for 10 minutes, reduce heat to 325 for 45 minutes or until crust is golden brown and filling is bubbly.

For a little added flavor to the crust you can sprinkle with a light mixture of Sweet and Low and cinnamon.

Cool on wire rack, serve with dollop of Lite Cool Whip or small scoop of vanilla ice cream if desired.

Sugar Free Chocolate Banana Cream Pie

---------------------------------FILLING---------------------------
- 1 pk Sugar free chocolate pudding
- 2 Bananas
- 2 1/4 c Milk

---------------------------------CRUST----------------------------
- 6 tb Peanut butter
- 1 tb Honey
- 2 c Rice crispies

---------------------------------TOPPING---------------------------
- 1 Cool whip light

Mix peanut butter with honey. Then mix in rice crispies. Press in pie plate with metal spoon, build up edge. Slice banana over crust. Then mix pudding with milk and spread over bananas. Top with Cool Whip.

Use Sugar free instant chocolate pudding mix.

Summertime Lemon Pie

1 Recipe

```
    2    Lemons, juiced
    1    Lemon rind, grated
  2 T    Corn starch
    3    Eggs, separated
1 1/2 c  Sugar
  3 T    Flour
  1 ts   Butter or margarine
  2 c    Boiling water
```

Sift flour, corn starch, and sugar into a saucepan. Add butter. Add the lemon juice to the egg yolks and beat with a rotary egg beater until they are thick and velvety. Add this to the sugar, corn starch, butter and flour mixture and stir until free from lumps. You may need to add a few tablespoons of cold water to make thin enough not to lump. Pour the boiling water over lemon mixture. Set on the stove and let come to a boil, stirring constantly. And here is a secret; Your pie will have a better flavor if it scorches just a tiny bit. Add grated lemon rind.

Let cool, stirring often. Pour into pie shell, and add meringue. Do not flatten the meringue, but let it stand in peaks. Brown slightly.

Sunny Cranberry - Raz Meringue Pie

   1/3 c Sugarp
    3 T Cornstarch
   1/8 t Salt
    3   Egg Yolks
   3/4 c Frozen Cranberry-Raspberry
        Juice Cocktail, thawed
   2/3 c Water
    1 T Unsalted Butter
    1 t Lemon Juice
        Frozen 9-inch Pie Shell,
        Baked according to pkg
        Directions

------------------------------MERINGUE TOPPING---------------
        Meringue Powder, prepare
        Topping according to pkg
        Directions

  Combine sugar, cornstarch and salt in medium size saucepan. Beat together egg yolks, juice concentrate and water in small bowl. Gradually stir into cornstarch mixture until smooth. Bring to boiling over medium heat, stirring constantly; cook 1 minute more. Remove from heat; stir in butter and lemon juice. Pour into pie shell. Preheat oven to 350 degrees. Using package meringue powder, prepare meringue topping according to package directions. Spoon some meringue topping around edge of filling so it touches inner crust all around. Heap remaining meringue in center. Bake in preheated oven about 15 minutes or until meringue is lightly browned. Cool on wire rack. Topping will weep after a few hours, so serve soon after baking.

Sunny Southern Pecan Pie

    4 lg Eggs
    1 tb Flour
  3/4 c Sugar
  1/4 c Dark karo corn syrup
    1 c Light karo corn syrup
    1 pn Salt
    1 ts Vanilla
1 1/2 c Pecans
    1 Pie crust, frozen; (9-inch), deep dish

Recipe by: Anita Douglas Preparation Time: 1:00 Thaw pie crust and pinch edges of crust. (Makes it look homemade.) Beat eggs. Add flour, sugar, corn syrups, salt and vanilla. Mix well. Pour into 9-inch deep dish pie shell.

Bake at 350 degrees for 10 minutes, and 300 degrees for 45 to 50 minutes.

Cover edges with thin strips of foil during first 30 minutes of baking.

Allow pie to cool before serving.

Sunroom Strawberry Cream Pie

9" pastry shell
1/2 c Sugar
   Small egg yolks
   1 tb Firm butter
1/3 c Flour
  2 c Milk
1/2 ts Vanilla
1 1/2 c Strawberries

    Bake and cool pastry shell. Blend flour and sugar in heavy saucepan. Slowly stir in 1 cup milk until sm Stir 1/2 cup of hot mixture into well-beaten egg yolks; stir together. Pour back in saucepan; cook and stir 2 minutes.
    Remove from heat; stir in v Pour half of mixture in pie shell. Layer strawberries; pour remaining mixtu

Sunset Chocolate Walnut Pie

    3 lg Eggs
1 1/2 c Sugar
    3/4 Stick (6 tablespoons) butter, melted and cooled
    2 t Vanilla
    3/4 c Flour
1 1/2 c Semisweet chocolate chips
1 1/2 c Chopped walnuts
Vanilla ice cream
Creme de cacao
Unbaked pastry for a 9 inch pie, fitted into pie pan and refrigerated.

In a large bowl, combine beaten eggs, sugar, butter (melted and cooled), vanilla and beat the mixture lightly until blended. Then add flour, chocolate and walnuts. Mix well. Pour filling into the shell and bake at 350 degrees for 1 hour to 1 hour and 5 minutes. Cake tester will come out almost clean. Top will be light in color and crusty. Pie is best served warm with vanilla ice cream and topped with creme de cacao. Sprinkle with shaved chocolate. Option: Substitute coffee ice cream for the vanilla ice cream and top with Kahlua.

Surprise Fruit and Cream Pie

    4 oz Cream cheese; softened
    1/2 c Powdered sugar
    1/2 c Cool whip; thawed
    6 oz Graham cracker crust
    1 pk 4 serving size gelatin
    1 pk 4 serving size cook and
      -serve pudding
1 1/4 c Water
    2 c Sliced fruit

Mix cream cheese and sugar in large bowl until well blended. Stir in cool whip. Spread in crust. Refrigerate. Mix gelatin, pudding mix and water in medium saucepan until smooth. Stirring constantly, cook on medium heat until mixture just comes to boil. Remove from heat. Cool 5 minutes. Stir in fruit. Spoon over cream cheese layer. Refrigerate 4 hours or until set.

Surrendering Sugar Cream Pie

1 1/2 c Brown sugar (do not pack)
6 tb All purpose flour
1 c Half and half
1 c Heavy whipping cream
pn Salt
1 ts Vanilla
Butter
Cinnamon

Mix together brown sugar and flour and put in bottom of an unbaked deep dish pie shell. Then mix together Half and half, whipping cream, salt, and vanilla. Slowly pour this mixture over the top of the brown sugar mixture.
 DO NOT STIR!!!!! Dot with slices of butter and sprinkle with cinnamon.
 Bake 10 minutes at 450 degrees. Reduce heat to 325 degrees and bake for 50 minutes. Serve slices of pie slightly warm.

**I have found that baking the pie in a glass pie dish has better results then using the pie shell already in a aluminum pan. The aluminum ready pie crust seems to over cook the brown sugar and make it hard instead of a gelatin type substance. Also Vanilla ice cream is a great accompaniment to the pie. Plus it will help ease some of the kick from the richness of the pie.

Susie's Soft Shortbread

- 1 c Butter, softened
- 1 c Flour
- 1/2 c Cornstarch
- 1/2 c Sugar, icing
- 1 t Vanilla

Preheat oven to 325 degrees F. Beat butter and vanilla until foamy. Add dry ingredients and blend. Do not over-stir.

Spoon onto an ungreased pan. Bake at 325 degrees F. until done (10-20 minutes depending on thickness)

Sway To Pavlova II

4 lg Egg whites
1 c Sugar, castor
1 t Cornflour
1 t Vinegar
1 t Vanilla flavour

Preheat oven to 250 degrees F. With an electric mixer beat the egg whites until soft peaks form, then gradually add the sugar. Beat until firm.

Add the cornflour, vinegar and vanilla. When combined, turn out onto a flat tray that has been greased and dusted with cornflour. Try a circular shape with slightly more mixture at the edges so that it may be served by placing goodies in its centre depression.

Cook in a pre-heated, cool (250 degrees F.) oven for one hour. When cooked, turn the oven off, leave the oven door slightly ajar, and allow to cool slowly in the oven. This slow cooling works to prevent the loss of too much height. Serve cold, with whipped cream and fresh fruit pieces, strawberries and kiwi fruit for example.

Sweet and Sour Milk Cake

- 1 1/2 c Flour, sifted
- 1 c Sugar
- 3 T Baking cocoa
- 1 t Baking soda
- 1/2 t Salt
- 1 Egg
- 1/4 c Butter (or margarine), melted
- 1 c Milk, sour
- 1/4 c Hot water
- 1 T Vanilla

Preheat oven to 350 degrees F. Sift together flour, sugar, cocoa, baking soda and salt into mixing bowl. Add egg, butter, sour milk, hot water and vanilla. Beat (preferably with an electric mixer) at medium speed for 2 minutes.

Pour batter into a greased 13x9x2-inch baking pan. Bake at 350 degrees F. for 20 minutes or until it tests done (a toothpick or fork comes out clean). Cool in pan.

Sweet As Maple Sugar Pumpkin Pie

- 16 oz Pumpkin, canned; solid pack
- 2 tb Flour
- 1/2 ts Ground cinnamon
- 1/2 ts Ground nutmeg
- 1/2 ts Ground ginger
- 1 tb Butter or margarine; softened
- 1 c Sugar
- 1 c Milk
- 2 tb Maple syrup
- 2 Eggs
- 1 9 inch pie shell; unbaked
- Whipped cream; optional

In a mixing bowl combine pumpkin, flour, cinnamon, nutmeg, ginger, butter, sugar, milk, syrup and eggs; mix well. Pour into the pie shell.

Bake at 425 for 15 minutes. Reduce heat to 350 degrees and continue baking for about 45 minutes or until a knife inserted near the center comes out clean. Cool to room temperature. Refrigerate. Garnish with whipped cream if desired.

Sweet Little Fruit Tart

   1   Pie shell (make your own, or buy the frozen, uncooked kind)
  1/2 c Water
   1 c Sugar
2 1/2 t Cornstarch
  10 c Fruit, sliced
        Cinnamon or nutmeg, ground (to taste)

Mash about 2 C of the fruit in a saucepan with the water, sugar, and cornstarch. Add another sprinkle of nutmeg or cinnamon. Boil until the liquid becomes clear (about two minutes).

Place the remaining fruit in the pie shell, and a sprinkle of the nutmeg or cinnamon. Pour the hot mixture over the fruit, and let cool for at least two hours.

Serve with whipped cream or ice cream as desired.

Sweet Treat Strawberry Glace Pie

- 1 1/2 c Raspberries
- 1 1/2 c Strawberries -- sliced
- 1   c Blueberries
- 1   Pie crust (9 inch) -- baked And cooled
- 3/4 c Sugar
- 3   tb Cornstarch
- 1 1/2 c Water
- 1   pk Strawberry gelatin powder Jello, 4-serv. pkg
- 8   oz Cool Whip -- 1 tub

Mix berries and pour into pastry shell.
Mix sugar and cornstarch in med. saucepan. Gradually stir in water until smooth. Stirring constantly, cook on medium heat until mixture comes to a boil; boil 1 min. Remove fromheat. Stir in gelatin until dissolved. Cool to room temperature. Pour over berries in pastry shell. Refrigerate 3 hours. Spread whipped topping over pie before serving. Garnish with additional berries, if desired.

Sweetheart Cookies

    2 oz Emisweet chocolate chips
   1/2 c Softened salted butter
    1 c White sugar
    2 lg Eggs
    2 ts Pure vanilla extract
1 1/2 c All-purpose flour
  1/2 ts Baking soda
    6 oz Semisweet chocolate chips
    3 oz White chocolate chips
1 1/2 oz Milk chocolate chips

Preheat oven to 375 F. Line cookie sheets with waxed paper.

In a double boiler melt the unsweetened chocolate and the first batch of chocolate chips. Stir frequently with wooden spoon or wire whisk until creamy and smooth.

Pour melted chocolate into a large bowl. Add butter and beat with electric mixer at medium speed until thoroughly combined. Add the sugar, eggs and vanilla. Beat on medium speed until well blended. Scrape down sides of bowl.

Add the flour, baking soda and the three types of chocolate chips. Mix at low speed just until combined. Chips should be distributed equally throughout the dough.

Roll a heaping tablespoon of dough into a ball, about 1 1/2 inches in diameter. Place dough balls onto paper-lined pans, 2 inches apart. With the palm of your hand, flatten each ball to 1/2 inch thickness.

Bake for 10-12 minutes. Transfer cookies with a spatula to a cool, flat surface.

Sweetie Pie

Ingredients

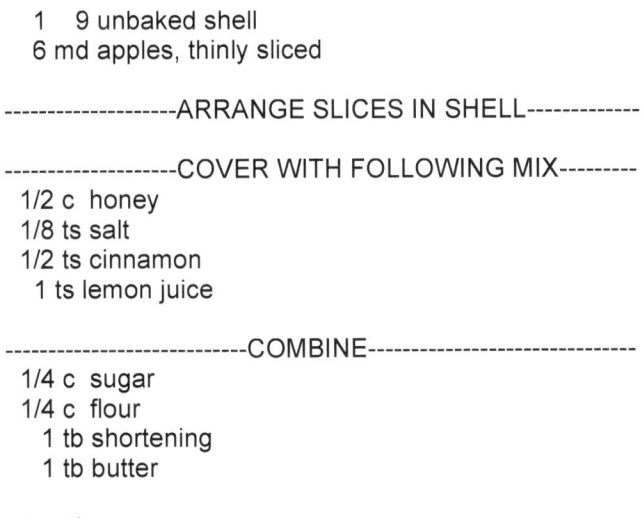

1   9 unbaked shell
6 md apples, thinly sliced

---------------------ARRANGE SLICES IN SHELL------------

---------------------COVER WITH FOLLOWING MIX---------
1/2 c honey
1/8 ts salt
1/2 ts cinnamon
1 ts lemon juice

----------------------------COMBINE------------------------------
1/4 c sugar
1/4 c flour
1 tb shortening
1 tb butter

Instructions

Sprinkle over apples. Bake at 400 for 20 minutes. Reduce to 350 and bake until apples are tender.

Suggestion: An excellent pastry for above recipe is the Cheese Pastry:

2 c. flour
1 ts. salt 3/4 c. shortening 5-6 T cold water 1/2 c. grated cheese.

Take A Bite Of Melomacarona

1 1/2 c Olive oil
  1/2 c Butter, unsalted
    -(at room temperature)
    1 c Beer
  3/4 t Cinnamon, ground
  1/4 t Ground cloves, ground
    Orange peel (use the grated peel of one orange)
    1 c Sugar
    2 c Semolina, finely ground
    6 c Flour
  1/2 t Baking soda
  1/2 t Baking powder
    1 t Salt
1 1/2 c Sugar (for the syrup)
1 1/2 c Honey
    1 c Water
  1/2 c Walnuts, chopped

    Put the olive oil, butter, beer, cinnamon, cloves, orange peel and sugar in a mixing bowl and beat until they are thoroughly blended.

    Sift about one cup of flour with the baking soda, baking powder and salt and blend into the mixture. Add the semolina, a cup at a time, into the mixture.

    Add the enough of the remaining flour, a cup at a time, until you get a rather firm dough (you may need a bit more or less than the amount mentioned in the ingredients list). Use your hands to do the mixing, as an electric mixer will be useless after the first two or three C of flour have been added.

    Roll the dough into cylinders, about two inches long and one inch in diameter, flatten them with your hands, and place them on cookie sheets greased with a little olive oil. Bake at 350 degrees F. for half an hour.
    Remove the cookies from the oven and let them cool for about half an hour.

    Make the syrup: mix the sugar, honey and water, and bring them to a boil.

Cook on low heat for three minutes and skim off the foam that forms on top.

Pour the hot syrup over the cookies, sprinkle them with the chopped walnuts and let them soak overnight.

Take Time For A Graham Cracker Quickie

1 servings

- 3 Eggs
- 1 c Sugar
- 1 c Chopped walnuts
- 1 c Graham cracker crumbs

Beat eggs thorougly and add sugar. Fold in walnuts and crumbs, also salt.

Spread in a 9 inch greased pie pan. Bake fo 25 minutes at 325 degrees.

Serve warm with whipped cream on top. Chewy and delicious.

Take Two Orange Pound Cake

- 1 lb Butter
- 1 lb Sugar, powdered
- 2 T Orange rind, grated
- 6 lg Eggs
- 3 1/2 c Flour (all-purpose), -sifted
- 1/2 t Mace
- 1/4 t Salt
- 1/4 c Orange juice
- 1 c Apricot jam, strained
- 2 T Orange peel, shredded

Preheat oven to 350 degrees F. Cream butter until light and fluffy.

Gradually add sifted sugar and rind. Cream thoroughly. Add eggs, one at a time, mixing well after each addition.

Sift the flour before measuring, then combine the dry ingredients.

Gradually add sifted dry ingredients to butter mixture. Add orange juice and combine thoroughly.

Turn into buttered and floured 10-inch tube pan. Bake at 350 degrees F. for 50-60 minutes or until toothpick inserted in center comes out clean and cake is golden brown. Cool for 5 minutes. Turn onto wire rack and cool thoroughly. Brush with jam and top with orange peel.

Tang Bang Lemon Meringue Pie

1 7/8 c Sugar
  1/3 c Cornstarch
  1/4 t Salt
    2 c Milk
     3 Eggs, separated, plus 1 extra egg white
1 1/2 t Grated lemon rind
  1/2 c Fresh lemon juice
    2 T Butter
     1 Baked 9" pastry shell
  1/2 t Cream of tartar

Combine 1 1/2 cups sugar, cornstarch, and salt in a heavy saucepan.
Gradually add milk, stirring until blended. Cook over medium heat, stirring constantly, until thickened and mixture comes to a boil. Boil gently 1 minute, stirring constantly. Remove from heat.

Preheat oven to 350 degrees. Beat egg yolks at hight speed of an electric mixer until thick and lemon-colored. Gradually stir about 1/4 of hot milk mixture into yolks; add this to remaining hot mixture, stirring constantly.
Cook over medium heat, stirring constantly, for 2 to 3 minutes. Remove from heat; stir in lemon rind, lemon juice, and butter, stirring until butter melts. Pour filling into baked pie shell.

Beat the 4 egg whites and cream of tartar at high speed of an electric mixer until foamy. Gradually add remaining 1/4 cup plus 2 Tbsp. sugar, 1 Tbsp. at a time, beating until stiff peaks form. Spread meringue over hot filling, sealing to edge. Bake for 12 to 15 minutes, or until browned. Cool before cutting.

Tasty Delight Pecan Pumpkin Pie

-----------------------------------CRUST----------------------------
  1   Pastry pie shell,
       -flaky, 9-inch
       -(uncooked)

------------------------------PUMPKIN LAYER-------------------
  3/4 c Pumpkin
  2 T Light brown sugar,
       -packed
  1 lg Egg
  2 T Sour cream
  1/8 t Cinnamon
  1/8 t Nutmeg, grated

------------------------------PECAN LAYER--------------------
  3/4 c Corn syrup, light
  1/2 c Light brown sugar,
         packed
  3 lg Eggs
  3 T Butter (unsalted),
       melted and cooled
1 1/3 c Pecans
  2 t Vanilla
  1/4 t Lemon rind, grated
1 1/2 t Lemon juice
  1/4 t Salt

Prepare pie shell. Keep chilled.

Whisk together until smooth pumpkin, about 2 T brown sugar, 1 egg, sour cream, cinnamon and nutmeg.

In another bowl, combine corn syrup, about 1/2 cup brown sugar, 3 eggs, about 3 T butter, vanilla, lemon rind, lemon juice and salt. Stir in pecans.

Spread the pumpkin layer into the pie shell, then carefully spoon the pecan mixture over it. Bake in the upper third of a preheated 425 degree F. oven for 20 minutes, then reduce to 350 degrees F. for 20-30 minutes more. The filling will puff slightly, but the center will not be completely set. Cool on a rack. Serve warm or at room temperature. Reheat in a preheated 350 degree F. oven for 10 to 15 minutes.

Tasty Kolachki

---------------------------------COOKIE DOUGH-------------------
- 1/2 lb Cream cheese (at room temperature)
- 1/2 lb Butter (at room temperature)
- 3 c Flour
- 1 x Walnut filling, below
- OR
- 12 oz Poppy seed filling (1 can)

------------------------------WALNUT FILLING-------------------
- 1 lb Walnuts, finely ground
- 1 Egg
- 1 c Sugar
- Water

Mix butter and cream cheese until smooth. Add flour and mix again until smooth. Making this dough is easy with a food processor, hard with a mixer.

Roll dough into 3 balls. Refrigerate dough to keep it from drying out. The dough can be refrigerated for 1-2 hours, but it is not necessary. Roll out 1 ball at a time and flour lightly. Roll dough out in flour or granulated sugar so it doesn't stick.

Cut dough into squares or circles using cookie or biscuit cutter. Add about a teaspoon of filling. Roll squares into "logs." Fold circles over and seal with a fork. Bake at 375 degrees F. for 10-15 minutes or until lightly browned.

MAKE FILLING: Mix all ingredients together. Add water to obtain a sticky consistency.

Tea Party Strawberry Chiffon Pie

```
 1 c  Water
 1    Env knox unflavored gelatine
20 oz (1 pk) kool aid unsweetened;
      Drink mix (strawberry flav.)
      -=OR=-
20 oz (1 pk) Wykler's unsweetened
      -flavored soft drink mix
 8    1 g packets equal sugar sub
 1    Recipe low cal whipped toppIng
 2 tb Instant dry milk
 9    Inch graham cracker crust
      (see diabetic recipe)
 9    Fresh strawberries
      (optional)
```

Combine water and gelatin. Let set for 5 minutes and then heat until gelatin is melted. Add Kool aid mix and sweetener to gelatin. Mix well and refrigerate until slightly thickened. Prepare whipped topping while gelatin is thickening. Refrigerate until needed. Add dry milk to thickened gelatin and whip at high speed until creamy and stiff. Remove beater and gently fold in whipped topping into whipped gelatin. Spread filling evenly into graham cracker crust. Garnish eack serving with a fresh strawberry, placing a fresh strawberry in the center of the pie. Refrigerate until firm. Cut into 8 equal pieces.

Teeter Totter Jam & Sour Cream Pie

---------------------------------PASTRY DOUGH------------------
8 tb Butter; unsalted;
cut into 1/4" bits; chilled
3 tb Shortening;Vegetable,chilled
2 1/4 c Flour; all purpose
1/4 ts Salt
  5 tb Water; iced; more as needed

---------------------------------FILLING----------------------------
  2 c Almonds; Finely ground
  4 ts Milk
  6 tb Rasberry Jam
  6 tb Cherry Jam
  2   Egg yolks
  1/3 c Sour Cream
  2 ts Cinnamon
  1 tb Butter;softened

Pastry: In a large mixing bowl, combine the butter, vegetable shortening, flour and salt. Working quickly, use your fingertips to rub flour and fat together until they blend and look like flakes of course meal. Pour ice water over over mixture all at once, toss together lightly and gather dough into a ball. If dough crumbles, add up to 2 more tablespoons per batch you are making, drop by drop until particles adhere. Divide the dough in half, dust each half lightly with flour and wrap separately in sheets of wax paper. Refrigerate at least 3 hours until firm.

Filling: Soak the almonds in milk for 5-10 minutes. With the back of a large spoon, rub the jams through a fine seive set over a large bowl. Then beat in it the egg yolks, sour cream, cinnamon, the nuts and their soaking milk. On a lightly floured surface, roll the dough into a 12" circle about 1/8" thick. With a pastry brush, coat the bottom and sides of a 9" false bottom tart pan with the softened butter. Gently press the pastry into the bottom and around the sides of the pan, being careful not to stretch it.

Roll the pin over the rim of the pan, pressing down hard to trim off excess pastry. Preheat oven to 425. Pour the filling into the pastry shell and roll out other half of dough into a 12" circle. Drape it over the rolling pin, lift it up and unfold it over the filling. Press the edges of the pastry layers together. Then crimp them with your fingers or press them firmly around the rim with the prongs of a fork.. With a sharp knife, cut 3 slits about 1" apart in the top of the pastry. Bake in the center of the oven for 30 minutes or until pastry is golden brown. Then set the pan on a large jar or coffee can and carefully slip off the outside rim. Let the pie cool to room temperature before serving.

Tempo Tart

** British Measurements **

----------------------------------THE PASTRY----------------------
6 oz Flour
3 oz Butter or margarine
1 oz Caster sugar
1   Egg yolk

------------------------------THE CUSTARD---------------------
1 tb Cornflour
1/2 oz Butter
5 oz Milk
1   Egg yolk
1 oz Caster sugar
2 dr Vanilla essence

------------------------------THE FILLING-----------------------
4 oz Marzipan
1 oz Almonds; flaked
1 oz Mixed peel; chopped

To make the pastry: Rub the butter into the flour, stir in the sugar and bind the mixture to make a firm dough. Line an 8-inch flan ring and reserve the extra dough for decoration.

To make the custard: Blend the cornflour with a little milk and stir in the remaining milk and sugar. Heat gently until it boils and simmer for a couple of moments before removing from the heat. Stir in the butter and let the custard cool a little before stirring in the egg yolk and vanilla essence. Leave it to cool.

To make the filling: Roll the marzipan to fit the base of the pastry.
Sprinkle over the almonds and peel. Spread the cooled custard over this.
Using the left over rolled pastry, cut circles of about 1-inch in diameter and arrange these in a pattern on top of

the custard.

Cover with a circle of greaseproof paper to prevent burning the custard and bake for 20 minutes at 400øF / 200øC / gas mark 6 and then for a further 20 minutes in a slower oven, 350øF / 180øC / gas mark 4.

Decorate by combining 1 ounce icing sugar with a little warm water and spreading over the pastry circles. Serve either hot and cold.

The Best Creamy Peanut Butter Pie

1 Servings

---------------------------------CRUST----------------------------
- 14 Oreo cookies
- 1/2 c (1 stick) unsalted butter melted
- 3 tb Finely chopped roasted peanuts

--------------------------------FILLING----------------------------
- 1 pk (8 oz) cream cheese room temp
- 1 c Sugar
- 2 ts Vanilla extract
- 3/4 c Plus
- 2 tb Creamy peanut butter (do not use old fashion ok or freshly ground)
- 1/4 c Finely chopped roasted peanuts
- 1 c Chilled whipping cream

--------------------------------TOPPING---------------------------
- 1/2 c Whipping cream
- 1/2 c Sugar
- 1/4 c Unsalted butter
- 2 oz Chocolate chopped
- 1/2 ts Vanilla extract

For crust: Preheat oven to 375 Line 9 inch metal pie pan with foil finely grind oreo cookies in processor, add butter and peanuts and blend until moise and crumbs form. Press mixture firmly onto bottom and sides of pie pan. Bake crust 5 min. freeze crust 30 min. Turn pan upside down, releasing crust gently peel off foiul. Return crust to pie dish. Transfere crust to refrigerator.

For filling: Using electric mixer, beat cream cheese in large bowl until smooth beat in sugar and vanilla. gradually beat in peanutbutter mix in nuts. In another bowl beat in chilled whipping cream to stiff peaks. Fold cream into peanut butter mixture in 4 additions. Transfer filling to crust mounting slightly. Refrigerae at least 6 hours or over night. For topping.

   Stir whipping cream and sugar in heavy med saucepan over med heat until sugar dissolves; Simmer without stirring until reduced to 2/3 c. about 6 min. Add buuter unsweetened chocolate & vanilla stir until melted and smooth. Let topping stand until cool but still pourable abut 15 min. Spoon topping over pie covering completely. Refrigerate until set at least 4 hours. Can be done a day ahead.

The Great Frozen Chocolate-PJ Pie

1 1/2 c Heavy cream
4 oz Semisweet chocolate squares
   cut-up
   Cocoa graham crust
   (recipe follows)
1 pk (8 oz) cream cheese; softene
1 c Powdered sugar
3/4 c Peanut butter
1/4 c Peanuts; chopped

Recipe by: 365 Great Chocolate Desserts - ISBN 0-06-016537-5 Preparation
Time: 0:42 1. In a small glass bowl, combine 1/2 cup cream and chocolate.
Heat in microwave on High 1 to 1 1/2 mins, until melted and smooth when stirred. Let cool slightly.

2. Spread half of chocolate mixture over bottom of Cocoa Graham Crust.
Freeze 1/2 hour, or until set.

3. Meanwhile prepare filling. In a medium bowl, beat cream cheese, powdered sugar, and peanut butter with an electric mixer on medium until well blended and fluffy, 1 to 2 mins. Whip remaining 1 cup cream until stiff; beat half of whipped cream into peanut butter mixture until well mixed, then fold in remaining whipped cream.

4. Spread filling evenly over chocolate mixture in crust.
Freeze 1/2 hour.
Then carefully spread remaining chocolate mixture over top and sprinkle peanuts over surface. Freeze 6 hours or overnight. Wrap tightly and store in freezer. Transfer pie to refrigerator 1 hour before serving. Cut into wedges to serve.

The Return Of The Macadamia Nut Pie

    3   Eggs
 2/3 c Sugar
 1/3 c Melted butter
    1 c Dark corn syrup
    1 c Macadamia nut bits
        Single crust 9inch shell

Prepare pie shell. Combine all ingredients and mix well. Pour into pie shell and bake at 350 degrees for 35-40 minutes, or until custard is set and crust is golden brown. Serve warm on warmed plates. This pie can be cooled and frozen. Reheat before serving in a 350 degree oven for 15 minutes.

The World's Greatest Meringue

  12 md Egg whites
  1/4 ts Heaping of cream of tartar
    2 c Powdered sugar

Preheat oven to 400F. Separate yolks from whites, being careful not to drip any yellow in the whites or they won't beat up. Put into a bowl, add the cream of tartar, and beat until stiff.

Add the powdered sugar and beat until it forms soft peaks.

Spread a layer of meringue on the pie. Make a good seal over the filling.
Spread until it meets the edge of the crust to keep the meringue from shrinking as it stands or bakes. Repeat until the meringue is used up, then gently swirl the top to make it pretty.

Bake about 15 minutes or until golden brown.

Time For Lime Summer Pie

3 Servings

1 Graham cracker crust
1 sm Can of limeade
1 cn Milnot
1 lg Cool Whip

Stir well, the limeade, Milnot and Cool Whip. Pour into pie shell. Chill for 2 hours before serving

Ting Tang Pie

- 1 14-oz can sweetened condensed milk
- 1 8-oz carton sour cream
- 1/4 c Tang instant breakfast drink
- 1 9-oz carton Cool Whip; thawed
- 1 10-inch graham cracker crust
- Mandarin oranges and banana slices (optional)
- Additional thawed Cool Whip; (optional)

Combine milk and sour cream; mix well. Stir in Tang (this will congeal rather quickly). Fold in Cool Whip. Add fruit, if desired. Pour into graham cracker crust. Refrigerate overnight. Garnish with additional Cool Whip, if desired.

Tip Toe Twinkie Pie

		Butter
9		Twinkies
3		Eggs -- large, seperated
1		Dash Cream of tartar
1/2	c	Sugar
1/2	t	Vanilla extract
6	oz	Chocolate chips -- semisweet
1	c	Pecans -- chopped
1	c	Heavy cream -- whipped

Grease pyrex square or rectangular casserole with butter. Cut 8 Twinkies in thirds, LENGTHWISE, and put one layer on the bottom of the casserole. Beat egg whites, with the cream of tartar and sugar, adding vanilla. Melt chocolate chips in the top of a double boiler. Add egg yolks to chocolate, slowly, continuing to stir over boiling water. Fold chocolate into egg whites. Spread over Twinkies, then sprinkle with about half of the nuts.

Layer on more twinkies, more chocolate, more nuts. Continue layering. Top with whipped cream and a single whole Twinkie. Chill and serve.

Tis' Chocolate Peppermint Angel Pie

  1 c Skim milk
  1 lg Egg
  1/3 c Light corn syrup
  2 ts Light corn syrup
  1/2 c Cocoa
  2 oz Lowfat cream cheese; in chunks
  2 ts Gelatin powder, unsweetened
  1 ts Vanilla
  1/2 ts Peppermint extract
  1/2 c Sugar
  1 tb Sugar
  2 lg Egg whites; at room temperature

Whisk 1/4 cup milk, egg, 1/3 cup corn syrup and cocoa till smooth. In large pot, heat remaining milk till bubbles appear at edges. Whisk some into cocoa mixture, then whisk back into milk in pot. Cook over medium, stirring constantly with a wooden spoon for 3-5 m in.. till slightly thickened. Remove from heat and whisk in chocolate and cream cheese till smooth. Set aside. Soften gelatin in 1/4 cup water and heat till dissolved. Whisk into chocolate mixture along with vanilla and mint. Set aside. Combine 1/4 cup water, 1/2 cup sugar and 2 tsp. corn syrup in small pot. Bring to a boil and cook at medium-high for about 5 min. (2 30 deg. - fine thread stage). Beat egg whites to soft peaks, add 1 Tbsp. sugar and beat till stiff but not dry. When syrup reaches 239 deg (soft ball stage) pour over whites, gradually while beating. Beat about 5 min, till stiff, satiny and cool. Whisk one cup of meringue into chocolate mixture, fold in the rest. Spoon into crust. Chill.

To The Rescue Pie Pastry

2 1/4 c Flour, all-purpose
3/4 c Shortening, well chilled
2 T Butter or margarine, chilled
5 T Or 6 water, well chilled

Sift flour and salt into bowl. Cut shortening and butter into 4 to 5 pieces and drop into bowl. Attach bowl and flat beater. Turn to Stir Speed and cut shortening into flour until particles are size of small peas, about 30 seconds.

Add water, a tablespoon at a time, until all particles are moistened. Use only enough water to make pastry form a ball. Watch dough closely as over mixing will result in a tough crust.

Chill in refrigerator 15 minutes. Roll to 1/8-inch thickness between pieces of waxed paper. Fold pastry into quarters; ease into pie plate and unfold, pressing firmly against bottom and side. Trim and crimp edges. Fill and bake as desired.

Yield: Two 8 or 9-inch single crust or one 8 or 9-inch double crust.

For Baked Pastry Shell: Prick sides and bottom with fork. Bake at 450F for 8 to 10 minutes until light brown. Cool completely before filling.

HINT: I also chill the wax paper and rolling pin.

Traffic Jam Oatmeal Cookies

    1 c Flour
    2 t Baking powder
    1/2 t Salt
    1 t Cinnamon, ground
    1/4 t Nutmeg, ground
    1/2 c Butter (softened to room temperature)
    1 c Brown sugar (packed firmly into measuring cup)
1 1/2 c Oats, quick-cooking
        (uncooked)
    2 lg Eggs (lightly beaten)
    1 t Vanilla extract
    1 t Almond extract
    1 c Raisins
    1 c Dates (chopped)
    1 c Pecans (chopped)

Preheat oven to 350 degrees F. Sift together flour, baking powder, salt, cinnamon and nutmeg until well blended.

In a separate bowl, stir softened butter with brown sugar until well mixed.

Stir sifted dry ingredients into butter-sugar mixture. Stir in dry oats and beaten eggs. Add vanilla and almond extracts. Mix thoroughly. Stir in raisins, chopped dates and chopped pecans. Mix well until batter is firm.

Drop small dollops (each about 1 heaping teaspoon) about 2 inches apart onto a greased cookie sheet. Bake for 18 minutes in 350 degree F. oven until golden brown. Remove from cookie sheet, lay flat, and cool for 10 minutes before serving.

Trick Or Treat Pumpkin Pie

2 ea Eggs,slightly beaten
1 3/4 c (16 oz) solid pack pumpkin
1/2 t Salt
1/2 t Ground ginger
1 ea 9" unbaked pie crust
1/4 t Ground cloves
3/4 c Sugar
1 t Ground cinnamon
1 1/2 c Milk, evaporated 12 oz
1 pk Ready-whip topping

Preheat oven to 425 degrees.Combine filling ingredients in order given;pour into pie shell.Bake 15 minutes.Reduce temperature to 350 degrees.Bake an additional 45 minutes or until knife inserted near center comes out clean.Cool;garnish with ready-whip topping.

Twisted Strawberry Lime Pie

    Baked 9" pie shell
6 oz Can frzn limeade concentrate
1 ts Grated lime rind
1 c Whipping cream; whipped
    Envelopes unflavored gelatin
1/3 c Sugar
1 c Diced strawberries
1 ds Green food coloring

Soften gelatin in 1/2 cup cold water. Combine limeaid concentrate, sugar, and 3/4 cold water in small saucepan; c Chill until syrupy. Stir in lime rind and strawberries. Fold in whipped cre Garnish with additional sliced strawberries. Yield about 6-8 servings. NOTE: I made this with a graham cracker crust, and it came out very tasty. However, it was a little on the sweet side.

Ultimate Frozen Peanut Butter Pie

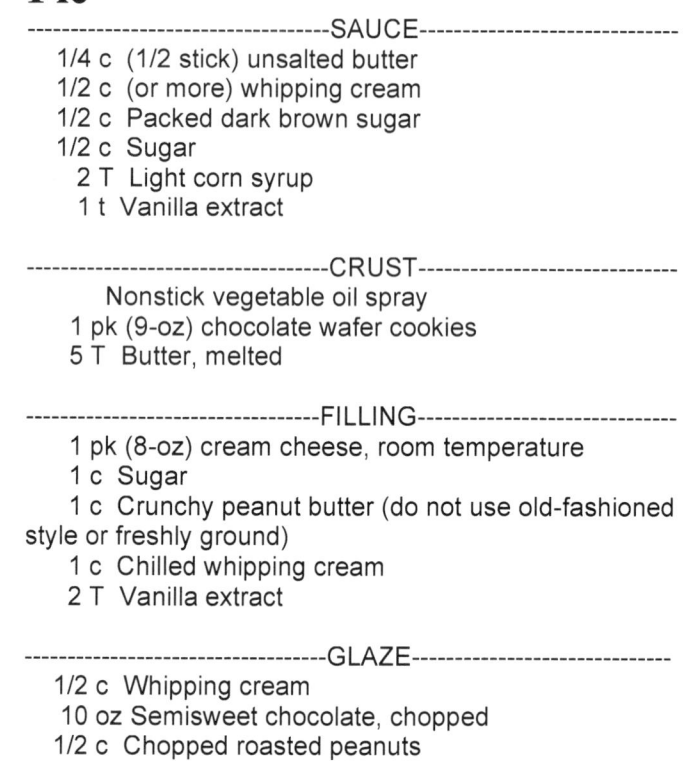

-------------------------------SAUCE---------------------------
- 1/4 c (1/2 stick) unsalted butter
- 1/2 c (or more) whipping cream
- 1/2 c Packed dark brown sugar
- 1/2 c Sugar
- 2 T Light corn syrup
- 1 t Vanilla extract

-------------------------------CRUST---------------------------
- Nonstick vegetable oil spray
- 1 pk (9-oz) chocolate wafer cookies
- 5 T Butter, melted

------------------------------FILLING--------------------------
- 1 pk (8-oz) cream cheese, room temperature
- 1 c Sugar
- 1 c Crunchy peanut butter (do not use old-fashioned style or freshly ground)
- 1 c Chilled whipping cream
- 2 T Vanilla extract

-------------------------------GLAZE---------------------------
- 1/2 c Whipping cream
- 10 oz Semisweet chocolate, chopped
- 1/2 c Chopped roasted peanuts

FOR SAUCE: Melt butter in heavy medium saucepan over medium heat. Add 1/2 C whipping cream, both sugars and corn syrup and bring to boil, stirring frequently. Reduce heat and simmer until slightly thickened, stirring occasionally, about 5 minutes. Mix in vanilla extract. Cool. (Sauce can be prepared 1 day ahead. Cover and chill.)

FOR CRUST: Spray 9-inch-diameter glass pie dish with nonstick vegetable oil spray. Finely grind chocolate wafer cookies in processor. Transfer cookie crumbs to bowl. Add 5 T melted butter and stir until moist crumbs form.
Press crumb mixture onto bottom and up sides of prepared dish. Place crust in freezer.

FOR FILLING: Using electric mixer, beat cream cheese and sugar in large bowl until smooth. Beat in peanut butter. Using electric mixer fitted with clean dry beaters, beat whipping cream and vanilla extract in medium bowl to stiff peaks. Fold cream into peanut butter mixture. Mound filling into chilled crust. Smooth top. Freeze overnight.

FOR GLAZE: Bring whipping cream to simmer in heavy medium saucepan. Add chopped semisweet chocolate and stir until melted and smooth. Cool to lukewarm. Spoon glaze over filling. Sprinkle with chopped peanuts. Freeze until chocolate sets, about 30 minutes. (Can be prepared 3 days ahead. Keep frozen.)

Let pie stand 20 minutes at room temperature. Using warm knife, cut pie into wedges. Place pie on plates. Bring sauce to simmer, thinning with more cream if necessary. Spoon warm sauce around pie and serve.

Uncle Karl's Caramel Apple Pie

  2   9 inch pie crust
  6 c Apples; peeled and sliced
3/4 c Sugar
1/4 c Flour
1/4 ts Salt
  2 tb Butter
1/3 c Caramel topping
  4 tb Pecans; chopped

Line 9" pie pan with pie dough.

Combine apples, sugar, flour and salt in a big bowl. Lightly toss. Spoon apple mixture into pie crust lined pan. Dot with butter. Top with the other crust and flute edges. Cut slits in several places.

Bake for 35-45 minutes or until apples are tender. Remove pie from oven.
Immediately drizzle the ice cream topping over pie and sprinkle with pecans.

Undercover Orange Meringue Pie

INGREDIENTS:
1 prepared 8 inch pastry shell, baked and cooled
3 1/2 tablespoons cornstarch
3/4 cup white sugar
1 pinch salt
1 1/4 cups boiling water
2 tablespoons butter
2 egg yolks, beaten
6 tablespoons frozen orange juice concentrate, thawed
4 teaspoons orange zest
2 egg whites
1/2 teaspoon vanilla extract
1/4 teaspoon cream of tartar
4 tablespoons white sugar

DIRECTIONS:
Blend cornstarch, 3/4 cup sugar, and salt in a saucepan. Gradually stir in the hot water. Cook over medium heat, stirring constantly until thickened. Reduce heat to low. Cook and stir 5 minutes longer. Remove from heat.
Mix butter or margarine, egg yolks, orange juice, and orange rind into the cornstarch mixture. Cook one minute more. Cover entire surface with clear plastic. Let cool just slightly, and pour into the cooled pastry shell. Cool to room temperature.
In a clean glass bowl, beat the egg whites with vanilla extract and cream of tartar until foamy. Beat in 4 tablespoons sugar gradually, and continue beating until meringue forms stiff and glossy peaks. Spread meringue in swirls over the filling; be sure to seal to the edge of the pastry.
Bake at 375 degrees F (190 degrees C) for 10 to 15 minutes, or till the meringue is tipped golden brown. Cool to room temperature.

V.I.P Apple Cinnamon Pie

1 c Knotts Berry Farm Light
    -Apple Cinnamon Syrup
1 c Hot water
1 ts Butter
3 tb Cornstarch
1 pn Salt
2   Egg yolks
1   Graham cracker pie crust
2   Egg whites
1 tb Knotts Berry Farm Light
    -Apple Cinnamon Syrup

   Combine syrup, hot water and butter and bring to a boil. Mix cornstarch, salt and enough cold water to make a thin paste, add egg yolks and beat well. Add cornstarch mixture to hot syrup gradually, return to heat and cook until thickened to the consistency of pudding, stirring constantly.
   Cool slightly. Pour into pie crust. Beat egg whites stiff, adding slowly the tablespoon of syrup. Pile on pie and brown in 400 F oven.

Valley View Vanilla Wafer Crust

2 tb Margarine melted
30   Vanilla Wafers
   1 3/4 inches in diameter
1/4 ts Pure vanilla extract

Prepare a 9" pie plate by rubbing inside, bottom and sides with 1 teaspoon of the margarine; set aside. Crush vanilla wafers to make very fine crumbs 1 1/2 cups. Place crumbs in a large bowl; combine vanilla and melted margarine and drizzle all over crumbs. Mix thoroughly with blending fork to make sure all is well blended. Remove about 2 tablespoons of crumb mixture and set aside to use as a garnish if desired. With back of a large spoon, press remaining crumbs evenly all over bottom and sides of prepared pie pan. Chill in refrigerator for 2 hours or longer before filling.

Variety Fried Pies

2 c Flour
1/2 c Shortening
1 x Fruit, stewed
1 t Salt
1/3 c Water, cold

Sift the flour and salt together, cut in the shortening and mix with hands.
Add water. Roll out about 1/8 inch thick on a floured board. Cut with a large cookie cutter about 4 inches in diameter. In each round, place 1 ½ Tbsp sweetened mashed fruit (dried apricots, peaches, prunes or thick apple sauce). Moisten edges with cold water, fold to make semi-circle and press edges together with a fork. Fry in deep fat.

Victoria's Vine Grape Pie

```
1 1/2 c  Graham cracker crumbs
    3 T  Sugar
　 1/3 c  Butter, melted
    3 t  Cornstarch
  2/3 c  Sugar
  1/4 c  Water, cold
　 2 lb  Grapes, seedless (green),
         -with stems removed
    1 T  Lemon juice
    1 c  Sour cream
    1 T  Sugar
    1 t  Vanilla extract
```

Preheat oven to 350 degrees F. Combine cracker crumbs, about 3 T sugar and butter. Reserve 1/4 cup of this crumb mixture and press the rest into a 9-inch pie pan. Bake at 350 degrees F. for 8 minutes. Allow to cool.

Dissolve cornstarch and about 2/3 cup sugar in cold water in saucepan. Add grapes and bring to boil, stirring constantly. Reduce heat and simmer for 5 minutes. Remove from heat and stir in the lemon juice. Cool.

Spoon this filling into the baked and cooled crust. Mix sour cream with about 1 T sugar and vanilla and spread over pie. Sprinkle with reserved crumbs. Serve.

Wafer Crust Pumpkin Pie

  12   Graham wafers crushed
   4 ts Margarine, melted
   1 pk Diet caramel instant pudding
      Skim milk
   1 c Canned pumpkin
 1/2 ts Cinnamon
 1/2 ts Cloves
 1/2 ts Nutmeg
 1/2 ts Ginger

Mix crushed wafers and margarine together in pie plate and press out to form crust. Mix pudding as directed on box with the appropriate amount of skim milk. Then mix in spices and pumpkin. Spread over crumbs. Let set a bit before serving.

Warm Butternut Biscuits

- 2 T Butter
- 1 c Sugar
- 1 Egg
- 1/2 t Cream of tartar
- 1 t Baking soda
- 1 pn Salt
- 1 1/2 c Flour, plain -(white)
- 1/2 t Vanilla essence
- 1 c Coconut, desiccated
- 2 T Golden syrup
- 1 T Milk

Mix all ingredients together well. Preheat oven to 250 degrees F. Roll dough into small balls. Bake for 15 minutes, or until brown.

NOTES:

* Golden syrup is not available in North America; it is a caramelized sugar syrup. North Americans can substitute dark corn syrup or a mixture of molasses and water.

Warm Elderberry Pie

2 1/2 c Elderberries
1/2 c Sugar
1/8 ts Salt
2 tb Flour
3 tb Lemon juice

Mix elderberries, sugar, salt and lemon juice. Sprinkle with flour and dot with butter. Put in an 8" pie crust and cover with another crust. Bake at 350 degrees for 30 minutes.

Serve warm with a scoop of vanilla ice cream.

Wedding Vow Cookies

```
2 c  Flour, all-purpose
1/2 t  Salt
3/4 c  Butter (or margarine),
       softened
1/2 c  Sugar
  1    Egg
  1 t  Vanilla extract
  1 c  Walnuts, chopped
       Confectioner's sugar
```

Preheat oven to 350 degrees F. Grease cookie sheets lightly with unsalted shortening.

Sift together flour and salt. Work butter in a bowl until creamy. Add sugar and beat until well blended. Add egg and vanilla and beat well.

Gradually add sifted dry ingredients, beating well after each addition.

Stir in walnuts. Shape dough into small balls about 3/4 inch in diameter.

Place balls about 2 inches apart on prepared cookie sheets. Bake 12-15 minutes or until lightly browned. Roll balls in confectioners sugar while still warm. Roll again in sugar when cooled.

Store these in a tight container. Powered sugar makes this recipe a little messy.

Welcome Home Oatmeal Pie

Amish Oatmeal Pie

1-1/2 c. milk
3 eggs, lightly beaten
3 tbsp. margarine, melted
2/3 c. rolled oats
1 1/3 c. dark brown sugar
2/3 c. flaked coconut
1 (9 or 10 inch) pie shell, unbaked

Preheat oven to 425 degrees. Combine milk, eggs, butter, oats, sugar and coconut in a large bowl. Mix thoroughly with a wire whisk. Pour into pie shell and sprinkle with additional coconut. Bake for 10 minutes. Reduce heat to 350 degrees and bake for an additional 30 minutes or until a knife inserted in the center comes out clean.

West Coast Carrot Raisin Bars

------------------------------BOTTOM LAYER-------------------

- 1/2 c Butter
- 1/2 c Sugar
- 1 c Flour

------------------------------TOP LAYER------------------------

- 2 Eggs
- 1 c Carrots, grated
- 1 c Brown sugar, packed
- 1 1/2 c Raisins
- 1/2 c Nuts, chopped
- 1 t Lemon juice
- 2 T Flour
- 1/2 t Baking powder
- 1 ds Salt

Preheat oven to 400 degrees F. Cream together the butter and sugar. Add the flour and mix well. Form into a ball, then press it down into a uniform layer in a 8-inch square baking pan. Bake until golden brown (about 15 minutes).

Combine ingredients for top layer, mixing well. When bottom layer is done, pour on top and spread evenly. Bake for 25 minutes.

NOTES:

* Chewy carrot raisin and nut bars -- This is from "The Carrot Cookbook," by Audra and Jack Hendrickson. As they say, this recipe is beta-carotene rich. In any case, they are a tasty treat. Serves 4-6.

Wetzel Lane Raspberry Tart

1 c Flour; all purpose
1 tb Sugar; granulated
6 tb Butter; cold
1   Egg yolk
1 tb Lemon juice
3 tb Cornstarch
3/4 c Sugar; granulated
1 c Raspberries; fresh

Pastry: In large bowl, stir together flour, sugar and salt. With pastry blender or food processor, cut in butter till it resembles tiny peas. In small bowl & using fork, stir together egg yolk, lemon juice and 1 Tbsp water; sprinkle over flour mixture. Stirring with fork, add a little more water if necessary to hold dough together. Using hands, gently shape pastry into ball. Press dough 1/8" thick into flan pan. Refrigerate while making filling.

Filling: Preheat oven to 425F. In small saucepan, stir together water & cornstarch till smooth. Stir in sugar. Add raspberries and cook, stirring, over medium-low heat for 10-15 minutes or till thickened. Let cool; spoon into shell, filling no more than 2/3 full.

Bake in 425F oven for 10 minutes. Reduce heat to 350F and bake 15 minutes longer or till pastry is golden brown. Let cool in flan ring 15 minutes before removing to rack.

Wheel Barrow Whipped Cream

   1 ts Granulated gelatin
   1 tb Cold water
2 1/2 tb Boiling water
  1/2 c Iced water
  1/2 c Instant nonfat dry milk
  1/2 ts Vanilla
   2 tb Vegetable oil
   3 tb Sugar = artifical sweetener

Chill a small mixing bowl and beaters. Meanwhile, soften gelatin in cold water, then disolve it over boiling water. Allow to cool to tepid. Placed iced water and nonfat dry milk in chilled bowl and beat until stiff peaks form. Continue beating, adding remaining ingredients and gelatin, until blended. Place bowl in freezer for 15 minutes, then transfer to refrigerator. Occasionally stir gently to keep mixture smooth and well blended.

Note Any artifical sweetener liquid or powdered may be used as long as it is equivalent to 3 Tablespoons of sugar.

Who's Ready Pumpkin Pie

  2 T Butter, melted
1 3/4 c Pumpkin (one standard can)
    2   Eggs
  2 T Flour
  1 c Evaporated milk
1/2 c Sugar, dark brown
1/2 c White sugar
  1 t Ginger
  1 t Cinnamon
1/4 t Mace
1/4 t Cloves, ground
1/2 t Salt
   1   Pie shell (standard), uncooked

Preheat the oven to 450 degrees F. Beat the eggs until frothy. Mix in the sugars and the flour. Mix in the spices and the salt. Mix in the pumpkin.

Mix in the melted butter. Finally, mix in the milk.

Pour the mix into the pie crust and bake at 450 degrees F. for 15 minutes.

Decrease heat to 375 degrees F. and bake for an additional 45 minutes.

Remove the pie from the oven and set it out to cool.

Will You Be My Brown Sugar Pie?

- 1 Unbaked 8 inch pie shell
- 1 c Brown sugar
- 3 T All purpose flour
- Speck of salt
- 1 12 oz can evaporated milk
- 2 1/2 T Butter
- Ground cinnamon

Preheat oven to 350 F. In the pie shell, place the brown sugar, flour, and salt. Mix with your fingers. Pour the evaporated milk over the flour and sugar, but do not stir or mix this in. Dot with butter, and drift cinnamon liberally over all. Bake for 50 min., or until the filling just bubbles up in the middle. The filling will never completely set, but that's the way it's supposed to be. This pie is better eaten at room temperature. If you refrigerate leftovers, reheat them in the oven before serving.
NOTE: Recipe can be doubled and prepared in a 10 inch pie shell. For that size, bake 1 hour and 20 min. (12 servings)

Winner's Circle Rum/bourbon Balls

    3 c Vanilla Wafers (crushed)
    1 c Sugar, powered
    1 1/2 c Nuts, chopped
    1 1/2 t Cocoa powder
    2 T Corn syrup, white (honey also works well)
    1/2 c Rum or Bourbon

Mix all dry ingredients and set aside.

Mix corn syrup or honey with rum or bourbon to thin the syrup. Blend wet mixture into dry ingredients with fork. Mix well. Allow to sit for 1-2 hours.

At this point, if you let it sit a couple of hours, you can come back and add another about 1/2 cup of rum or bourbon and let sit again. This process may be repeated a few times to your taste. The last time, the mix should sit a couple of hours so it's not really moist. There's a good midpoint between too moist and too dry where rolling into balls won't be difficult (too wet) or cause crumbling (too dry).

Roll into balls, then roll in powered sugar to make a sugar coating. When rolling in powered sugar, the moister they are, the more sugar will be absorbed over time. They may need another roll in the sugar right before serving.

Winter Wonderland Oatmeal Squares

- 1 c Flour, self-raising
- 1 c Rolled oats
- 1 c Coconut, desiccated
- 1 c Sugar, raw
- 1 Egg
- 1/2 lb Butter
- 1 T Golden syrup

Combine flour, oats, coconut, sugar and egg. Melt butter and add golden syrup, then pour over combined ingredients and mix. Spread over flat baking dish (about 1/2-inch thick), and cook for 25-30 mins at 350 degrees F. Slice when warm.

Wisconsin Cranberry Pie

      Pastry for double crust pie
   3 c Halved cranberries
 1/2 c Water
1 3/4 c Sugar
   5 tb Flour
 1/4 ts Salt
 1/2 ts Almond extract
   2 tb Butter

  Prepare pastry for pie. In saucepan add cranberries and water and bring to the boiling point. Mix dry ingredients and slowly add to cranberry mixture. cook on low heat until mixture thickens. Remove from heat and add extract.
  Cool filling completely. Pour into 9 inch pastry lined pan. Dot with the butter. Add top crust as a lattice crust or as a whole top crust, crimping edges and pricking top in several places. Bake in 425 oven for 35 to 40 minutes or crust light golden. Serve room temperature or cold with ice cream or whipped cream. A no nonsense delicious cranberry pie.

Wishful Hazelnut Cherry Tart

---------------------PASTRY---
- 1/2 c Plain flour
- 1/8 t Salt
- 2 oz Hazelnuts, roasted ground
- 2 T Sugar
- 2 oz Butter
- 1   Egg yolk
- 2 t Water

-------------------CUSTARD FILLING----------------------------
- 4   Egg yolks
- 1/4 c Sugar
- 1 t Vanilla extract
- 1 3/4 c Cream
- 3 t Gelatine
- 2 T Water

--------------------------------TOPPING---------------------------
- 2 lb Cherries, canned
- 2 t Gelatine
- 2 t Rum (see note)

MAKE PASTRY: Sift flour and add all dry ingredients together, with the sugar in the centre, on a pastry board. Add the butter (softened), egg yolk and water. Work the liquids into the sugar, until it is creamy.

Now work in the flour mixture, as you would for any sweet pastry. Press the dough into a greased 9-inch flan tin. Prick the base of the pastry all over. Refrigerate for 30 mins, then cook in a moderate oven (375 degrees F.) for 15 to 20 mins (until golden brown)

MAKE FILLING: Put egg yolks, sugar and vanilla into a bowl and beat until thick and creamy. Heat cream carefully until almost boiling.

Combine the two mixtures, beating until smooth, then add the result to the top of a double boiler and simmer until it thickens (STIR CONSTANTLY).

Dissolve the gelatine in the water and add to the cream mixture, stirring well until it is well mixed. Allow this mixture to cool completely before adding to the pastry case. Refrigerate until it sets.

MAKE TOPPING: Drain the cherries and reserve about 1 cup of the syrup. We don't use commercial canned cherries. I would suggest a "light" syrup.
Arrange the pitted cherries artistically over the top of the tart.

Put the reserved syrup, gelatine and rum (we usually use cherry brandy or kirsch) into a saucepan and heat (stirring) until gelatine dissolves. Cool the liquid and pour over the cherries. Refrigerate until set.

Yes You Flan

- 3/4 c   Sugar
- 2   Eggs
- 2   Egg yolks
- 2 c   Milk
- 1 t   Vanilla extract

In a small kettle, heat about 3 T of sugar with about 1 t of water until the mixture turns brown. Pour the mixture into 4 gelatin molds. Move the molds around so that the mixture coats the interior. Set aside.

Mix the eggs, sugar, milk and the vanilla extract. Pour the mixture into the molds. Put the molds over a deep pan with water (double boiler or bain marie technique) for 1 hr in a 350 degree F. oven. Keep the water in the pan at the same level by adding boiling water. Cool and put it in the refrigerator. Unmold the flan before serving.

You Can Do It Corn Flake Crust

1 Recipe

   1 c Finely crushed cornflakes or Bran
1/3 c Melted margarine
1/4 c Honey

Mix honey and crushed cereal. Mix well with the shortening and press with the palm of your hand against the bottom and sides of the pie pan. It is well to chill this crust thoroughly, but if you are in a hurry, you may bake it at once in a moderate oven about 350 degrees for 15 minutes.

Yummy C.C. Peanut Butter Pie

- 3 Eggs; beaten to blend
- 1 c Dark corn syrup
- 1/2 c Sugar
- 1/2 c Creamy peanut butter
- 1 ts Vanilla extract
- 2/3 c Salted peanuts
- 1 Unbaked 9-inch pie shell; chilled
- 1 c Semisweet chocolate chips

Preheat oven to 400 degrees. Using electric mixer, beat first 5 ingredients
Sprinkle pie shell with chocolate chips. Pour filling over. Bake 15 minutes

Yummy Cream Cheese PB Pies

- 2 Graham cracker crust pie -shells (9-inch)/baked)
- 1 c Chunk-style peanut butter
- 8 oz Cream cheese; softened
- 1/4 c Margarine; softened
- 1/2 c Plus 1 tb sugar, divided use
- 1 ts Vanilla
- 1 c Whipping cream
- 1 pk Instant chocolate pudding (prepared as directed on box)
- 2 tb Chopped peanuts
- 1 Spray can whipped cream

In large bowl beat peanut butter, cream cheese and margarine with electric mixer until blended. Gradually add 1/2 cup sugar. Beat about 1 minute, until soft and fluffy. Beat in vanilla. In another bowl, whip cream with 1 tablespoon sugar until soft peaks form when beaters lifted. Fold into peanut butter mixture until thoroughly blended. Pour into pie shells. Frost pies with a half-inch of chocolate pudding. Sprinkle chopped peanuts on top. Cover with plastic wrap or with inverted pie crust covers. Chill at least two hours.

Zesty Bavarian Pie

    1   Envelope unflavored gelatin
3/4 c Sugar, divided
1/4 ts Salt
    3   Eggs, separated
3/4 c Milk
  2 T Fresh lemon juice
  1 ts Grated fresh lemon peel
  1 ts Grated fresh tangerine peel
  1 c Diced tangerine sections
1/2 c Heavy cream, whipped
    1   Baked 9-inch pastry shell

  Mix gelatine, 1/2 cup sugar and salt in saucepan. Divide eggs; beat egg yolks with milk and stir into gelatin mixture. Stir over low heat until gelatin dissolves and mixture thickens slightly, about 5 minutes. Remove from heat and chill, stirring occasionally, until thick enough to mound slightly when dropped from a spoon. Stir in lemon juice, lemon peel, and tangerine peel. Peel tangerines and separate into sections. Remove white stringy portion, seeds, and membranes. Cut into small pieces. Add diced tangerine sections. Beat egg whites until soft peaks form; gradually add remaining 1/4 cup sugar and beat until stiff. Fold into tangerine mixture; fold in whipped cream. Turn into baked pastry shell. Chill until set.
  Garnish, if desired, with whipped cream and tangerine sections. Makes 6 to 8 servings.

Zesty Lemon Custard Pie

1 servings
-----cookie pastry-----
1 Unsalted butter; at room temperature
1/4 c Sugar
1 Egg
1 1/2 c Flour
-----filling-----
1/2 Unsalted butter
4 Eggs
1 c Sugar
1 tb Grated lemon peel; (1 large lemon)
2/3 c Fresh lemon juice
Powdered sugar; for garnish

Beat butter and sugar until light and fluffy, about 2 minutes. Add egg and flour and mix until smooth dough is formed. With hands, shape into a ball and flatten into a disc. Wrap in plastic wrap and refrigerate until chilled. Preheat oven to 350. Make pastry and roll or press dough evenly over bottom and up sides of 9-inch pie pan. Melt butter in microwave; set aside. Whisk eggs and sugar in medium-size bowl until blended. Add peel and slowly stir in butter and lemon juice until incorporated. Pour into crust. Bake for 30 to 40 minutes or until top of custard is lightly browned. It will not test clean and will look underdone, but will set as it cools. When cool, refrigerate. Before serving, sprinkle powdered sugar on top.

Zeta Sorority Apple Pie Cake

1 pk Cake mix; yellow
3 Eggs
1/2 ts Lemon extract
1 Jar apple pie; filling
Topping
1/4 c Butter; or marg.
1/2 c Sugar
1/2 c Flour
Cinnamon(optional)

Mix the Cake mix, eggs,lemon and Apple pie filling.
Pour batter into a 13x9 greased pan.
Bake at 375 degrees for 22-28 minutes

Zeus Is Loose Dirty South Apple Pie

--------------------------------PIE--------------------------------
22 oz Tart apples
1 1/2 c Sugar
1/4 c Flour
3 c Sour cream
2 Eggs, beaten
1 t Vanilla
2 Pastry shells,
-deep-dish, about
-9 inches wide

--------------------------------TOPPING--------------------------
1 1/8 c Sugar
3/4 c Flour
1 1/2 t Cinnamon
1/2 c Butter

Preheat the oven to 400 degrees F. In a large bowl, combine the sugar, flour, sour cream, eggs and vanilla into a smooth mixture. Core, peel and chop the apples. Boil them in a small amount of water with a little lemon juice for 3 to 5 minutes until they begin to get tender. Drain apples and add to the mixture. Pour into two 9-inch pastry shells. Bake at 400 degrees F. for 30 minutes. While pies are baking, crumble topping ingredients into a bowl and mix with a pastry cutter or two knives. Remove pies from oven and cover with topping recipe. Put pies under broiler for 1 to 2 minutes until the topping begins to bubble.
Don't take your eyes off the pies while they're under the broiler. A moment's inattention can mean burned pie!

Zig-Zag Apple Cranberry Pie

1 x Double Crust Pie Crust
3/4 c Sugar
1/4 c Corn starch
1 t Cinnamon
5 c Peeled apple slices
2 c Cranberries, fresh or frozen
1/3 c Corn syrup, light or dark
1 T Butter or margarine
1 x Milk
1 x Sugar

Prepare pie crusts for filled two-crust pie using 9-inch pan. Heat oven to 450F. In a large bowl, stir sugar, corn starch and cinnamon until well mixed. In another large bowl, mix apples, cranberries and corn syrup. Add fruit to sugar mixture. Mix to combine. Spoon into pie crust-lined pan. Dot with butter. Top with second crust; flute. Cut four 4-inch slashes in center of crust forming a criss-cross design. Peel back center points and press lightly in crust to hod and form 8 petals. Brush crust with milk; sprinkle with sugar. Bake at 450F for 10 minutes. Reduce temperature to 350F; continue baking 40 to 45 minutes or until golden brown. Cool completely on wire rack. Store in refrigerator.

Zippy's Crab Apple Pie

Pastry for 2 crust pie
1 c Sugar
1 tb Flour
1/4 c Salt
6 c Crab apples *1
1 ts Vanilla
1 1/2 tb Lemon juice
1/3 c Water
1 1/2 tb Butter
*1 finely chopped, unpeeled.

Combine sugar, flour and salt, toss together with apples. Pour mixture into pastry lined 9 inch pie pan. Sprinkle with mixture of vanilla, lemon juice and water. Dot with butter. Cover with top pastry, flute edges and cut vents. Bake at 400 F. 50 minutes or until filling is tender and crust is browned.

Zoltar Baklava

1 Batch

----------------------------------DOUGH---------------------------
1 lb Strudel dough
-(or fillo leaves)
1 lb Butter, unsalted,
-well-melted (salted
-butter (or margarine)
-is not acceptable)

----------------------------------FILLING---------------------------
1 lb Walnut meat,
-chopped medium-fine
1/4 c Sugar
1 t Vanilla (or use
-vanilla sugar)

----------------------------------SYRUP----------------------------
4 c Sugar
2 c Water
1 t Lemon juice

Heat oven to 300 degrees F. to 325 degrees F. MAKE THE SYRUP: Boil the water and sugar for 15 minutes. Add lemon juice, boil 10 more minutes, set aside to cool. MAKE THE FILLING: Mix all ingredients well. I prefer the walnuts fairly coarse; some people like them quite fine. BUILD THE BAKLAVA: Cut the dough with scissors to the size of the tray.
Handle the dough very carefully; do not press hard on it at any time. Cover with wax paper and damp towel.
Take out one sheet of dough at a time and place it in the pan. Brush the dough with melted butter between each layer. Continue until you have about 12 sheets buttered. Small and broken pieces of dough can be used in the center, but there must be butter between every two layers.
Spread walnut filling across the tray. Put on a sheet of dough, brush on butter and continue until all the dough is used up.
Cut into diamond shapes: cut into quarters with cuts parallel to the long axis, then cut diagonally across.

Don't press hard!
Bake for about 1 1/2 hour, until golden brown. Be careful not to burn the bottom or the walnuts, especially with a glass pan.
Let cool on rack for 5 minutes. Add syrup which should have cooled to room temperature. Let cool for at least two hours before eating.
NOTES:
* An incredibly sweet and wonderful Balkan dessert -- Baklava is claimed by almost every Balkan state as its own invention; most people in the United States first encounter it in Greek restaurants. If the truth were known, it's probably the Turkish who invented it, as is the case for many other "typically Greek" dishes. This recipe comes from my Bulgarian grandmother and follows Bulgarian tradition, in that the filling is very simple. Makes two small pans.
* Probably the hardest thing about this recipe is waiting those last two hours!
* Depending on where you go, you'll hear the name of this dish pronounced different ways. I pronounce the name with all /ah/ sounds, with accents of equal intensity on both the first and third syllable. The second syllable is quite faint. Greek-speaking persons typically put a heavy accent on the second syllable.
* Many variations on the filling are to be found. A simple one was mentioned above, regarding the coarseness of grind of the walnuts in the filling. They may even be ground. Spices such as chopped cloves or cinnamon may be added and the filling may be included in several layers instead of just one.
* A large (14 x 10 inch) pan is almost too big to handle. I typically make this recipe in two 7 3/4 x 11 inch pans, which is just about the size of a half sheet of the dough I buy. By the way, if you can make your own strudel dough, it will be even better... but much more effort.
* It is best to have a partner help you prepare the pans. One person handles the dough and places it in the pan, while the other applies the butter. It is very important that sufficient butter be placed between layers so that each layer gets flaky, rather than having them stick together. Pay particular attention to the edges and corners.
* In case you haven't noticed, this is very sweet stuff. It goes great with a fine cup of coffee, espresso, or Turkish coffee, even with sugar.

Two pieces will probably fill anyone up; it refrigerates and freezes quite well. This recipe requires a lot of effort, but it's well worth it.

Zone 105 Sour Cream Apple Pie

Crust:
2/3 c Butter
1/4 c Pure maple syrup
1/2 c Cream cheese
1 Egg
1 tb Orange rind
1 ts Vanilla
2 1/4 c Unbleached flour
1/2 ts Baking powder
Filling:
2 lb Green apples
Topping:
1/2 c Sour cream
1/4 c Pure maple syrup
2 tb Lemon juice
1/4 ts Nutmeg

For the crust, blend together butter, maple syrup, cream cheese, egg, orange rind.
Roll to 1/3-inch thickness. Fit or pat the dough into 7-inch pie plate.
Sprinkle nutmeg on top. Bake at 350 degrees for 30 minutes.

Zoo Keeper's Baked Apples

4 md Green apples (crispy, tart; Granny Smiths are good)
Cinnamon stick (3-inch),
　broken and ground
　OR use 1 1/4 t powdered
14 Allspice berries, ground
　OR about 1/2 t allspice
1/8 t Nutmeg, grated
1/2 c Brown sugar
3 T Butter (grate if cold)
Lemon juice (from
1/2 medium lemon)
3/4 c Golden raisins
1/4 c Prunes, dried, pitted
3/4 c Walnuts, chopped
(or other nuts)

Preheat oven to 400 degrees F. Butter a deep baking dish that has a lid.
Core the apples but do not peel them. Arrange them in the dish. Cut apples to fit, if necessary.
Combine all remaining ingredients in bowl. Mix well (this is where grating the butter comes in handy). Stuff this mixture into the holes and spaces in and between the apples.
Bake covered at 400 degrees F. for about 30 minutes. Serve hot with vanilla ice cream (spoon extra sauce over ice cream).
NOTES:
* A quick substitute for apple pie.
* Grind the cinnamon stick and allspice berries with a coffee grinder; makes interesting coffee afterwards.
Alternative: Use about 1 1/4 t powdered cinnamon and 1/2 t allspice.

Zoom Upside Down Apple Pie

Ingredients:
3-4 large Granny Smith apples
4 tbsp butter
3 tbsp sugar
One sheet puff pastry dough
Splash of warm rum
Vanilla ice cream (optional)
Method:

Peel 3 to 4 Granny Smith apples and slice. Melt butter in saucepan (2 tbsp) with a few tbsp. of sugar. Arrange apples around deep sauté pan; arrange in circular pattern, place apples overlapping each other and then add a few slices to the middle of pan. When finished, this will be the top of your torte.

Drizzle butter/sugar mixture over top of apples. Cook on medium heat until apples start to get soft and the butter/sugar mixture begins to caramelize. Remove apples from stove and then bake in oven, uncovered for 10 minutes at 425 degrees.

Remove from oven and put one sheet of rolled-out puff pastry dough on top, cutting edges and then tucking them under the apples around edge. Bake in oven for 20 minutes at 425 degrees. Remove from oven and place large serving plate on top and flip over. Drizzle warm rum over the top and serve each piece with a scoop of vanilla ice cream.

Serves 8